IMPERIAL PATRIOT

CHARLES ALMA BAKER
AND THE HISTORY OF LIMESTONE DOWNS

Charles Alma Baker in court dress for the presentation of his CBE at
Buckingham Palace, 1919. MRS ALMA CURTIN

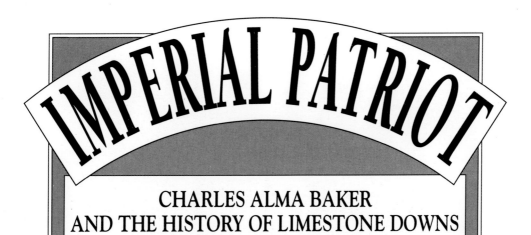

IMPERIAL PATRIOT

CHARLES ALMA BAKER
AND THE HISTORY OF LIMESTONE DOWNS

Barrie Macdonald

First published in 1993 by Bridget Williams Books
Limited, P.O. Box 11-294, Wellington.
© Barrie Macdonald, 1993
This book is copyright under the Berne Convention.
All rights reserved. No reproduction without permission.
Inquiries should be made to the publishers.
ISBN 0 908912 56 0
Design and production by R & B Graphics
Printed by GP Print

CONTENTS

For Maureen

ACKNOWLEDGEMENTS

My exploration of the life of Charles Alma Baker began in 1987 when I was asked to comment on historical material about Baker and Limestone Downs that had been gathered with a publication in mind. It quickly became evident that many aspects of Baker's life still remained obscure and that the life, in so far as it was known, was sufficiently interesting to justify an attempt to fill the gaps. In undertaking this task, I have received professional and personal assistance from many sources. In particular, I wish to acknowledge the support given by the trustees of the C. Alma Baker Trust – Norman Boyes, Robin Boyes and Roger Moore – and its New Zealand Committee, the latter being chaired by the Hon. L.W. Gandar. Both bodies have contributed to the cost of undertaking the research and publication, but have been scrupulous in respecting my professional independence. Kevin Lowe, a specialist in farm management at Massey University and supervisor at Limestone Downs, was of enormous assistance with the research relating to the farm, read drafts without complaint and spent many hours explaining the philosophy and process of farm development at Limestone Downs. Warwick and Doreen Deighton were always hospitable and helpful during my visits to Limestone Downs.

Librarians and archivists too numerous to name have been unfailingly helpful in answering queries put in person or by correspondence as I have tried to garner details of Baker's life not just in New Zealand, but also in Australia, Britain, the United States and Malaysia. A major source of the study has been material gathered by Judith Fyfe of the New Zealand Oral History Archive; these recorded interviews, many with people who had known Baker or had worked at Limestone Downs in the 1920s and 1930s, provided invaluable insights into a life that was always difficult to penetrate. Family members have also supplied information and photographs without which this book could not have been completed; particular thanks are due to Mrs Alma Curtin, Valerie and Eric Gray, Ms Kahukore Baker, Harland Harland-Baker and the families of the late Roderick and Lionel Whitaker. Through the publication process, it has been a pleasure to work with Bridget Williams (publisher), Anna Rogers (editor), and Bruce Blair (designer). I thank all three for their interest and professionalism.

I wish to acknowledge continuing collegial support from within the Department of History at Massey University and the particular assistance of Mrs Rama McGee. As usual, my family, and especially Maureen, have tolerated my preoccupation, and have borne the burden of living with me while I have lived with Charles Alma Baker; thank you all.

Barrie Macdonald
June 1993

LIST OF ILLUSTRATIONS

INTRODUCING CHARLES ALMA BAKER

Charles Alma Baker lived an interesting life. Born in Otago in 1857, he was raised in Oamaru where his parents, recent immigrants from London, established the first hotel in the district. Baker, Barney to his friends, was trained as a surveyor and, having moved to Auckland, worked extensively in the Waikato and Bay of Plenty areas. In Auckland, he began to move in higher social circles and married Florence, the daughter of Sir Frederick Whitaker, lawyer, land speculator and a leading politician of his day. Baker also fathered a son by Maria Nikora, a high-born woman of the Whakatohea tribe, while surveying in the Opotiki district. Leaving New Zealand in 1890 soon after, but not necessarily because of, this latter event, he moved to Perak, one of the Federated Malay States where, over a period of thirty years, he made successive fortunes from contract surveying, tin mining and rubber planting.

Baker was an imperial patriot, committed to the cause of King and Empire. During the First World War, in Malaya and Australia, he contributed heavily, in both time and money, to a campaign for the purchase of military aircraft, for which he was awarded a CBE. From about 1920, and for the remaining two decades of his life, Baker travelled the world. In 1923, having effectively retired, he returned to New Zealand for the first time since 1890 and discovered the joys of big game fishing at the Bay of Islands; it was he who persuaded Zane Grey, the famous novelist and outdoors man, to visit New Zealand and he was subsequently embroiled in the controversy over fishing methods that caused Grey to fall out with local fishermen. From New Zealand, in the autumn, Baker sailed to Catalina Island off the Californian coast for more fishing, to London for the summer, to Malaya to check on his mines and plantations, and to Australia where he had pastoral interests, some of them in partnership with 'Cattle King' Sir Sidney Kidman. By January, Baker was back in the Bay of Islands, and by March fishing for trout on the Tongariro River. And so the circuit would begin again, with Baker, determined to avoid winters, circling the globe administering his various enterprises by letter and telegram. His entourage was considerable. His wife Florence (known as Floss), and his daughter Julitha (known as Judy), usually accompanied him, together with a companion for his wife and daughter and one or two servants.

Until 1926, Baker's annual visits to New Zealand were recreational but he then entered into a partnership with Eric Baker, a nephew, to farm Te Karaka, a property south of Port Waikato. He also bought a much larger adjoining property which he called Limestone Downs. Although partly cleared, both properties (then with a combined area of some 9,500 acres) were mostly bush-covered, a mixture of hill country suitable for grazing and a swampy area bordering the Kaawa Stream that was potentially valuable once it had been extensively cleared, drained and fenced. Over the next fifteen years, Baker poured a small fortune into expanding the properties and into farm development; his aim was to make Limestone

Downs a highly profitable venture, but also a showpiece for innovative stock breeding and the production of beef and wool of the highest quality.

His interest in agriculture did not stop with the development of his plantations and farms. From the turn of the century, Baker had been interested in the properties of soil, the biological processes of plants and animals, and the dangers of what he called 'de-natured foods'. Drawn towards Rudolph Steiner's principles of biodynamic farming, he propounded his own distinctive views in a series of publications in the late 1930s. In these, Baker warned that the future of the British Empire was threatened unless agricultural practice was reformed and the quality of food improved. He also experimented with his own diet, and put Worcestershire sauce in his tea. He had only limited success, however, when trying to put his theories into practice through agricultural experiments. His attempt to revive his aging rubber trees with composting rather than the introduction of vigorous new plant stock through bud grafting, and his animal breeding experiments at Limestone Downs, were the despair of his managers and had a serious impact on longer-term profits. In his twilight years, he was convinced that all living things were affected by showers of cosmic dust; he would hold his hands to the sky to absorb the cosmic forces that he believed would revitalise his aging body.

Some of Baker's ideas were unconventional, but in many ways he was ahead of his time. His basic concern to protect soils, to increase food production through natural processes and to improve food quality can all be related to modern views of agricultural sustainability and the dangers of junk foods. He was among the earliest to see the potential for the growing of plantation rubber in the Federated Malay States, and the fundamental sound-ness of many of his cultivation practices, rejected at the time, was later recognised. His views on the future of aviation – military and civil – expressed during the First World War can only be described as visionary. It was his recognition of the potential of game fishing at the Bay of Islands that brought his friend Zane Grey to New Zealand and contributed, in turn, to international attention and a new tourist industry. Baker was also a man of his time. He made his money as an entrepreneur on the frontiers of empire, and this was reflected in his attitudes towards race and politics which were conservative, sometimes reactionary. But, for Baker, the empire was more than an economic opportunity; it embodied an ideal to be protected at any cost.

In his prime, Baker was a tall, imposing man. He spoke little, but with authority, and he expected to be heard. As a young man he cultivated an 'aristocratic' accent that tended to obscure his colonial origins and his parents' background in London trade; he wore a monocle, though for show rather than from necessity. In later years he was often described in the press as an English sporting gentleman, an image that he did little to dispel. Although he could be a good conversationalist, and would carry on a discussion at an anecdotal level, he was always reticent in speaking of himself or his own affairs. He was not a demonstrative man, and would not discuss his feelings with others, even when Florence died of cancer in 1934. When he died in 1941 at the age of eighty-four none of those who had handled his affairs, not even Florence's nephew, who had worked for Baker for twenty years and lived in his household for much of that time, could supply Baker's birth date, or even year of birth, for his grave. In personal affairs, Charles Alma Baker was an intensely private man, but in business he was aggressive, opportunistic and determined to be in control.

Baker was generous with his wealth, paying for trips for Whitaker and Baker relatives, and granting small pensions to a number of family members who had limited means. When he died, he left a considerable surplus of assets over debts, but very little cash. Despite the implications, he had been a patriot to the end, seriously affecting his estate with gifts totalling £30,000 to the RAF for the war effort. By this time, his major assets were two rubber plantations in Malaya and the two farms in New Zealand. Te Karaka was left conditionally to Eric Baker, and the rest of the estate was heavily encumbered. Although generous in remembering relatives, friends and long-serving employees, Baker's major concern in his later years, and in his will, was to provide for his daughter, Judy, who had a slight intellectual impairment and had been widowed for a decade after a brief and difficult marriage. There is no mention in Baker's will of his son, just as there is no evidence of any contact between the two during his life; indeed, it is not clear whether Baker even knew that his son had been born in 1889.

Baker drew a clear distinction between his private and public lives, remaining reticent about the one and, although not necessarily motivated by the desire for publicity with the other, accepted this when it came and even sought it on occasion. Letters of appreciation for his fund-raising from imperial leaders, for example, quickly found their way into the press, and in later years he regularly signed himself 'C. Alma Baker, C.B.E.'. To assist in securing resources from governments, donations for public causes, or buying stock for his farms, Baker cultivated the acquaintance of powerful members of the establishment. Nor was he averse to modest personal monuments: his published *Souvenir* of the battle plane fund published after the First World War was a tribute to the generosity of donors, but also gave incidental prominence to Baker's role. In the Second World War, his donation of six aircraft to the RAF was made publicly, *pour encourager les autres*, but he also asked that the planes carry his own name. Only he knew that the gift, made just months before the death he expected, would effectively cripple his estate in the short term.

Baker made four separate wills – one each for his properties in Australia, Malaya, New Zealand and Britain, with the executors for the last having ultimate control. For thirty-five years, the estate was managed largely for Judy's benefit; by 1976, when she died, other assets had been realised, leaving only Limestone Downs, by this time a major sheep and cattle station, under the control of trustees – Norman Boyes, son of Baker's London solicitor, his son Robin, and Enid (Poo) Harington, Baker's former secretary.

In his will, Baker had envisaged that, when Judy died, Limestone Downs would be sold and the proceeds distributed (mostly for agricultural research or to charity), but his executors sought approval through the courts to retain the property and apply the income to charitable purposes in the spirit of Baker's will, and with a particular emphasis on agricultural research and education. From its original inaccessible, bush-covered state, Limestone Downs had been transformed over the years into some 6,920 acres of farm land and a 1,035-acre bush reserve. The swamps had been cleared, drained and fenced to provide a prime area for the fattening of beef. From 1981 most of the assets of Baker's estate were transferred to a new charitable trust that was based in England but focused on Limestone Downs. Farm management was placed in the hands of a New Zealand-based committee, which appointed a farm supervisor from Massey University.

To that time, Limestone Downs had been managed along conventional lines for a station property on the North Island hill country. It carried some 12,000 sheep and 1,200 cattle. Under the new regime, there was a radical change in policy with the adoption of intensive farming methods and their adaptation for a large-scale operation. Over the next decade, the property was transformed. Limestone Downs was subdivided, using electric fencing, into small paddocks, a water reticulation scheme was installed and a strict system of rotational grazing introduced. New stock purchasing and breeding programmes were adopted, and stock culled on the basis of performance that was systematically measured and recorded. In little more than a decade, the value of the property was increased by 73 per cent, the carrying capacity by more than 50 per cent and its net earnings increased by $465,000 a year in 1992 terms. Limestone Downs has become a talking point in the district and a model for the development of similar properties.

As its sub-title suggests, this book has two major components: a biography of Charles Alma Baker, and a history of Limestone Downs. The two overlap most strongly in the period from 1926, when Baker purchased the farm, until his death in 1941, but the links are maintained through to the present with ownership of Limestone Downs being vested in the C. Alma Baker Trust and its surpluses being used for agricultural research and education.

Baker himself had neither the power of a politician nor the fame of a movie star, but he knew politicians and movie stars and he used both to further his business interests and to promote his ideals. Above all, Baker was dedicated to the imperial cause, working on the colonial frontier in New Zealand and embarking on new ventures in Malaya. His writings on agriculture were driven very largely by a belief that the empire's future was at stake. This same theme runs through ventures that brought him wealth and those that he knew would cost him money. The philosophies and colonial systems that supported Baker's activities are no longer fashionable or politically correct. He grew rich as a colonial entrepreneur simply because he was the product of his age; he represents a type of colonial settler who can be found in most frontier societies in the late nineteenth and early twentieth centuries, and who was at the forefront of the introduction of a western capitalist economy, and profited from it. But Baker was more than this. Although he was an international investor, his life also reflected the local histories of the areas where he lived and worked, and his investments had a significant effect on their economic development. He was one of the early promoters of fishing as part of the New Zealand tourist industry and a public benefactor of some note. And Baker was fascinated by agricultural research and food production, and by their links to human health and prosperity and the future of the empire.

The major events in the life of Charles Alma Baker can be readily established and are easily recorded, but motives and meanings are more difficult to determine. Baker left no diaries, and no personal correspondence has been found either in his own papers or those of his correspondents. There are fragmentary references, but that is all, and this absence stands in marked contrast to his business life, where a wealth of instructions, policies, reports and accounts gives a good insight into concerns and priorities. There are also copies of correspondence with governments to be found in official archives, and recorded reminiscences from those who knew him in his later years. A series of wills and instructions dating from the 1920s and 1930s are of some help, but there is little more. On matters of business, Baker is clear and articulate; on personal matters, he is silent.

To a significant extent, then, the picture of Baker presented here is based heavily on the interpretation of actions, public and private, and on business and official papers, rather than on Baker's own recorded thoughts and feelings. But the process of reconstruction has not been as haphazard as it might seem, partly because of the quantity of business and official papers, and partly because of the nature of the life itself. Baker's career falls into clearly marked phases, each characterised by an interest or enthusiasm that absorbed much of his time, money and energy. Each new phase provides additional insights into personality and reveals new facets of character; each phase thus advances the biographical story in a chronological sense while throwing an illuminating beam of light on the life as a whole.

BORN IN OTAGO

When Charles Alma Baker was born on 6 January 1857, he was the fifth child and third son of a family that, from modest origins, was beginning to prosper in colonial Otago. Andrew and Matilda Baker were recent immigrants to Dunedin, having arrived in 1853. They showed little interest in pursuing the dream of rural independence that drove so many early New Zealanders but remained urban-based, first in Dunedin, then in Oamaru. Despite the potential disadvantages of being English among Scots, and Anglican among Presbyterians, the Bakers were to prosper. Both Andrew and Matilda worked hard to establish their own businesses and were then prepared to invest in new ventures; once secure, they began to speculate in land. The household in which young Charles was raised was comfortable without being opulent. The family enjoyed and extended connections that linked it to both land and commerce in a way which helped its members to find marriage partners and employment reflecting the social fluidity and economic opportunities of frontier towns in the young colony.

Although incomplete, and sometimes contradictory, the fragmentary records available on the family's early history in New Zealand tell a story of thrift, hard work and remarkable good fortune. Andrew Baker was born in Salisbury, Wiltshire, in 1821 but by the time of his marriage to Matilda Headland in 1840 he was living in London. The birth of their daughters Elizabeth Christiana (1840) and Matilda Catherine (1843) at Islington and Clerkenwell respectively, suggest that the young couple (both were nineteen at the time of their marriage) remained close to the area of Matilda's Cockney upbringing. William Andrew, their first son, was born in May 1852, less than a year before the family sailed for Dunedin.[1]

The Bakers sailed on the *Maori*, a vessel of about 800 tons that had been built just two years before. Already she had a reputation for being a slow sailer, generally taking about 120 days between England and New Zealand, but on the 1853 voyage, to the relief of her passengers, she took just 93 days 'land to land'. The voyage had seen the usual seasickness, and passenger complaints over food and service but, even so, most of the new settlers signed a testimonial to the captain assuring him of the 'pleasant sensations' with which they would remember the voyage. Most of the 105 passengers left the ship at Nelson, but the Bakers

The sailing ship *Maori*. Artist unknown. ALEXANDER TURNBULL LIBRARY

stayed on board to Dunedin where the ship was to deliver her main cargo carried on behalf of Captain William Cargill, the New Zealand Company's agent in Otago and leader of the fledgling community.[2] Andrew and Matilda Baker arrived in Port Chalmers on 19 August, together with their three children and Matilda's sister, Amelia.[3]

On the *Maori*, the Bakers travelled 'intermediate' class (between 'passengers' and 'steerage'), which suggests at least modest savings. Within a few months they were able to pay £30 (albeit with the assistance of a mortgage) for their 10-acre 'suburban' block outside the town in the area then known as the 'Upper Harbour – West Side', and now part of the suburb of Ravensbourne.[4] Then, it was a doubtful investment. The land was steep and not particularly fertile, it missed the sun, and was exposed to biting southerly winds; and it was accessible only by a rough bush track over the hills from Dunedin or by boat from the harbour. The land was cheap, but experience soon showed that it was not cheap enough. Andrew Baker was the second to purchase land in the area, but there were no other takers until the price was dropped from £3 to 10s an acre, at which point Andrew Baker bought four adjoining blocks to give him a total holding of about 50 acres.[5] At this price the land sold well, and by 1856 a number of houses were under construction, including 'a substantial three-roomed' dwelling for Andrew and Matilda Baker.

News of the outbreak of the Crimean War had first reached New Zealand late in 1854. The Battle of Alma, where British and French troops defeated the Russian Army, and the ensuing siege of Sevastopol, were given prominent coverage in the newspapers, prompting the New Zealand colonial citizenry, still close to 'Home' though on the other side of the world, to respond with their usual patriotic fervour. Within a short time there were at least two Mount Almas, an Alma River and numerous 'Sebastabol' Streets in honour of the victory. Not to be left out, Andrew and Matilda Baker called their new home Alma Cottage and, a few months later called their next child, the first to be born in the cottage, Charles Alma Baker. Even at that time, this was an unusual choice because then, as now, the name Alma was more commonly bestowed on girls than boys. Charles faced few difficulties on that score, however, because by the time he was a young man, if not before, he was 'Barney' to his friends and, with a subtle shift, set himself aside from other Bakers by combining 'Alma Baker' as though it were a surname.

After buying the land on the harbour, there was still enough capital left over for Andrew to set up as a storekeeper while Matilda made good use of her training as a milliner and haberdasher. Both seem to have been self-employed from the outset, which again suggests capital, and were well placed to join in the growing prosperity of Dunedin and its pastoral hinterland. By early in 1854 Matilda was advertising goods for sale to the 'Ladies of Dunedin' from rented premises in Princes Street and, by the time that another son, Alfred, was born in June 1855, she was employing an apprentice to help with the business.[6] Dunedin prospered in the 1850s with the rapid growth of sheep farming throughout the province together with cropping for the Australian and domestic markets. As the settlement neared the end of its first decade, it lost some of its pioneering character and its leading citizens were anxious to keep up with the fashions of Home. As well as supplying fabrics, ribbons, lace and ready-made hats, caps and bridal bonnets, Matilda Baker expanded into dressmaking and the 'straw bonnet business'.[7]

Andrew Baker's business also grew. Soon after the family moved into Alma Cottage, he became a carter as well as a storekeeper. The rapid growth of the settlement in the 1850s, and the expansion of trade as the region developed, meant lucrative trans-shipment opportunities for harbour lighters and road transport between Port Chalmers and Dunedin.[8] As well as ploughing profits back into business expansion, the Bakers were able to invest in other areas. By 1859, most of their land on the harbour had been cleared, a set of stockyards built and a jetty suitable for use at all tides constructed to take advantage of the harbour steamers that had recently begun to operate. By that time, too, Andrew Baker also owned two town sections in a prime location between Royal Terrace and Queens Drive in the suburb of Maori Hill. They had cost £13 each, which was expensive for the time, but they were well placed, with a view of the green belt on one side and the harbour in the distance on the other.

These were all relatively minor investments, however, compared with the new Princes Street premises, near the heart of the central business district, into which the family moved early in 1859. The Bakers now owned a 'new and substantially built' seven-roomed house with stabling for two horses and, at the front of the house, accommodation for Matilda's thriving millinery business.[9] From modest beginnings this all represented a substantial achievement. Neither Andrew nor Matilda Baker were yet forty, they had two daughters, nearly grown up, and three young sons. They had prospered and, although not part of the wealthy elite, they had, in a very real sense, 'arrived' as colonial townsfolk, after a journey from 'London trade'. Rather than consolidating their position, however, Andrew and

Princes Street, Dunedin, about 1860. *CYCLOPEDIA OF NEW ZEALAND*

Matilda Baker chose to move on, to take up a new pioneering challenge.

In June 1860, 'Mrs. Baker, being about to leave Dunedin', advertised a cost-price sale of all her stock, including 'the newly-arrived Assortment' of coloured and bridal bonnets, white and black dress caps, half caps and head dresses, artificial flowers, silk laces, ribbons, velvets, chenille, '&c. &c. &c. &c.' that had just arrived on the *Clontarf* and the *Elizabeth*. She also wished to sell several articles of household furniture. The same newspaper carried advertisements for the sale of the Princes Street property, the two town sections and the harbour land, including Alma Cottage, which had been leased since the family had moved to town in the previous year. This latter site, with its quarter-mile of water frontage, and with jetty access that brought it within thirty minutes of the town by harbour steamer, was urged upon buyers as being 'well adapted for the erection of a superior class of Villa Residences'.[10]

At a land auction in May 1859, Andrew Baker had bought three town sections at Oamaru, then a new settlement on the coast about 80 miles north of Dunedin. Although access from Dunedin was made difficult by the need to cross the Kakanui Mountains, it was already evident that Oamaru was destined to become the main commercial centre of North Otago. The district's identity was shaped by mountains to the south and west, the ocean to the east and, in the north, the swiftly flowing Waitaki River that formed Otago's northern boundary with the Canterbury province. The area had been part of the Crown's huge Ngai Tahu purchase (for token payment only) of 1848, and by the early 1850s the first runholders had established their flocks on leaseholds that covered much of the natural grasslands of the North Otago plains. For example, in 1857 W.G. and R.A. Filleul had added the Oamaru run to their Papakaio holdings, giving them total leaseholds covering some 75,000 acres on which they grazed more than 20,000 sheep. Farming on this scale did not last, however, as the 'proclamation of hundreds', which forced leaseholders to purchase the freehold or make way for those who could, brought an era of closer settlement and opened the way for the development of Oamaru.

When the Bakers arrived in Oamaru the township amounted to no more than a score of buildings – about half were dwellings and the remainder commercial premises of one sort or another – straggling away from the harbour. There were a couple of stores, stables and a number of tradesmen including a butcher, a baker, a carpenter, a bootmaker and a blacksmith.[11] Access to the new settlement was either by sea (though landing could be hazardous when a south-easterly was blowing) or by horseback. For those seeking somewhere to stay there was a rough 'accommodation house'; for those with a thirst there was a choice, albeit a difficult one: 'either to consume the watered-down whisky or "highland dew" distilled by one Donald McLean in Test Street, or to sample the "fermented mixture of bilgewater, cabbage tree juice and boiled matagouri roots" concocted by the Maoris who manned the landing facilities at the fledgling port'.[12]

A month after the sale of his Dunedin properties in July 1860, Andrew Baker was supervising the construction of the Northern Hotel at Oamaru. A two-storey building of baltic pine on the corner of Tyne and Wansbeck Streets, it stood on a site leased from the Filleul brothers, and immediately adjacent to his own land. Baker's Northern Hotel was the first licensed premises in Oamaru and, being located closer to the port landing than its later rivals, was well placed from a business point of view.

Within a year, two competing hotels (the Star and Garter and the Oamaru) had been established but the Northern still had the best location; it was closest to the harbour and stood on Wansbeck Street, the main road into the town from Dunedin. The Northern also offered superior accommodation and meals compared with its rivals and so won the continuing patronage of the wealthy runholders. The Northern boasted a billiard room that was 'second to none in the Province – provided with one of Thurston's best tables, and … under the management of an efficient marker', 'Saddle Horses, Buggies, Dogcarts, and Gigs' were available for hire and, when Cobb & Co. started to run coaches between Dunedin and Oamaru (arriving late in the evening and leaving early in the morning), there was more business for the Northern, which served as the Oamaru terminus and offered 'HOT COFFEE and other refreshments for passengers leaving by the early coach'.[13]

From the outset, the Northern could make good its claim to be 'the leading hostelry' in Oamaru. In common with the rest of the town, it also did extremely well out of a small gold rush to the Lindis Gorge, about 100 miles north-west of Oamaru, in 1861. Although, in the words of one historian, 'nobody found more than they might have earned', there were still rich profits for the Oamaru businesses as the prospectors bought stores, and drank and gambled on their way to the diggings. Two months later the district also benefited indirectly from the major gold discoveries in Central Otago as miners arrived in their thousands, the pastoralists enjoyed a premium market for their stock and the province

Andrew Baker, probably 1860s. Artist unknown.
OTAGO EARLY SETTLERS' MUSEUM

boomed under the impact of its new-found wealth.[14]

There were many signs of the Bakers' growing prosperity and of the centrality of the Northern Hotel to the development of Oamaru. As well as being the informal gathering place for merchants of the town and the district's runholders, the Northern was the venue for the annual dinner of the local Agricultural and Pastoral Association, and for the early meetings of the Oamaru Town Board where the members found 'a comfortable room, a bright fire burning in the grate, [and] the whisky was as a rule fairly good'.[15]

While the district's leading figures enjoyed their home comforts in the parlour, most of the local populace might well be enjoying the public entertainment in the Northern's 'Assembly Room' – a large corrugated iron annexe on the southern side of the hotel that could seat 200 people. Built in 1863, because the existing public room at the Oamaru Hotel had become associated with 'the rather noisy revelry of shearers and bullock-drivers on their visits to town', Baker's Assembly Room quickly found favour for public meetings, and for local concerts, but it really came into its own and attracted large crowds when itinerant entertainers visited the town. In just a few months in late 1864 and early 1865, for example, a wide range of attractions was offered: 'Mr Ryan, The Popular Comedian and Author', gave his 'much-admired and truthful rendering of Dickens' Christmas Carol, improved,

Matilda Baker, probably 1860s. Artist unknown.
OTAGO EARLY SETTLERS' MUSEUM

revised, and interspersed with appropriate Music'; Mrs Chas. Fanshawe Evereste delivered her 'highly popular and amusing lectures on '"FLIRTATION," ITS EVILS AND REMEDY' and 'LOVE, COMIC AND SENTIMENTAL'; and patrons paid 5s for reserves, 3s for back seats (children half-price) for the 'GRAND MOVING DIORAMA OF BURKE AND WILLS'S EXPLORING EXPEDITION', which occupied no less than 2,500 feet of canvas that was trundled between a pair of revolving drums for the entertainment of the audience.[16]

Although Andrew Baker was undoubtedly a successful and respected local businessman, and took his turn with the other hoteliers in organising sports meetings on public holidays, he participated in few other public activities. The Bakers seem to have steered clear of local community organisations and they appear in the local newspapers only as hotel proprietors. Of Matilda Baker's life in these years, we know virtually nothing except that two more children were born to the family in Oamaru – Walter Headland (known as Valentine) in January 1862, and Herbert James in July 1864. But the business did well, and by 1866 Andrew Baker was in a position to sell the Northern's hotel licence and to retire, at the age of forty-five and still with young children, to a small farmlet on the northern outskirts of Oamaru. Since his arrival in the town, Andrew Baker had invested steadily in urban property, competing with gold-rich investors; at a single sale in 1863, he had bought no fewer than seven town sections.[17] Apart from a brief venture running 'Express' cabs in 1869, he does not appear to have worked subsequently, though his town sections were gradually sold. In the list of freeholders for 1882 he is shown as still owning land to a value of £6,400, sufficient to generate a substantial income. Being of independent means and 12,000 miles from England, Andrew Baker was now described in the directories of the period as a gentleman.

Andrew and Matilda Baker had prospered in their new country. Such success in the bush or on the urban frontier was not uncommon, and the wider links built by the family over the first decade or so of their residence in New Zealand contributed to the world in which Charles Alma Baker spent his formative years and emphasised the fluidity of social organisation in colonial New Zealand.

It had been more than a shrewd eye for an opportunity that had attracted the Bakers to Oamaru. When the couple and their family arrived on the *Maori* in 1853, they were accompanied by Amelia Headland, Matilda's sister. In January 1854, just five months after reaching Otago, Amelia had married Edward Bland Atkinson who, having come out on the *John Wickliffe* in 1848, had been one of Dunedin's founding settlers. It is possible that he was a distant relation, because Amelia's mother had been born an Atkinson, in which case the marriage may have been anticipated or even arranged before the voyage to New Zealand. After spending a year in charge of the New Zealand Company's stores, and securing a place in local history as the first man to undertake ploughing in the province, Atkinson had acquired interests in the emerging pastoral industry. In 1854 he bought the leasehold of the Clifton Falls run of some 14,000 acres about 12 miles north-west of Oamaru township. Sheep numbers on the property increased rapidly to reach 20,000 by 1864.[18] It seems reasonable to suppose that the Bakers were made aware of the potential of North Otago development by the Atkinsons and a factor in their decision would have been the prospect of bringing the sisters, who evidently were close, near enough for regular contact. It also allowed the Bakers to consolidate through family ties their business relationship with the land-owning elite of the district.

One of Atkinson's employees at Clifton Falls in the late 1850s was Alfred Headland, brother of Amelia and Matilda. Headland, a printer's assistant in London before emigrating from England on the *Agra* in 1858, also worked for the Filleul brothers on the Papakaio run, in the north-east of the province. He was described by a fellow worker at Papakaio as 'a regular cockney, desperate as regards his "h's," knew nothing whatever about sheep or dogs, but like many others soon learned enough to be of service as a boundary-shepherd'.[19] The comment helps to establish the social background for the Headlands, and for the Bakers, but it also demonstrates the potential for social mobility in colonial society because Headland, too, made the most of his opportunities in Otago.

After living for some time with his wife and children in a sod hut on a remote part of Papakaio, and then a spell at Clifton Falls working for Atkinson, Headland moved to Oamaru. Like Andrew Baker, he bought land at the first Oamaru sale of May 1859. Before establishing his own grocery and ironmongery store, he worked for the much larger firm of Traill & Roxby, located across the road from the Northern Hotel. Like Headland, Traill

The Northern Hotel, Oamaru, about 1873. The building to the left is the 'Assembly Room' used for public entertainment. NORTH OTAGO MUSEUM, OAMARU

had worked on Papakaio, and he struggled to establish Oamaru's first store until he joined with Roxby, a recent immigrant whose capital and connections allowed the business to import directly from England. According to one of Oamaru's early historians, Eustace Wriothesley Roxby 'was a gentleman by birth, education and manners'; in August 1861 Roxby and young Matilda Baker, then aged eighteen, were married. In the following year Elizabeth, the elder of the Bakers' daughters, married James Wilson, a prominent Dunedin businessman who owned the Wellpark Brewery on the Water of Leith. In 1869 he bought from Andrew Baker the leasehold of the land on which the Northern Hotel stood. The women of the family had all married 'well' and probably 'up' in colonial society, establishing links to both commerce and the land.

The Baker sons had rather more varied fortunes. Of William, the eldest, we know nothing except that, as a lad of eleven, he nearly drowned while swimming in the Oamaru Creek. He was saved by a passing youth who 'heroically rushed to the rescue', and was later rewarded with 'a handsome gold chain' presented to him by Andrew and Matilda.[20] By the turn of the century, if not before, the family had no knowledge of William's whereabouts. Alfred was the only one of the five sons to remain in Oamaru. He had a variety of occupations over the years, among them carter, tea dealer, grocer's assistant, storekeeper and hawker. He was the subject of a bankruptcy petition in 1881, but paid his debts before being declared insolvent. Walter (Valentine) joined the British Army, rose to the rank of major, and eventually retired to Birmingham on a small pension. Herbert, the youngest son, moved to the North Island where he worked for New Zealand Railways for many years before buying Te Karaka, a bush-clad farm near Port Waikato which he developed with the assistance of Eric, his only son. Matilda and Andrew Baker lived out their lives in Oamaru; he died in 1885, she in 1900.[21]

We know very little about the childhood of Charles Alma Baker. He was one of the early pupils at the Oamaru District School where, although not a star pupil, he did win a general prize at the age of eight, and a reading prize three years later. From school he moved to Dunedin where he worked as a surveying cadet with the real estate firm of Connell & Moodie, a career choice which, by implication, reveals something of the family's circumstances.

In the late nineteenth century the surveyor was regarded as a professional gentleman, and often mixed with the cream of colonial society.[22] To become an 'authorised surveyor' he first had to spend time as a cadet, working for at least two or three years under the direction of an established surveyor, learning the laws, regulations and procedures, as well as meeting a high standard in mathematics. The requirements of the training demanded a relatively high level of education, and of social standing, by colonial standards. Contemporary accounts also show that the cadet was a gentleman-in-training, as well as a surveyor. Usually, he was not paid for his services, but had to pay a fee of as much as £100 for his tuition, and to find all his own equipment as well. But because of his social and professional status the cadet would usually avoid the less pleasant chores; hired labourers were expected to carry the heavy equipment and to clear the survey lines. The cadets would also have their own tent, separate from both the surveyor and the labourers. Having completed his training, Baker became an authorised surveyor in July 1881.

Despite the lack of information about Charles Alma Baker's early life, a number of significant features about the environment in which he grew up are important to understanding his subsequent career. First, his parents presumably migrated in search of a better world which, through hard work and good fortune, they achieved. They were pioneers, not only in Dunedin, but again in Oamaru, and they profited from being pioneers and risk-takers. Second, Charles Alma Baker was just three years old when the family moved to the Northern; his earliest memories would therefore be of a small, rough frontier town with unformed roads, crude buildings and few services. By the late 1860s, the population of Oamaru was only about 1,500, with twice that number in the surrounding district. By colonial standards, the Northern Hotel offered a degree of comfort, and perhaps even gracious living, that relatively few homes could match. Third, through his Atkinson and Roxby relations, and at the hotel, he became accustomed to dealing with those who were by birth his social superiors, and subsequent evidence suggests that he soon adopted their manners, attitudes and customs. And throughout his life, after a childhood at the Northern with 'one of Thurston's best tables', he was to retain an enthusiasm, bordering on passion, for a fine billiard table and the enjoyment that it could offer. As soon as he had secured his professional qualifications, Barney Baker left Otago and, so far as can be ascertained, never returned, even for a visit. His departure for Auckland at the age of twenty-four has all the marks of a young man going off to seek his fortune.

CHAPTER 2

THE HANDSOME CAB

In the early 1880s, Auckland offered many attractions for a young man with ambition, a pioneering spirit and shrewd commercial instincts. As the new colony's administrative capital from 1841 to 1865, Auckland flourished on government spending, but even more important to the town's prosperity was the growth of a range of extractive industries in a hinterland that spread up the North Auckland peninsula, reached down the western side of the island through the Waikato Basin to Taranaki and then spread across to the East Coast through the Matamata Plains and the Bay of Plenty. Much of the land in this region had been acquired from its Maori owners by European speculators – some was bought or leased, some confiscated by the government after the wars of the 1860s – and extensive areas had to be surveyed before title could be given or the land could be sold.

From the 1860s, especially, commerce in Auckland was dominated by a 'limited circle' of businessmen led by Thomas Russell who, in many of his business dealings, was closely associated with his legal partner, Frederick Whitaker. More noted for his entrepreneurial flair than his legal caution, Russell was instrumental in forming the Bank of New Zealand and, soon to rival it in size, the New Zealand Loan and Mercantile Agency Company. These organisations he enmeshed in the affairs of innumerable companies and syndicates; only later did investors discovered that many of these ventures, most of which were concerned with land speculation in one form or another, rested on dubious financial and legal foundations.[1]

Whitaker, the senior member of the partnership in law but the junior in business matters, was also English born. The son of a deputy-lieutenant of Oxfordshire, he had studied law, but migrated to New Zealand when the family suffered a financial reversal and had to mortgage Bampton, the family seat. Whitaker served as a member of the Auckland Provincial Council in the 1850s and, in central government, in either the Legislative Council or House of Representatives, for most of the period from 1853 until his death in 1891. He served often as a Cabinet minister and had two brief terms as Premier. As a politician he was, according to one biographer, 'pertinacious, intelligent and extremely hard-working; he found it easy to dominate more indolent and less single-minded men'.[2]

Both Russell and Whitaker used political power for personal ends, their policies generally reflecting the interests of Auckland business. When Whitaker was Premier in 1863-64, for example, the colonial government waged war against the Waikato tribes in a conflict that was essentially over the Maori challenge to European dominance and, more specifically, resistance to the encroachment of white settlers on Maori land. Victorious, the government embarked on a policy of land confiscation. The original intention had been to secure peace through the acquisition of 'rebel' land for military settlements and, at the same time, to punish the various Maori tribes through confiscation to the extent of their 'guilt'. Whitaker and the Auckland merchants who dominated his ministry were, however, more concerned to confiscate for the profit of European capitalists, and turned the policy to the advantage of their own kind.[3]

There were opportunities for investors and speculators in the acquisition of military allotments from settlers who had no desire to take them up, and in the leasing and purchase of land direct from its Maori owners. But the chance for the richest pickings of all lay in the apparent willingness of the new Vogel government to pass confiscated lands on to its friends at little more than nominal values. In 1873 a syndicate headed by Russell, and including Whitaker among its members, acquired the 80,000-acre Piako Swamp in the Waikato Basin and passed it on to the Waikato Land Association of which they were both directors. Russell, in partnership with John Studholme, also controlled the more remote 90,360-acre Te Akau Run that occupied the 30 miles of coastal land between Port Waikato and Raglan Harbour.

After a brief downturn in the colonial economy in the late 1870s, Auckland, which was experiencing rapid population growth, embarked on a boom period with capital flowing in from Britain to finance urban housing, commercial buildings and the development of the speculators' large landholdings in South Auckland and the Waikato. The clarification of title, subdivision, roading and the laying out of the new townships all created a demand for surveyors, forcing the government to hire contractors to supplement the staff of the Surveyor-General. The rewards were greatest for those with a pioneering spirit who were prepared to spend months on end in the bush, and to face the prospect that survey parties might be harassed or attacked by Maori who saw them as symbols of an oppressive government intent on land seizure.

This was the world that Barney Baker entered when he moved north in August or September 1881. For the next three years he worked as a bush surveyor across the southern part of the Auckland Province. His first few jobs were relatively small – some were on the south-eastern fringes of Auckland and included, for example, the definition of school reserves near Waiuku and Patumahoe for the Board of Education. Within a few months, however, his contracts reached southwards into the Waikato, leading to a series of plans from the northern end of Lake Waikare on the fringes of the Piako Swamp. He then became heavily engaged in surveys in the eastern Bay of Plenty, working along the coast from Opotiki to Cape Runaway and reaching inland to the foothills of the Raukumara Range and the tributary streams of the Motu River. Most of his work was in remote hill country where the terrain was difficult and the heavy bush cover made for laborious work clearing trees for the survey lines.[4] Access to the Bay of Plenty from Auckland was generally

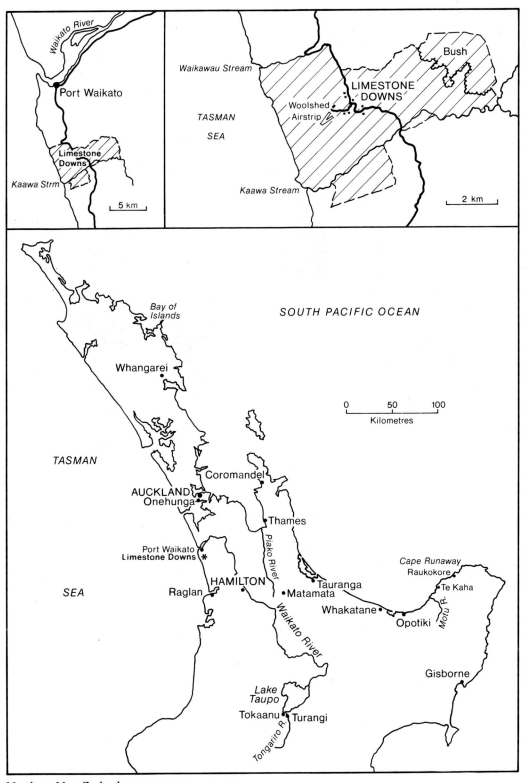

Northern New Zealand

Surveyors' bush camp, 1890s. TYREE COLLECTION, ALEXANDER TURNBULL LIBRARY

by coastal steamer, but reaching the port nearest to the survey area was the least of the surveyor's difficulties. Each job represented a major undertaking that might keep him out in a camp for weeks or months on end. He therefore needed horses for himself and his gang, and to pack equipment and stores into the survey area.[5]

From the fragmentary evidence provided by Baker's surviving field books, it seems that he organised his business like most of his contemporaries although he did not, apparently, train any cadets. So his party, depending on the job, might include up to half a dozen men – a chain-man employed on a regular basis, and a cook who was also responsible for making and moving camp and packing in the supplies. Some surveys might permit the establishment of a base camp which would be used for several weeks but, given that many of the surveys were of blocks of several thousand acres, regular movement of the camp was inevitable. The labourers, whose major task was to clear the bush from the survey lines, would usually be recruited locally; many were Maori.

It was in these years that Charles Alma Baker earned the sobriquet of 'the handsome CAB' among his contemporaries in Auckland. He was also admitted into the social set dominated by the 'limited circle' of Auckland businessmen and their families, perhaps through his friendship with surveyor Arthur Harington. By this time Russell was living in England, but Whitaker was still prominent in Auckland's legal and business world and in 1884 he had been knighted after serving as Premier for a few months in 1882-83. At a

'The Handsome CAB'. Charles Alma Baker in Auckland, 1886. MRS ALMA CURTIN

'fashionable wedding' in August 1884, Charles Alma Baker married Florence Isabel, the youngest daughter of Sir Frederick Whitaker.

According to the press reports, 'St Paul's Cathedral was thronged with eager spectators' long before the appointed hour. 'The bride looked charming in a gown of white satin, profusely trimmed with rich old lace and sprays of orange blossoms, with wreath to match and Tulle veil' and was accompanied by four bridesmaids – her sister, Emily; her niece, Augusta Minnett; Eva, daughter of the Hon. Henry Chamberlain; and Lilian, daughter of Mr J. Lawford, Manager of the Bank of Australasia. The ceremony was 'most impressively' performed by the Right Reverend Bishop Cowie, assisted by the Reverend C.M. Nelson, the incumbent of St Pauls. Among the guests were many members of the Whitaker and Shepherd families (the latter being the relatives of Lady Whitaker) as well as numerous Whitaker friends and business acquaintances. Alfred Whitaker, brother of the bride, was Baker's best man. No relatives of the groom are mentioned. The newly married couple, Barney and Floss as they were known to friends and family, spent their honeymoon at Whitaker's country residence near Lake Takapuna (now Lake Pupuke) on Auckland's North Shore.[6]

The suggestion from the reports of the wedding that Baker had married a family and not merely a bride is borne out by the little we know of the next few years. The newly-weds did not establish their own household but, until 1890, lived at either the town or country

Florence Baker, 1916. MRS ALMA CURTIN

residences of Sir Frederick Whitaker. At the latter, according to the *Observer* which made a habit of mocking the lifestyle of the business community, they could enjoy the '*rus in urbe*' and the other privileges of the leisured classes 'and also the delicious plums, peaches and nectarines of that favoured locality'.[7]

There is no record of Baker undertaking any survey work over the next two years. It is to be assumed, then, that he either took some other employment in the city, worked as an agent for one of the many Whitaker business enterprises or lived a life of leisure. His later boast that he had never in his life worked for anyone else except as a self-employed contractor, suggests that he remained within, and worked for, the Whitaker family as its fortunes changed. As it turned out, the wedding of Barney and Floss was one of the last symbols of a Whitaker lifestyle that was crumbling from 1885, as depression reached into the world of Auckland business and exposed the follies of the speculative ventures of the previous fifteen years. According to Russell Stone, the historian of the Auckland business community, Whitaker, together with Russell and others, 'could no longer meet the crushing interest burden of indebtedness from past speculations …. [and] Their financial distress was kept quiet by the deeding over of properties and other securities to mortgagees, assignees and creditors'.[8]

In 1886 prices for both rural and urban land slumped even further and by the time Russell arrived on a visit from London in April 1887, it was clear that little could be salvaged. Frederick Whitaker, son of Sir Frederick, land-buying agent for Russell, speculator on his own account and, like his father, a former Member of Parliament, shot himself while depressed over the hopelessness of his financial position.[9]

The following year, land prices fell even further. In December 1888, as the final symbol of his business failure, Whitaker was forced to put up for sale his Takapuna country house – 'That magnificent property … containing 23 acres of choice land, laid out in gardens, orchards and paddocks, together with the 7-roomed residence thereon'. It was, said the auctioneers, 'admirably situated commanding Magnificent Views of Lake, Sea and Auckland Harbour and well adapted for Villa residences', but even so, it attracted a top bid of only £1,250 and was subsequently sold by private sale.[10] Rumours circulating in Auckland suggested that Whitaker owed at least £42,000 at the end of the decade.[11]

By that time Baker had returned to his surveying. Even before Russell had brought his message of doom in April 1887, Baker was back in the Bay of Plenty surveying on the Coromandel Peninsula and in an area south of Opotiki near the Waioeka River; he spent Christmas Day surveying in the vicinity of Mount Puketaru.[12]

The volume of work completed by Baker suggests that he spent most of the time between February 1887 and November 1888 in the Opotiki area while Florence remained with her family in Auckland. During this period, or perhaps before, Baker formed a liaison with Maria Nikora, a high-born member of the Ngati Rua hapu of the Whakatohea tribe with connections to marae at both Omarumutu (near Opotiki) and Raukokore (towards Cape Runaway). Accounts from Maria's family suggest that this was not a casual affair but a sustained relationship which led to Maria becoming pregnant in about August 1888. Shortly afterwards, Maria went, or was sent, to her mother's people in Hawke's Bay. A son, given the name of Pita Heretaunga Baker by his mother, was born in May 1889 at Waiohiki, a Maori settlement some 6 miles from Napier. Baker himself left the Opotiki district late in 1888. It is not known whether he subsequently found out about the birth of his son, or even if he was aware of the pregnancy, although the family memory of Maria's people does suggest that he left under a cloud. He completed no further surveys around Opotiki.

Pita Baker was raised by his mother and later cared for by his step-brother, Maria's elder son by some eighteen years, Hamiora Hei. 'Sam' Hei was the first Maori to practise law in New Zealand and it was he, as guardian, who sent Pita to Te Aute College, which he had himself attended. Pita excelled at rugby and cricket but also came under the sway of the long-serving principal, John Thornton, who had a major influence on a generation of Maori leaders, including Sir Apirana Ngata and Te Rangi Hiroa (Sir Peter Buck). After leaving school Pita was employed as a shepherd by Hei, who owned a 4,000-acre farm near Te Kaha in the eastern Bay of Plenty.[13]

Throughout 1889, Baker continued surveying, but in the Kennedy Bay area, near Coromandel, and on the fringes of the Te Akau Block north-west of Raglan. By March, the last of his surveys had been completed and the plans submitted for payment; uncharacteristically for Baker, and probably as a result of haste, two of his last three plans were returned for corrections before he was paid.[14]

The haste is easily enough explained, because Barney and Floss were planning to emigrate; less clear is the reason for their departure. It is not certain whether Baker knew of his son's birth, or whether this may have been a factor in the decision. And, despite the sinking fortunes of the Whitakers, there is no evidence that Baker was financially affected by the difficulties of his in-laws. Indeed, as a surveyor, he had been doing rather well, and would have been able to accumulate his own capital. Inconsistent methods of payment and incomplete records make it difficult to determine just how lucrative surveying was, but authorised surveyors working for the government were paid salaries of about £200 in the 1880s, and were provided with basic equipment. Contractors, like Baker, received more for their surveys, but had to provide their own equipment and horses and to pay for labour out of the fees collected. But we do know that for the year 1888-89 Baker received at least £700 as final payment for his work on the Oamaru Block south of Opotiki where he completed two major surveys, and that over the next few months he was paid £356 17s 4d for surveying 6,600 acres in eight sections – 'Nearly all forest country' – in the Raglan area.[15] The evidence suggests that at least half of the amounts paid would represent Baker's fee, a very substantial income at that time.

The Whitakers' situation may have been important in a general way. Like most of the other family members who had been in and around the Whitaker household in Symonds Street from the mid-1880s, Florence and Charles Alma Baker may have decided to establish their independence. By early in 1890, Alfred Whitaker had established his own law practice in Auckland; Edward, who had been trained in mining technology and the assaying of minerals, had migrated to South Africa; Harry was in Melbourne, and Herbert, who had been employed by the Colonial Sugar Refining Company of which his father was a director, had been transferred to northern New South Wales. Lady Whitaker had died after a long illness, and only Emily remained at home to take care of her father, who returned to the law and to politics, again serving as Attorney-General, until his death in 1891.

Floss and Barney sailed for Sydney on the *Te Kapo* at the end of March 1890, intending to make India their destination for a new life.[16] At Singapore, they missed their connection for Ceylon, and became aware of the demand for surveyors in the tin-mining areas of the Malay States on the west coast of the Malayan Peninsula. The voyage to Ceylon was abandoned as they moved to build a new life as colonial pioneers.

CHAPTER 3

PLANTING STONES

The Malayan state of Perak became Baker's home, in so far as he had one, from 1890 until his death in 1941. From the outset, Baker easily found contract work for the government, surveying and supervising the construction of new roads to service the rapid expansion of commercial agriculture and tin mining. With British policies committed to encouraging entrepreneurial enterprise and the development of the state through Chinese immigration, the explosive growth of the Kinta Valley area in particular placed the small colonial administration under extreme pressure as it attempted to ensure that mining development was orderly and based on a clear definition of title. In a bid to take pressure off the overstretched Lands Department, the government appointed Baker on contract as surveyor for the whole Kinta Land District from 1892 until 1897 when, dissatisfied with some aspects of his work, the British Resident terminated the agreement. Despite his differences with the government, Baker had by this time become a prominent member of European society in Perak; rather than having an adverse effect on his income or lifestyle, his departure from government service created new opportunities for his commercial ambition and led to a further consolidation of his social position.

When Florence and Charles Alma Baker arrived in Perak in 1890, the state was still a recent addition to the British Empire. Until the 1870s, the main British presence in the region had been in the Straits Settlements of Singapore, Malacca and Penang but the commercial potential of the peninsula hinterland, and the disorder that was preventing it from being realised, led to intervention in Selangor, Perak, Negri Sembilan and Pahang in the 1870s and 1880s; the four were brought under a single administrative umbrella as the Federated Malay States in 1895. Perak had become a protectorate in 1874 after several years of internecine warfare among factions, each of them comprising coalitions of Malay and Chinese interests, over control of the northern tin-mining district of Larut. British intervention brought an arbitration on mining rights, the recognition of one chief by the others as Sultan of the state and the appointment of a British Resident who, once peace and order was established in the 1880s, effectively controlled government policy, except in matters affecting Malay custom and religion. The state was divided into administrative districts, each headed by a district magistrate who was responsible to the Resident. Batu

Colonial Malaya

Gajah, a small mining town 13 miles south of Ipoh, and 54 miles south of Taiping, the state capital, was the administrative centre of the Kinta Land District.

In the 1890s, Batu Gajah offered little in the way social amenities for Europeans other than the entertainments and clubs that they organised among themselves. For Europeans, living in Perak was still very much a pioneering venture. In September 1894 there were complaints that 'Tigers appear to be on the increase and almost daily reports are brought in of their depredations'; and in the same month there was a collision between a train and an elephant on a newly opened line in the south of the Kinta Valley.[1] Pythons were occasionally sighted, and cobras were common. Crocodiles could be seen in the Perak River. In 1891, the year after the Bakers arrived in the state, the European population of Perak was only 366, with about one-quarter of that number being women. Batu Gajah had a European population of about twenty or thirty including, perhaps, half a dozen women.[2] Florence Baker was not completely isolated, however. In the 1890s she was joined by her sister Emily, who, within a short time, had married Noel (later Sir Noel) Walker, a senior official in the government of the Federated Malay States based at Kuala Lumpur. Walker and Baker shared a common interest in horses and racing, the former often riding as an amateur at meetings throughout the state.

By the 1890s, the Kinta Valley was assuming some prominence in the Perak economy as the British administration imposed its peace on warring tribes and factions and settled disputes over the ownership of known areas of stanniferous land. With tin to be found from the topsoil down to the richest layers of wash-dirt 15 feet or more below the surface, the deposits could easily be exploited either by large-scale operators using the latest hydraulic mining technology, or by individual miners using the *lanchut kechil*, a portable, coffin-shaped wash-box that was readily and cheaply available.[3] By 1888, the steady stream of miners entering the district had become a flood. Between 1879 and 1901, the population of the state quadrupled, from 81,000 to 326,000, with the number of Chinese increasing from 20,000 to 150,000.[4] More was needed, however, as the district was 60 miles inland, and lacked easy access to a port. This meant that cargoes of tin had to be carried either by elephant or by bearer and, as well as the expense of transport, had to face the imposition of duties by a succession of local rulers. As a consequence, the government was forced to develop road and rail networks.

It was this development that provided Baker with his first surveying work in the state, including a contract to survey and construct part of the road running north from Taiping towards Penang. Generally, Baker ran his own business, but for some of these contracts, he worked in partnership with W.K. Kellie Smith, a fellow entrepreneur who remained a friend but was later to become a social and business rival. Roading work offered reasonable but not spectacular returns, although with the details of the route determined by the surveyor, and payment by the chain, there was always room in the contract for a little 'padding'; early European settlers and the surveyors used to debate whether the gentle gradient of rural roads in Perak was designed to ease the task of oxen or to line the pockets of the surveyors.[5]

To encourage the activities of small mining operators, and to break the dominance of

Nineteenth-century survey party, Malaya. NATIONAL ARCHIVES OF MALAYSIA

Chinese capitalists, the government permitted any miner who could raise $M100 for survey fees and rent to apply for a previously unclaimed area of up to 25 acres and to start mining as soon as the boundary stones had been laid by the surveyor. To prevent speculation, each licence-holder was required to employ a minimum number of labourers, depending on the nature of the claim, and had to forfeit the land unless it was worked within a specified period. In the Kinta Valley, however, the licensing system soon collapsed and, as the Resident reported, 'it was found necessary, owing to the mining rush, to enter into a contract with a New Zealand Surveyor (Mr. C. Alma Baker) to survey the applications which were poured into the Land Office, and, to preserve uniformity, this contract system was extended to agricultural lands'.[6]

In theory, Baker had a simple task. All applicants for mining or agricultural land lodged their documents with the Lands Office and paid their fees to the Treasury. When the requisite survey had been completed, the government paid the surveyor and issued a lease to the applicant, who was thereupon free to occupy the land. In practice, however, the working of the system was more complicated. Applicants had to ensure that their preferred area was not already subject to lease or a pending claim; all surveys, once complete, had to be marked on a district map that indicated all areas subject to lease or confirmed as being under ancestral Malay tenure. The surveyor, in completing his work, and the government in checking it, had to eliminate all gaps and overlaps along boundaries and to ensure that the individual surveys were connected and were consistent with the survey outline for the district. Each month, in order to assess the payments due under the contract, the government expected a tracing showing all surveys completed as well as the individual survey plans.

Although Baker conducted a number of the individual surveys himself, especially in the early years, he was obliged, under his contract, to employ a sufficient number of other surveyors (usually about six) to ensure that the required surveys were performed 'rapidly, accurately and continuously'.[7] He also employed draughtsmen in his office at Batu Gajah, where the general work of connecting the individual surveys and preparing the general maps was completed, and a number of 'demarcation gangs' to mark out and clear boundaries before the detailed surveys were carried out.

In practice, it proved almost impossible to recruit and retain professional staff from either Britain or India at the prevailing rates, so making it even more difficult for Baker to fulfil the terms of the contract. As the Collector of Land Revenue complained: 'It is notorious that most of Mr. Baker's surveyors are utterly unreliable & that surveys are continually sent in where the [boundary] stones shown on the plan are not in on the ground, boundaries are not cut, land is cut out in a different place to that authorised or of an excessive area ....'[8]

Although the work of the contract surveyor was often difficult, there is little doubt that it was lucrative. Under Baker's contract, a scale of fees was fixed specifying payments, according to 'chainage', for each original survey line, and each line reopened in connection with a subsequent survey; there were further payments for each boundary stone laid, and for the connection of each survey to the district scheme. It was a scale that worked very much to the advantage of the surveyor. In 1897, in every district of Perak other than Kinta, the average cost to a cultivator of the demarcation of a 5-acre plot and its identification by boundary stones was $M2; under his contract with the government, Baker was paid $M18 for identical work. Of the fees collected by Baker one-quarter, on average, went to pay his sub-contracting surveyors and, from this, each paid for his own equipment and field staff. Moreover, the implication running through the records is that, despite the one-sided division of the fees, the sub-contracting surveyors still did rather better than their equivalents in government service. From his three-quarters of the total fees, Baker maintained the office in Batu Gajah, and paid his clerks and draughtsmen. In each of the years from 1894 to 1896, the average amount paid to Baker in survey fees (before deductions to pay his surveyors) was over $M62,000, or about £7,000 a year (at a time when a career colonial servant with ten years' service – the local Lands Officer, for example – would earn something less than £500). The indications are that Baker's earnings had been even higher in the early years of the decade.[9]

By the mid-1890s, Baker was maintaining a lifestyle that could be matched only by the elite of the colonial service, most of whom enjoyed a private income as well as a salary, and to which few planters or mine owners could aspire before the rubber boom of the early 1900s. In August 1894, the *Perak Pioneer* reported that 'Mr Alma Baker is building a fine house facing the Race Course, to be called, probably, Goodwood or Ascot, or some appropriate name of the kind – or maybe, "the Bakeries"'.[10]

Baker's new mansion was set in extensive trees and gardens in Changkat Road and firmly located in the small European enclave on the ridge above Batu Gajah where it was designed to challenge the splendour of the District Magistrate's residence. The ground floor of the house was mostly taken up with a large living room that accommodated with ease a dining table which would comfortably seat a dozen people (cooled by a *punkah*), several sofas and easy chairs, and a full-sized billiard table. In later years, the room was adorned with trophies from Baker's hunting and big game fishing excursions. To the rear of the house there was a suite of offices and to the side a large kitchen and a servants' wing. Upstairs, there were five bedrooms (most with their own dressing-rooms and bathrooms) opening off a huge sitting room (some 60 feet long and half as wide) that extended into the area above the pillared entrance and offered a view of the main gardens.

In accordance with the conventions of a time in which the maintenance of high standards of living by Europeans was regarded as integral to the preservation of British prestige and power, such a household required a large number of servants. At a minimum, an average European household would employ one or more houseboys, a water carrier, a cook and someone to do the washing as well as a coachman and gardeners for outside work; given the size of his house, Baker might well have employed twice that number. It was, perhaps, with her brother-in-law in mind that Emily Walker, in a cookbook and house-keeping guide written for Europeans in Malaya, observed that 'There is no doubt that as soon as a man arrives in Malaya, his ideas of what he *cannot* do without become very much enlarged'.[11]

Baker's view of his own place in Perak society had certainly 'enlarged' in the few years he had lived in Batu Gajah – his business was flourishing, he was rich in local terms and he had built a house to match his achievements and ambitions. The house was large, even by the standards of the colonial elite, and he had brought his own builders from Ceylon for the task. Baker designed the house himself to provide for local conditions and his own interests. For example, the roof had overlapping layers for improved ventilation; the breeze could circulate above the bedrooms, with hot air escaping through the small latticed attic that capped the building. This latter feature proved doubly advantageous, as it often became a private grandstand from which Baker could watch the training of his own horses, as well as the race meetings held on the track of the Kinta Gymkhana Club on the other side of Changkat Road.

With Baker, horses – their training, appearance and performance as racing animals, circus performers, polo ponies or in carriage harness – were an obsession that came a close second (with fishing) behind his affection for billiards. He was a keen polo player and, naturally enough, a leading member of the Kinta Gymkhana Club. A founding member of the club, Baker contributed generously to its development and virtually ran its affairs for many years. His name also appeared regularly as a starter, timekeeper or steward at race meetings in Ipoh or Taiping. In 1903, one of the local newspapers noted that he was 'among many well known sportsmen' in Kuala Lumpur for the races.[12] He owned and trained a number of horses which, in between formal race meetings, he would pit against those of other owners for a private purse.[13] Later, however, when the Gymkhana Club at Kinta amalgamated with that at Ipoh, by then a much larger town, and Baker was deprived of the

Baker's residence, Changkat Road, Batu Gajah, Perak. C. ALMA BAKER TRUST

pleasures of a racetrack that at times seemed almost his personal preserve, he severed his links with both clubs being, according to his nephew, the sort of person who always liked to be in control and had little time for anything not organised to his liking.[14]

In the reports of his sporting activities throughout the 1890s, Charles Alma Baker was increasingly referred to as 'Mr Alma Baker', and he took to signing letters simply as 'Alma Baker', a change from the 'C.A. Baker' that can be found on earlier correspondence. Although government officials in Malaya persisted in referring to him as 'Mr Baker', and he later appeared in *Who's Who* and similar publications under the Baker surname, from this time, and where he was in control, he seems to have adopted 'Alma Baker' almost as a family name. When his daughter was born, she was baptised Julitha Winifred Alma Baker. But it was merely a usage that he adopted, rather than a formal change, and it is intriguing to note that his wife continued to sign her letters simply as 'Florence Baker'.

At the end of 1894, while waiting for their house to be completed, Floss and Barney completed the voyage to Ceylon that had been interrupted four years before and, shortly after their return, the *Perak Pioneer* noted that 'Mr and Mrs Alma Baker and a few friends are on a two days picnic to the sulphur springs near Tanjong Rambutan' north of Ipoh.[15] In this early colonial society there was, of necessity, a great deal of private entertaining, an area in which Florence excelled, but little that was organised and, as might be expected, women were considerably restricted in what they might or might not do. They generally entertained one another privately because they were usually admitted only to special functions at the social clubs, most of which catered almost exclusively for men. Baker was a member of the Kinta Club, the Ipoh Club, the Perak Rifle Association and, as has been mentioned, of all of the racing clubs within reach of the town. Florence organised bridge parties at home.

But although Charles Alma Baker may have been a joiner, he was not universally popular, especially among the Europeans at Batu Gajah, many of whom were employed in the colonial administration. The senior members of the colonial service were distinguishable not only by their professional standing but by their social class at Home. Baker could soon compete with their wealth, and seems to have acquired their manners, but he none the less remained a 'colonial' in their eyes.[16] Baker's position as a self-employed contractor did provide some entrée to the social circuit, as would his link with the Walkers and his friendship with Ernest Birch, Secretary and later British Resident of Perak, but there seems always to have been an implicit tension in his dealings with officials and officialdom.

In the small town of Batu Gajah, especially, there was jealousy of the income Baker earned from what was essentially a government position and he had little option but to mix socially with those who, from a professional perspective, were critical of his business activity. In reporting on the construction of Baker's new house in 1894, the 'Kinta Correspondent' for the local newspaper reflected the attitudes of both civil servants and a planting community that was struggling through a period of depressed prices with a gratuitous sneer: 'It appears that boundary stone planting in these parts is a more profitable job than tea or coffee planting, or even tin-mining'.[17]

The Kinta Alphabet, a piece of doggerel published a few months later in the *Perak Pioneer*, offers further insights into the European community at Batu Gajah:

> A is for Arndt on raffles intent
> B is for Baker who to Ceylon went
> C is for Cologan working a mine
> D is for the Demarcator who drinks good wine …

This woeful effort prompted the appearance of the *Kinta Alphabet No. 2* in the next issue, 'With apologies to [Bob] the author of No. 1', from a poet with a more acerbic turn of phrase:

> A is for Alma Baker – the money making man,
> B is for Bob – who would be a poet if he can ….[18]

From the government's point of view, it was the surveying practice rather than the money earned from it that was the major cause for concern, and there was a running battle between Baker and officials of the Kinta Lands Office throughout the duration of the contract. At issue was the extent to which Baker was fulfilling his contract concerning both the accuracy of surveys on the ground and the subsequent completion of the mapping requirements. Despite this, however, Baker secured two renewals of his original contract, with only relatively minor procedural changes and, until 1897, when an official inquiry was held, maintained his monopoly on surveying in the Kinta Land District. Part of the explanation for this might lie in the fact that senior officials discounted the credibility of

Downstairs living room of Baker's residence at Batu Gajah. The billiard table is at the far end.

complaints emanating from the local lands officer, W.P. Hume, because of his known hostility towards Baker, and part might lie in Baker's friendship with Birch.

The relationship between Baker and the government had followed a difficult path. Within a year of the first surveying contract being signed, the government had amended the clause which provided for one-third of the fees to be paid at the time a survey was requisitioned, because it was found that requisitions issued were getting well ahead of surveys delivered, and thereafter it paid only upon completion. As early as June 1893, at the height of the tin rush and just after the government had seriously contemplated dismissing Baker, Hume had reported that 'There is no doubt … that Mr. Baker has hitherto utterly failed to cope with the work'.[19] Two years later, another official in the Kinta Lands Office complained that any attempt to co-ordinate Baker's surveys was a 'waste of time' because of errors of up to 5 miles in the locations given for some blocks.[20] In cases of proven deficiency, of which there were many, Baker's fees were cut until the matter was made good, but in a few cases where he was sure of his ground he appealed to the British Resident and, having proved his case, added to the impression that he was the victim of official harassment rather than being seriously behind or incompetent in his work. The complaints emanating from the local Lands Office were merely irritating pin-pricks to be brushed aside: 'My time is much too occupied, & I consider the time of the Resident much too valuable, for me to write on trivial subjects'.[21]

After a procedure requiring surveys to be completed in the order of their receipt was abandoned because of the cost and inconvenience to the surveyors of constantly moving around the district, Baker could apparently exercise little control over his sub-contractors and

> the surveyors could and did pick and choose what they would and what they would not do and would extort money very frequently from applicants for doing out of the way blocks or any particular blocks before the rest .....
>
> The reiterated outcries raised by Mr. Baker, whenever the L.O. [Lands Office] attempted to bring pressure on him to overtake arrears or do any particular work that was the least distasteful to him, necessarily created, sometimes, an impression that he was being harshly treated and this impression, with the confidence the Govt. always reposed formerly in his bona fides and in his assumed knowledge of and desire to meet all the requirements of his surveys, rendered it comparatively easy for him to satisfy the Govt ....[22]

But by 1897, the accumulated exasperation had reached the point where Birch, despite reaching the conclusion that Baker 'did a great mass of work and the great mass of it is good', decided to terminate the contract in favour of appointing government surveyors as in other districts. To end the wrangling for once and for all, he appointed a committee of inquiry to examine all outstanding matters in dispute between the parties.[23] The inquiry established the difficulty of maintaining up-to-date surveys under the conditions prevailing in the state, and was critical of the government's failure to supervise Baker more closely (ironic in the light of the steady stream of complaints from the Kinta Land Office since 1892). In turn, it was also critical of Baker's failure to supervise his surveyors, to ensure accuracy and to provide the co-ordinated survey plans as provided for in the contract.[24] As a final settlement for all outstanding and disputed surveys, the government agreed to make a payment of £3,600 (an amount equivalent to three times the annual salary of the British Resident).

In his seven years as contract surveyor for the Kinta Land District, Baker and his employees had submitted some 7,500 individual survey plans, as well as district plans and topographical maps to the government of Perak. The settlement determined by the committee of inquiry left Baker believing that he had been short-changed and still threatening, even a decade later, to lay his grievance before the Secretary of State in London.[25] But it was a gesture, rather than a threat, and Baker felt largely vindicated by the inquiry, which had acknowledged his pioneering role under difficult conditions. And although he had not succeeded in securing the full amount to which he felt he was entitled, and there was no prospect of future surveying work with the government, he was not particularly concerned. He had already become absorbed by the prospects for tin mining which, within a few years, would prove even more lucrative than the planting of stones.

CHAPTER 4

A FORTUNE FROM GUNONG LANO

Baker's failure to fulfil all the terms of his surveying contract, and his conflict with the government, were caused partly by his growing preoccupation with new forms of investment. As he had accumulated capital from the mid-1890s, he had taken up the concessionary access to land available to European settlers in the Federated Malay States. He took out prospecting rights over small areas of likely-looking tin-mining land and, on a larger scale, made an abortive investment in plantation land during the first enthusiasm for rubber in the late 1890s. By the time his surveying contract with the government had been terminated at the end of 1897, with a consequent loss of income, he had already acquired major mining concessions in the Kinta Valley district. These ventures made satisfactory returns for the first few years, and Baker then made his fortune with the discovery of rich deposits on his land at Gunong Lano, a fortune that he multiplied in the years before the First World War by reinvesting his massive mining profits in the rapidly expanding rubber industry.

Baker's first mining investments date from 1894 and 1895, when he was permitted by the British Resident to select up to 150 acres of mining land; this he did, over the next few years, naming eight parcels spread through the Kinta Valley from Ipoh in the north to Kampar in the south. Still concerned with surveying, and actively exploring the prospects for rubber, he did little to develop his mining leases until the turn of the century. At first he considered plantation development on a 640-acre concession he had secured on the River Kwang, near Chemor, north of Ipoh, but he then secured permission to switch the land from agricultural to mining use, so that prospecting could proceed. He then sought exemption from some of the usual restrictions, reminding the British Resident that 'In my case, certain privileges have been granted in order to promote dredging', which was then still at the experimental stage.[1]

At the Perak Mining Conference held at Ipoh in 1901, Baker had chaired a sub-committee appointed to consider new methods of mining, especially hydraulic mining and dredging, to supplement existing small-scale operations and various forms of open-cast mining. The introduction of centrifugal pumps from the 1870s had allowed deeper excavation than was possible with chain-pumps but, in general, mining methods and government regulations still encouraged the unsystematic exploitation of the richest pockets and, in practice, continued to preserve the advantages of Chinese miners.

By the turn of the century it was believed, correctly as it turned out, that most of the main tin deposits in the Federated Malay States had been discovered and the government of Perak wanted to ensure the fullest exploitation of its mining resource. World tin production had increased rapidly in the last two decades of the nineteenth century in response to the demand for tin-plate and the use of tin in the manufacture of alloys, but by 1900 supply was exceeding demand and the price for ore fell sharply. To protect its own longer-term interests, the government of Perak changed the mining regulations to favour the large European mining companies which were using methods that enabled previously uneconomic areas to be worked. These changes, combined with new technology and the richness of the Kinta deposits, retained the profitability of the Perak mining industry at a time of failure elsewhere. Most of the companies adopted hydraulic mining methods, which involved damming a river or stream above the mine and then using high-pressure hoses to break down the tin-bearing soil so that the ore could be concentrated. Although this method was highly efficient, it was applicable only to areas in or near the hills where the required water pressure could be achieved at a reasonable cost.

For the alluvial plains of the Kinta Valley, Baker was one of the earliest advocates of using a dredge that could advance across flat land, swampy or not, in a pond of its own making. It was this method he proposed for the Chemor land, apparently being willing both to provide the capital and take the risk that would be involved in pioneering a new method of mining for the Federated Malay States. As it happened, he was not called upon to do either, since his Chemor concession carried no tin. His similarly innovative plan for the dredging of a 10-mile stretch of the Kampar River in the south of the Kinta Valley was also abandoned. Forsaking innovation for safety, Baker then put his efforts into other mining leases on land more easily worked under conventional arrangements.

Until the large overseas companies became established on the Perak mining scene in the decade before the First World War, very few owners of mining leases actually did the work themselves. It was more common for the owner, in return for *chabut*, or tribute, to sub-lease to a mining contractor. The contractor would then purchase the required machinery, and engage labour under a further contract with an 'advancer', who would provide capital in return for an agreed share of the proceeds and the right to profit further from the provision of food, supplies and opium for the miners. Although clearing bush or removing topsoil might be performed on piece rates or for wages, by the early years of the twentieth century the labourers, too, worked for a fixed share of the proceeds or a payment for each picul (or 130 pounds) of ore produced.

Under a second prospecting concession granted by the British Resident in 1897, Baker quickly accumulated at least twenty mining leases covering some 500 acres scattered throughout the Kinta Land District. After a period of prospecting, half of the leases, with a combined area of 300 acres, were relinquished.[2] The others seem to have been worked on a tribute basis, with Baker taking no part in the mining himself, nor risking capital as advances to the mining contractors. Most of his mines, however, were relatively modest

Early tin dredge, Malaya. NATIONAL ARCHIVES OF MALAYSIA

affairs, with one 20-acre block near Kampar employing about thirty labourers from 1899 to 1902 but none after that time, whereas another, an open-cast site near Ipoh, employed, on average, fewer than ten labourers a year but lasted from 1903 to 1920.[3]

It was clear, however, that Baker had ambitions to mine on a larger scale and to play a more active part in the industry. Over the next few years, his attempts to secure mining rights to as much land as possible, while paying the government as little as possible, called for considerable skill in juggling the various demands to maintain minimum labour levels, arrange surveys, pay licence fees and land rents and select his mining lands within the specified prospecting period. Inevitably, too, there was a renewal of the ill-feeling that had characterised his earlier relationship with the officials of the Kinta Lands Office.

In 1901 Baker was granted a prospecting concession over two 800-acre blocks, with the right to take up mining leases of up to 200 acres in each block, or 400 acres in either. On the first block, a dredging concession near Batu Gajah, he spent some £500 on boring exploratory shafts, only to find that the land was too poor to mine on a commercial scale. On the second block, which was similar to the first, the prospecting licence clashed with a Sakai (local Malay) claim to title over 700 acres of the land in question under ancestral tenure.[4] In vain, Baker asserted the importance of his own claim, and tried to invoke superior authority by informing the Assistant District Officer that he 'had interviewed the Resident who said there was no reason for any delay in this matter'. He then 'expressed his surprise that the development of the country should be delayed on account of a few dirty Sakais'.[5]

Unmoved by the pressure, the official wrote that he was 'not inclined to accept, without verification, the statement that he has spent $M7,000 [£816] on prospecting this block' and suggested that in any case no action should be taken until Baker had paid all of his outstanding rents.[6] After a further eighteen months, Baker's claim to the land was finally rejected, as was his claim that he should be permitted to select an alternative block of land even though the Kinta 'mining book' had been closed since 1898 because of the need to complete outstanding surveys. He appealed to the Resident-General in Kuala Lumpur, but without success. After a nearly a year, he raised the matter yet again, urging that special consideration be given to his case, because he had not been able to exploit either block under the concession and because 'I have for many years taken a very keen interest in the dredging method of mining and have been most anxious to begin dredging in this country'. He added that 'I intend visiting the tin dredging fields in Australia and Tasmania at the end of this year and am most anxious to have an area of reasonable prospects to begin on'.[7] Again, he was unsuccessful. It would appear that, although Baker was undoubtedly enthusiastic about the prospects for dredging, the renewed claim was speculative and prompted more by the proposed trip to Australia than because the area in question was vital to his future plans.

Several months spent in Australia towards the end of 1905, and a trip to England in the following year with agents left in charge of his business, are both indications of Baker's increasing income from mining and reveal a growing interest in the international travel that was to become a feature of the rest of his life. As an indication of his future intentions, he took a long-term lease on an estate at Newton Abbot in Devon. Despite his enjoyment of the fishing and hunting rights included with the lease, he would not buy that property or any other in Britain – not even when Bampton, the Whitaker family home in Oxfordshire, came on to the market – because it would make him liable for the payment of British taxes.[8] He could certainly afford to travel now, and was no longer tied by the need to supervise his surveyors; his mining interests were secure under marketing arrangements that secured the tribute of mine owners. The travel also seems to have followed from changing family circumstances. After eighteen childless years of marriage, Florence had given birth to a daughter, Julitha, in 1903. From this time family travel, usually accompanied by either servants, a nurse or a companion for Florence and Judy (as the baby was usually called), became more frequent.

Upon the family's return from England, a new venture soon lifted Baker's wealth to a higher plane. Among his mining leases, there was one near the base of a limestone outcrop known as Gunong (or Mount) Lano. Lano was near Simpang Pulai in the Sungei Raia district, about 6 miles south of Ipoh and 10 miles north-east of Batu Gajah. A hill rather than a mountain, Lano covered less than a square mile and stood about 1,300 feet above sea level, but only half of that height above the valley floor. Its jungle-covered cliffs, which rose steeply from the surrounding plain to a plateau, were broken by sharp gullies and ravines. In such country, some prospecting was conducted by sinking shafts to seek the heavy concentrations of tin ore that had accumulated between the granite base and the limestone formations that capped the hill, but equally rich deposits could also be found in the labyrinth of caves running through the limestone.

Chinese mining village, Perak, late nineteenth century. NATIONAL ARCHIVES OF MALAYSIA

Most of the limestone hills in the northern part of the Kinta Valley had been prospected and abandoned as worthless by the turn of the century, but Baker himself had carried out the early surveys in the Lano area and had secured a mining lease over about 40 acres by 1900. This land was worked by between fifty and eighty Chinese labourers between 1899 and 1901, and then abandoned. After a new discovery, the mine was reopened in 1903 and Baker, alone and in partnerships, quickly acquired another 120 acres of the cliff land running around the base of the hill. There were practical difficulties in mining such land, especially in locating deposits, establishing sets of wire cables to convey the ore to the plain for concentration and, where there were adjacent claims with boundaries defined on the surface, deciding just who owned the tin, sometimes in rich seams, being removed from the underground caves. Most miners avoided the limestone hills, and the cliff land in particular, but from about 1904 Baker made it his speciality.

Early in 1905, he applied for a mining lease to cover most of the remaining area of the hill, seeking a further 170 acres that would have given him control over almost all of Gunong Lano. Because it was outside his concession, he had to tender for this and pay a premium to the government. But when it came to having the land surveyed there were difficulties, some posed by the land, others by officials who carried old grudges and had become irritated by Baker's policy of delay. As far as mining was concerned, there were the practical difficulties of surveying, and the uncertainty of return, making it difficult for the government to set the premium. As the Warden of Mines reported:

I consider it absolutely impossible for anyone to report as to the value of this land, as without a very thorough prospecting it is purely a matter of guessing. In the first place anyone acquainted with mining in limestone hills must be aware that such work is most precarious and although at times rich pockets are struck, they are worked out in a very short time & it may or may not [be] to the luck of the miner to find fresh ones. At any rate when a fresh pocket is found it means that all wire ropes and other mining implements have to be shifted to the new scene of operations which entails extra expense, & that every few months (should fresh pockets be discovered) the miner has to repeat this expense which means that no permanent improvement is ever effected, & he is never in the same position as his fellow miners who work flat land, & who from systematic boring can tell whether they have a property the life of which can be more or less determined.[9]

For these reasons, and because 'The hill lands to the north are known to be very poor indeed', only a small premium was recommended, despite the knowledge that Baker was 'getting very high chabut' from his existing leases at Lano. Baker claimed that by this time some £7,000 had been invested in mining equipment for Lano, although officials estimated its cost at closer to £2,000 or £2,500. Either way, it was not Baker's money that was involved but that of Chew Boon Juan and his brother Chew Boon Sing, who held the sub-lease, provided the equipment, employed the miners and paid Baker his *chabut* for the Lano mines.[10] By early in 1905 they had several hundred miners employed on the existing Lano leases, which showed their confidence in the future of the mine and suggested that, despite the Warden's uncertainty, Baker and his contractors already knew the location of rich deposits within the leased area.

Baker's problem was to have the survey on the remaining lands completed by officials who seemed no more able to have the work done quickly than they had been when he was the surveying contractor. And Baker was now at a disadvantage; he was a supplicant, needing the work done, rather than a speculator trying to keep alive as many options as possible. Officials who had criticised his work and resented his wealth were disinclined to move quickly to ease the way, and refused even to consider conducting the survey until Baker had paid all the outstanding demands for rents and survey fees on his leases.

One official complained that 'Mr. Baker is notorious for giving trouble to the Land and Settlement officials' and wished 'to put on record that all delay with regard to Mr. Baker's land affairs is entirely due to himself and that he has none but himself to thank for the fact that they cannot be finished before he goes home'.[11] A sharp letter refusing any further action by the Lands Office and threatening forfeiture of some leases unless outstanding matters were settled was intended to make Baker 'attend to his land affairs instead of constantly procrastinating'.[12] But the issue remained unresolved when he left for England in mid-1905, and little progress was made while Baker was away, despite a further reminder from the firm that acted as his agents. The District Officer replied tersely that 'the survey is not nearly ready. It is a shocking locality and Mr. Baker can have the consolation of knowing that it is his bad work that is responsible' for the delay.[13]

This was extreme provocation, especially in the light of Baker's continuing grievance over the 1897 inquiry. Upon his return, he protested angrily to the British Resident about the slur on his professional reputation, and had the satisfaction of having the remarks ruled 'irrelevant and unnecessary'. Further enquiries drew the concession from the Survey Department that 'the portion of the Lano survey done by Mr. Baker was excellent but that portion done by Mr. Shaw's surveyors was bad work'.[14] Birch was clearly aware of the official obstructionism towards his friend, and penned a savage minute observing that 'If the Govt. had not been stupidly advised by its professional men and if they had given the information which can in all other countries be bought for very small sums, Mr. Baker might have been saved much trouble'.[15]

This incident was typical of many confrontations between Baker and officialdom. In his dealings with the government Baker was always prickly, litigious and opportunistic. At the same time, however, and as a matter of policy, he sought the maximum area for prospecting while trying to avoid any financial commitments until the land in question showed promise for mining; he husbanded his resources (and thus widened his options) by deferring as long as possible any payments due to the government. It must also be remembered that wider issues were involved. It was the role of colonial officials to reconcile 'native interests', as they were called, with the provision of opportunities for commercial entrepreneurs, whose activities were expected to ensure the development of the territory and thus the eventual prosperity of its people. There was, therefore, some tension in the relationship between officials and settlers, with the latter convinced that their interests should prevail. This view they justified not simply because their presence contributed to 'productive economic development', as distinct from mere subsistence occupation of the land, but also on the grounds of racial and moral superiority. Baker's attitudes towards mining and commercial development were by no means unique but merely reflected the prevailing realities of empire.

This particular dispute was eventually resolved to Baker's satisfaction. Early in 1907 the lease was confirmed, Baker paid his premium and was then in full possession of Gunong Lano. Thereafter, apart from renewing his leases as they came due, he had very little to do with the operation except to collect his tribute.

Among the limestone hills dotted across the Kinta Valley plain, Lano was typical in that it was difficult of access, surrounded by steep cliffs and expensive to work; but it was unique, it would seem, in the richness of its tin deposits and the profits that it generated. Gunong Lano was worked continuously until the mid-1920s, employing more than 200 men through until 1913, then about 100 for the next seven years and steadily declining numbers for the remainder of the twenty-one-year lease. Although Baker's richest mine, Lano was by no means his only productive lease. In 1911, for example, when a particularly rich deposit was found, the workforce on another lease reaching to the base of Lano, leapt from about a dozen to nearly 200 and back again within the space of two years.[16] By 1915, Baker's mines, which covered more than 740 acres, about half of them on or around Gunong Lano, were employing only 227 men down from 425 in 1913. By 1919 the number had dropped to about 100, and by 1923 it was less than thirty.[17] As the leases expired during the 1920s and

1930s the land, no longer producing, was returned to the government. After mining at Lano, Baker took up little new land, because there were few rich new deposits to be found, and both the scale and technology of mining activity meant that the industry became the preserve of large firms and small-scale prospectors, with little room for individual entrepreneurs. Baker, unwilling to compromise his independence, quickly lost interest.

Baker did well out of all the mines he worked between 1904 and the end of the First World War, but he did best of all out of Lano. In its first six years, this mine alone had produced 2,500 tons of tin which was sold for $M1,463,693 (£171,000).[18] Of this, Baker's share as mine owner would have been not less than 10 per cent, and was probably closer to 15 or 20 per cent, in the light of the Warden of Mines' comment that Baker was getting 'very high chabut' from Lano because of the richness of the deposit. Baker's annual income from this mine alone would be within a range from £2,850 to £5,700. Given that he also had other mines in production before Lano, that Lano itself continued to produce well into the 1920s and that only in the initial prospecting stages around 1905-06 did Lano employ more than half of the labour on Baker's leases, his mining income between 1898 and the end of the First World War might be conservatively estimated at more than £100,000, after the payment of all land rents, mining fees and other expenses. Given, too, that almost all the required capital was advanced by his mining partners, Baker's share of the profits from the various mining enterprises was all available for investment in the development of other projects.

Baker's last mining venture came in March 1916, with a bold and visionary scheme that would have transformed tin mining in Perak. He sought a prospecting licence over some 1,700 acres of the Ulu Johan Valley which lay a few miles west of Ipoh and north of Batu Gajah, running north from Papan township to the foot of the Keledang Mountains. Baker wanted control over the main Johan Valley, together with its tributary streams and valleys, including all the undulating hill country that surrounded it. The area had originally been designated as a mining area but, even with mining concentrated on the valley floors, the disposal of tailings had proved an insuperable problem, and all mining activity had been terminated. Earlier prospecting had apparently shown the existence of rich hill deposits on the eastern side of the main valley and a number of smaller deposits on the west, but none of these had be mined previously because of insufficient water.[19]

Baker's plan aimed to solve all of these problems. He pointed out that at several points the Johan Valley narrowed considerably, providing natural sites for dams that could be used both to prevent tailings from flowing on down the valley and to conserve water. He proposed to use the dams to collect storm-water which could then be pumped to higher levels to create the pressure required to open up the whole valley for hydraulic mining. Government officials thought 'there is no doubt he can supply the capital or raise it for a large scheme like this' but there were doubts on the technical side; the Senior Warden of Mines conceded that 'The scheme as outlined is no doubt on the right track but involves the erection of works requiring the supervision of experienced civil engineers'.[20]

The Resident certainly wanted to see more detail before the scheme could proceed, but finally it was not the technical viability of the scheme that determined whether the ban on mining would be lifted. Rather, it was the attitude of officials towards Baker himself. Most agreed with the Senior Warden of Mines who observed that: 'Mr. Baker … has worked his lands with the absolute minimum of risk to himself & can no way be considered to be deserving of special consideration'.[21] The District Officer for the Kinta District agreed, commenting that 'Mr. Baker has never been a real miner himself – he has always sublet his land for others to work'.[22] But there was another element involved, the constant official suspicion of individual entrepreneurs, who were few in number, and the government's preference for large-scale enterprise. Despite a few gestures towards small capitalists, mining in Perak in the nineteenth century had been dominated by Chinese capitalists; from the early twentieth century it was increasingly the preserve of large European firms – and both grew rich from the toil of Chinese labourers.

As is clear from his correspondence, Baker, like most Europeans living in Malaya at this time, recognised the contribution of the Chinese to commercial development, but dismissed the Chinese labourers collectively as 'coolies' and the Malays as 'Sakais', although he had rather more sympathy for the former than the latter because of their willingness to work in the capitalist economy. The Malays, with a lifestyle dominated by subsistence agriculture, were seen as a lazy people with little interest in wage labour or commerce, and more often than not their presence (and particularly the protection of their lands) was seen as inhibiting the country's development. This perception both explained and justified British policies that promoted the immigration of Chinese and Indians to serve the interests of British capital.

But, in a changing environment increasingly dominated by companies and outside capital, Baker stood apart from most of his fellow Europeans involved in mining in Perak because he chose to operate as an independent proprietor when most other wealthy investors put their money into companies and stayed away from the frontiers of empire. Baker was independent from choice or, rather, from conviction. He preferred the risks and profits of individual enterprise, and he insisted on being in control. He was also unusual in that most other European entrepreneurs in Malaya at the turn of the century preferred the role of planter to that of miner; Charles Alma Baker was both and, in the presence of the growing company of planters, who rarely shared the social background or educational accomplishments of the Malayan colonial service elite, he felt rather more at home.

CHAPTER 5

THE MOST WONDERFUL
OF ALL TREES

While on his way to Ceylon in December 1894, Baker had bought a copy of *All About Para Rubber* from the bookstall of the Penang Railway Station. By the time that he reached Colombo, he was convinced that there was a future for rubber planting in Malaya. He shared this enthusiasm with two friends in Ceylon, Edward (later Sir Edward) Rossling, Chairman of Directors of the Ceylon Planters' Association, and Ronald Farquharson; both men owned large tea plantations on which they also grew the Brazilian rubber tree, *Hevea brasiliensis*. Impressed with Baker's apparent knowledge of Malaya's soil and climate, and of labour conditions in South-east Asia, they agreed to share in a pioneering venture and between them committed £20,000 to the project. Then, from the Botanical Gardens at Colombo and a range of private estates, the trio filled ten gunny-sacks with *Hevea brasiliensis* seeds for Baker to take back to Malaya.[1]

Upon his return, Baker applied for 10,000 acres under agricultural lease – 5,000 acres of hilly country a few miles south of Batu Gajah in the Kinta Valley district, and 5,000 acres in the low-lying Krian district of Upper Perak. This was, in fact, the first application for plantation rubber land in the Federated Malay States. Since the 1870s, experiments had been conducted at Kew Gardens, and a few plants sent to both Colombo and Singapore, but not even the enthusiastic advocacy of rubber by N.H. Ridley, Curator of the Botanical Gardens at Singapore, had won acceptance for rubber in competition with sugar and coffee. As late as 1894, after six years in the job, Ridley lamented that he 'had not succeeded in inducing a single planter to take up the industry'.[2] As Baker himself noted, as far as *Hevea brasiliensis* was concerned, 'No one knew anything about it and cared less. No one appeared to appreciate the growing commercial value of this, the most wonderful of all trees.'[3] It was not until he returned to Malaya in 1895 that Baker himself was aware that flourishing trees could be found around the Selangor Residency at Kuala Lumpur and even in the grounds of the District Officer's house and the Police Barracks at Batu Gajah.

Ernest Birch, now Resident of Perak, recommended that Baker's proposed leases be approved on quite generous terms: for ten years the land would be rent-free, thereafter 2s 4d per acre per year; export duty would not exceed a farthing per pound; a proportion of the land was to be cleared and planted each year. The proposal ran into trouble, however, when

Clearing land for rubber, early twentieth century. NATIONAL ARCHIVES OF MALAYSIA

it reached Birch's superior, Sir Frank Swettenham, Acting High Commissioner for the Federated Malay States. As Resident of Perak in 1884, Swettenham had planted out some 400 rubber trees and it was supposedly because of low-tapping yields that, as Baker noted, he 'objected entirely to the planting of Hevea Brasiliensis in Malaya' and for plantation land would sanction only the *Gutta rambong* and *Caera* varieties of rubber, and a creeping latex-yielding plant native to the Selangor district. Ridley also maintained that 'it was due to Sir Frank that Para rubber was not planted in abundance ten years earlier than it was'.[4]

The unofficial explanation current in the planting community was more colourful, however: Swettenham's critics maintained that it was because his horse had been poisoned by eating *Hevea brasiliensis* leaves in Perak that Swettenham was so opposed to the new variety of rubber. (The cynics among them also noted that Swettenham's prejudice did not prevent him from accepting a number of lucrative directorships in rubber companies when he retired.) Be that as it may, with *Hevea brasiliensis* still unproven, Swettenham was certainly not prepared to countenance Baker's new venture. Unable to overturn the leaseholds already granted by Birch, he chose to exercise his right to impose additional conditions: if any of the land remained unplanted by the end of the rent-free period, then the whole of the 10,000 acres would revert to the government without compensation for improvements; and under no condition could *Hevea brasiliensis* be planted on any of the land in question.

Faced with 'these stipulations [which] were so unexpected and so impossible to carry out', Baker abandoned the project and, while the government and planting community gradually learned how to grow and tap 'the most wonderful of all trees', Baker returned to surveying and to the development of his tin-mining interests. But he did persist with his interest in rubber. Despite the failure of most of the seeds he had brought back from Ceylon (because the sacks had been stored on deck and exposed to salt and damp), he did get some trees to grow and these, together with other local stock, he planted on the 20-acre block around his new house at Batu Gajah.

At the turn of the century, having lost his surveying contract with the government of Perak, Baker again tried agriculture, and again in a joint venture. With Sir Graham Elphinstone, he acquired a block of several hundred acres about 15 miles north of Ipoh and beside the new railway line to Taiping, which was then nearing completion. After prospecting for tin, and finding nothing, the partners proposed to import young oxen from India and raise them for subsequent sale to local transport operators wanting to capitalise on the tin-mining boom. That scheme was thwarted by an outbreak of cattle disease in India, whereupon they decided to clear the land for rubber for which, by that time, there was a strong demand. Baker himself took charge of the development work, camping in the new and as yet unused Chemor railway station. As he later recalled:

> The felling went on apace; the Sakais are good bushmen, but one day Mr. Hanson, the General Manager of the Railway Department, with Mr. Barnard, decided to give an engine and guard's van a run from Chemor to Kuala Kangsar on the new railway line. This they did but it proved to be the end of my Sakai band. Like a flock of wild duck they made straight for their ancestral halls in the Cameron Highlands, and they left their dried food stores of monkeys, rats, mice etc. hanging on strings in the sun before their attap shelters.[5]

This took place towards the end of 1906 and, as he was about to depart for England, Baker did nothing more about the land, which he sold shortly afterwards to one of the agency houses for amalgamation with a neighbouring plantation. The sale did not represent the end of his interest in rubber, however. Rather, it marked a new beginning, for it was about this time that major tin production from Lano began, providing the capital he needed to fulfil his ambition of becoming a major presence in the rapidly growing rubber industry.

From England, Baker applied for selection rights over 3,000 acres of agricultural land for himself, and an adjoining block of 640 acres in the name of John Harwood, a friend from Newton Abbot. Having a detailed knowledge of the Kinta Valley, Baker was specific in his request, asking for a block a few miles south of Batu Gajah, just north of the intersection of the road to Teronoh with the Tanjong Tualang Road. He reminded the Resident that this was part of the same block that he and his Ceylon partners had tried to develop for rubber a decade before, and could not resist adding that 'had the Government met me in any reasonable way my partners and myself together with the state would long 'ere now have reaped substantial benefit from the industry'.[6]

As might have been expected, the officials in the District Office at Batu Gajah dismissed this further Baker application for land as merely speculative, but Birch, despite some reservations, was prepared to allow Baker 2,000 acres on the usual conditions, which meant an initial payment of 4s 8d per acre, a rental of 2s 4d per acre for the six-year development period, followed thereafter by 9s 4d per acre, and with one-third of the land to be planted within five years. Once the lease had been approved, however, Baker still dickered and delayed over the final boundaries of the block, provoking Birch, whom Baker still counted as a friend, to comment: 'Tell him that I lose patience with a man who does not know his own mind but chops & changes every week & in this latter case every day & whose chief desire seems to be to upset someone else's selection ....' [7]

The matter was not resolved for another nine months, but Baker's main concern was to identify and secure the best rubber land. He thus chose the well-drained undulating land and, in the light of the experience of the early planters, rejected swampy land on the lower side of Tanjong Tualang Road. Ironically, in winning the right to finalise his own boundaries, he had eliminated valuable alluvial tin deposits from his estate, deposits that were later mined using the very dredges he had been so keen to introduce just a few years before. But he still had nearly 2,000 acres for rubber, and he quickly acquired Harwood's land, which had probably been secured on his behalf anyway, together with several other small adjacent blocks, formerly used for mining. In all, he had acquired 3,165 acres of uncleared jungle which he called the Kinta Valley Estate.

It soon became clear that, on this occasion at least, the District Officer had misjudged Baker's motives. The establishment of the Kinta Valley Estate was no mere speculation and over the next few years Baker invested heavily in the development of the plantation, using the profits from Lano. This enabled him to resist selling out, or taking in partners, when he needed to raise the large amounts of capital required to clear and plant the land and then to prevent it from reverting to jungle for five years until the trees came into production.

Because his land was not yet producing, Baker was unaffected by the depression in rubber prices in 1907-08 and could still meet the development costs of about £30 per acre from his tin revenues. He also resisted selling during the boom that followed immediately after, when rubber prices on the London market leapt from their 1908 average of 4s 3d per pound to a high of 12s 9d in April 1910, making even uncleared plantation land worth from £5 to £7 an acre. In part, the increase was the result of attempted price-fixing by Brazilian producers, but more important was the phenomenal growth in motor vehicle manufacturing in the United States and the consequent demand for pneumatic tyres. [8]

In the first two years of Baker's ownership, more than 1,000 acres of the Kinta Valley Estate was cleared and planted in rubber. Progress was not always straightforward, however, because Baker was inclined to experiment, and to reject some of the conventional wisdom on the growing of rubber trees. This predilection quickly drew him into conflict with both his managers and with government officials, the latter able to criticise because of Baker's use of government development loans. In March 1908, a loan of more than £4,000 was approved, but reduced to £2,300 at Baker's request. A few months later, when he applied to have the original amount restored, he was told that 'little hope can be held out .... unless it is seen that there is a marked improvement in the condition of the Estate which should be put under proper management'. [9]

It seems, however, that officials were too quick to condemn. Baker protested that an adverse report by a government inspector was unfair and out of date. Since March, when the first instalment of the loan was made available, he had completed 'first class lines' for 100 labourers; the original labour force of thirty had been increased by eighty labourers brought in from India, with thirty more to follow on the next boat; the manager's bungalow had been completed, more than 200 acres of trees clean-weeded, 30 acres 'holed and planted'; 100 acres of jungle had been felled, and numerous patches of *lalang* (coarse grass, weeds and brush) cleared. Baker himself had surveyed the estate into 50-acre blocks that became the basis of his management and recording systems; he then subdivided each block into 2.5-acre lots, to facilitate the setting of tasks for individual labourers. Because of the 'very unsatisfactory state' of the tin market, he now wanted the additional loan to sustain the momentum of development and to complete the weeding and maintenance of the 600 acres already in rubber until the next planting season.[10]

This work was all carried out under the direction of the new manager, Robins, 'a thoroughly experienced planter', but here, too, trouble was in store.[11] Within a few months of taking up his position Robins had left the Kinta Valley Estate, complaining that 'no planter can do any good there, because Mr. Baker has so many theories he wishes tried & gives so many contradictory instructions, that no ordinary Manager can take an interest in the place & deliberately see good money wasted'.[12]

Officials agreed, and wanted any further advances to be conditional on estate management being taken out of Baker's hands and placed in those of a competent visiting agent. The incident is also revealing in that it represents the first indication of the 'theories' of agriculture which were to become a feature of Baker's management style, causing disagreements with managers and bringing criticism from 'experts'. Although some of Baker's theories eventually proved their worth, most were unsuccessful and costly when put into practice.

It seems that with tin prices down, and with £12,000 of his own funds already committed to the development of Kinta Valley Estate, Baker was stretching his resources rather thinly. He sought a loan against the Lano mine, and even tried to defer paying some £300 in land rents, complaining that 'Owing to the great financial depression prevailing throughout the country it is absolutely impossible to get money in'.[13] The additional loan was eventually granted and, although the economic situation of the country did improve over the next few months, it was the stream of Lano profits that paid off the entire loan by the end of 1909, an achievement that both helped to restore Baker's credibility with senior officials, at least, and reduced criticism of his methods.

It is not difficult to find the origin of these conflicts between Baker and the officials of the Kinta District Office and Lands Department in the 1890s disagreements over the surveying contract. Even though, as the Resident himself conceded, Baker's surveying work had, by 1906, 'been recognised as not so bad as it has at times been painted', the rancour remained with the long-serving officials at Batu Gajah who had constantly been outmanoeuvred and were resentful both of Baker's wealth and of his success in locking up large areas of land for speculative purposes. As those who had to deal with him on a day-to-

Rubber processing factory at Kinta Valley Estate, 1916. The rollers were driven by steam power.
MRS ALMA CURTIN

day basis, they had to cope with the consequences of his vacillation, a trait that seems incompatible with Baker's general decisiveness. More often than not the apparent vacillation may have been, as the officials half-suspected, merely one more device to delay any expenditure that did not generate an immediate return.

Rubber planting in Malaya was in its infancy; it was only from the turn of the century that plantation rubber exports exceeded those from the harvesting of 'wild' stocks. The rubber plantations in Malaya were among the first in the world, making experimentation a necessity and failure a regular occurrence. But the growth in demand ensured rapid development for the industry and by 1910 Malaya was producing more than half of the world's plantation rubber; by 1914, it exported more than all the South American producers of wild and plantation rubber combined; by 1918 more than half of the world's rubber was produced in Malaya.[14]

In the early years of the rubber industry in Malaya, the government had a considerable stake in the new industry through the provision of land on concessionary terms and the granting of development loans. Through its officials it tried to maintain 'orthodox' methods of cultivation, even though the orthodoxy itself was unproven. For example, the orthodox view placed great stress on 'clean-weeding' between rubber plants during their growth to maturity and throughout their productive life. In the early years of the twentieth century the standard of weeding almost became a litmus test for the quality of plantation management; it was not until the 1920s that this practice gave way to the planting of groundcover to promote the development of humus and to prevent erosion.

In such matters, because of his growing interest in the properties and 'behaviour' of soil, Baker was well ahead of his time. As early as 1908 he was rejecting the 'absolute clean weeding' advocated by the government because

> This had the disastrous effect of exposing our once fertile soil to the evil of erosion through wind, sun and rain .... The result of clean weeding was that our beautiful fertile top soil which had taken thousands of years to accumulate in the jungles was washed into the swamps and eventually into the sea, thus leaving for our planted rubber trees nothing but the starvation diet composed of what was held by the upper clays.[15]

Thirty years later, Baker was to advocate composting on a massive scale to overcome the problem of declining productivity, but when establishing his plantation in the years before 1914, he placed most emphasis on the digging over of the ground between the trees with the *changkol* (a deep shovel introduced to Malaya by Chinese tin miners), a practice that eventually drew the support of the previously critical Inspector of Plantations:

> the trees on the whole property are looking healthy and making most satisfactory growth .... as regards the older rubber land an excellent [type] of work has, in my opinion, been introduced lately. This consists in digging over the whole of the land a chankol deep in big slabs and turning over all the weeds into the soil which not only tends to fertilise the ground but also prevent wash from rains from carrying off the topsoil.[16]

Even at this early stage of Baker's involvement in agriculture, we can discern a number of features characteristic of his later theories and policies on agricultural development. Most important was his willingness to experiment, not just with 'changkoling', as he called it, but in other areas as well. In another section of the Kinta Valley Estate, he planted grass around the rubber rather than clean-weeding, anticipating the later common practice of providing groundcover, and he then grazed sheep among the trees. In yet another area he planted some 15,000 camphor trees among the rubber as a cash crop to be harvested until the plantation matured. Underlying all of these developments lay Baker's ideas on what he called 'the living soil', and his concern with establishing management strategies to protect natural fertility and soil quality. In many ways, Baker's plantation practices foreshadowed the principles of biodynamic farming that were to gain currency in the 1930s. And he was prepared to stand out against conventional wisdom and to publicise his own views. On rubber planting, for example, he published before the First World War at least one, and perhaps two, brief manuals in which he urged the adoption of changkoling. This, he argued, would not only reduce erosion, retain moisture and protect fertility, but also help to eradicate termites and disease through the burying of the debris that harboured them.[17]

At a time when government policy in agriculture, as in mining, favoured development through major companies, the Kinta Valley Estate was one of the largest private rubber estates in Malaya, but not *the* largest. Baker's main rival in this, as in so many other things (down to the appearance of carriages and horses), was W.K. Kellie Smith, his former road-

Judy, Floss and Barney beside the factory water supply pond, Kinta Valley Estate, 1916. MRS ALMA CURTIN

making partner, and now the owner of the nearby Kinta Kellas Estate. Having completed the planting of the minimum third of the Kinta Valley Estate as required by the leasehold, Baker then purchased the 2,600-acre Pondok Tanjong Estate near Taiping, on the road that he himself had constructed in the early 1890s. He thus became the proprietor of the largest private rubber holdings in the Federated Malay States. He did not boast of holding the largest private estates, nor did he discuss his motives for the purchase, but the size of his landholdings was common knowledge and those close to him were convinced that this was the reason for the acquisition of a second estate and firmly believed that he derived great private satisfaction from his pre-eminent position among the proprietary planters.[18]

Although the estates were large, neither was fully developed until after the Second World War. The development of the Kinta Valley Estate was suspended in about 1910 after the first 1,000 acres had been planted and funds diverted to the purchase of the Pondok Tanjong Estate, which had about 800 acres in rubber when it was bought by Baker.[19] Both estates therefore met the minimum leasehold requirements that one-third be planted in rubber within five years, but that is all. Having established his plantations, for many years Baker showed little interest in any expansion of their planted areas. He was not short of capital and had little difficulty in meeting the additional demands for the construction of process and packing facilities for the latex as the early plantings came to maturity. It was as though he had more than sufficient income to maintain his chosen lifestyle, and had little interest in making more.

Baker with a fortnightly consignment of rubber ready to leave Kinta Valley Estate, 1916.
MRS ALMA CURTIN

Although some rubber may have been tapped earlier on the house site at Batu Gajah, the first rubber from the Kinta Valley Estate was produced in 1911; with the proceeds Baker bought a necklace and brooch for Florence 'who had daily visited the Estate with me and taken a great interest in its development'.[20] By 1914, with all of the planted area coming into full production, it was necessary to move beyond makeshift arrangements and build a new factory, smoke-houses, and ponds for water supply. Although not reaching the heady levels of 1910, when the London price peaked at 12s 9d per pound, there were still good profits to be made through until the end of the First World War. Even so, the average price fell to 5s 5d per pound in 1911, 4s 9d in 1912 and 3s in 1913.

Throughout the war, prices ranged from 2s 3d to 2s 10d, with most rubber companies estimating the cost of production, collection, and processing (that is, excluding the initial plantation establishment cost) at between 9d and 1s 8d per pound.[21] Baker's costs were almost certainly at the bottom end of the range, however, and perhaps even lower than any of the company figures because he financed his venture from tin profits, thus avoiding the crippling interest charges faced by some growers, and he did not have to support the London office infrastructure that burdened most of the commercial companies. And, in the early 1920s, he could still tap at a profit (when few others could do so) with prices as low as 9d per pound, meaning that, at least until the depression of 1921 and 1922, he had a fair margin to spare.[22]

By 1919 he had invested a total of £70,000 in the development of the Kinta Valley Estate and £60,000 in Pondok Tanjong, although the estates were worth at least twice these sums under the prevailing market conditions. In 1919, Kinta Valley alone produced 227 tons of dried rubber sheet; production had increased steadily across the decade and some of the trees had still not reached full maturity. With Pondok Tanjong adding a further 140 tons a year by this time, Baker was able to make very large profits indeed.[23] Even with the price as low as 2s per pound in 1919, the evidence suggests that his profits for the year could have been as high as £50,000. In the preceding five years or so, when production would have averaged about half of this level, but prices were rather higher, his returns from rubber would still have been in the order of £20,000-30,000 a year (aside from any mining profits he might have made). With Baker's volume of production, he stood to gain £450 a year for every 1d by which the price of a pound of rubber on the London market exceeded the cost of production. To put these figures into context, at this time his brother-in-law, Sir Noel Walker, as Registrar of the Supreme Court of the Federated Malay States, was earning a salary of £1,200.[24]

Given the obvious profitability of rubber planting it is, perhaps, surprising that more of the estates were not cleared and planted during the years of high prices. A further 800 acres had been planted at the Kinta Valley Estate between 1916 and 1918, but plans to clear and plant a further 1,000 acres between 1919 and 1924 were dropped in the face of declining returns. But it might also be suggested that more than commercial factors were involved.

Even by this stage, Charles Alma Baker's life can be seen as falling into phases, each characterised by an 'enthusiasm' to which he would give his full attention while the interest lasted. His career as a surveyor effectively ended in 1897, and his interest in tin mining, and especially the development of Lano, absorbed most of the next decade. By 1914, with the rubber estates nearing full production, and processing facilities built, the development cycle was complete. In the future it would simply be a case of maintaining production, perhaps expanding plantings, and establishing a routine. It was almost as though Baker looked for challenges and then, once his goals were achieved, lost interest.

So far, the achievements had always brought profits, but Baker seems to have been little interested in profits for their own sake. Rather, he sought wealth for what it could do. Subsequent enthusiasms were to cost money, rather than to make it, but to bring the less tangible benefits of public recognition. With Baker's income secure, there was time now for other things. Charles Alma Baker was more than a colonial pioneer or an opportunistic entrepreneur; he was also a British patriot and imperial enthusiast, dedicated to the expansion and preservation of the British Empire. The threat to the empire posed by the war with Germany prompted him to commit substantial amounts of time and money to the cause of imperial defence in a fund-raising campaign that gave material assistance to the war effort, and brought him widespread recognition for public service.

CHAPTER 6

IN DEFENCE OF EMPIRE

In mid-1915, Charles Baker issued 'An Appeal to all Britishers, men and women of Greater Britain, and to those living in safety under our Flag' to contribute to a Malayan Air Squadrons Fund. The appeal, seeking funds for the purchase of aircraft for the Royal Flying Corps, brought together Baker's commitment to the British Empire and his belief that the future of civil communications and military power lay with aircraft. By the end of the war, he had raised more than £200,000 in Malaya and Australia, sufficient for the purchase of ninety-four aircraft for the war effort.

By 1915, Baker was a prominent member of European society in the Federated Malay States. Having operated his tin mines (albeit at second hand) for a decade, and established large rubber plantations, he was no longer vulnerable to the charge of being a mere opportunist and speculator and there was less cause for friction with officialdom. Moreover, planters now matched officials in number and, following the rapid and very profitable development of the rubber industry in the early years of the century, there was a much larger group of private settlers who could match the incomes and lifestyle of those serving at the upper levels of the Malayan Colonial Service. The inherent tensions between the two groups remained, however, but the growth in the European population of the Federated Malay States – from 700 in 1891, to nearly 3,300 by 1911, and 5,700 by 1921[1] – allowed greater individual preference in social relationships and generated more organisations and activities. Baker lunched on occasion with Sir Edward Brockman, Chief Secretary of the Federated Malay States; he was the President of the Ipoh Chamber of Mines (later the Chamber of Commerce), a member of the Town Guard of Batu Gajah, and still retained extensive hunting, fishing and racing interests. The house at No. 3 Changkat Road was the centre for wide-ranging social and commercial relationships fostered by the dinners, luncheons and bridge parties organised by Florence. Judy, now a teenager, was an enthusiastic member of the Girl Guides in which Florence also served as Commissioner for the Federated Malay States. So Baker's patriotic fund-raising initiative came from a man securely based within colonial society, who enjoyed easy access to those of wealth and power in both the official and commercial sections of the community.

Baker's first step in his new fund-raising venture was to seek official blessing, which he did by asking Sir Ernest Birch, the former Resident of Perak now living in retirement in London, to approach the Imperial Army Council. The council gave its approval in March 1915 and promised that any aircraft donated would be divided equally between the Naval and Military Wings of the Royal Flying Corps and that the donor of each machine would be identified by a plate fixed to its chassis and also kept informed of any 'good work' done by the aircraft. Before going public with the scheme, Baker persuaded the members of the Chamber of Mines to donate one aircraft, and secured the promise of another from Eu Tong Sen, a wealthy Kinta mine owner.[2]

The first Malayan appeal for the Air Fleet Fund in March was brief and to the point – 'I now earnestly appeal to all British subjects ...' – but Baker soon found that a simple statement of need was not enough; he had to emphasise the dangers of German power. Before long, he had developed a much more emotive propaganda style, and tried to personalise the implications of war for the people of the Malay States. In particular, he attacked the notion that this was Britain's war and should not be a burden on the colonies; he therefore appealed to imperial sentiment:

> It must be remembered that this war is costing Great Britain, roughly, £2,000,000 daily, and that the greater part of this is being paid by the people living in the British Isles, while we out here are left to enjoy in safety commercial prosperity and comparative luxury, with no extra taxation, while the greatest war the world has seen is raging round us ....
>
> It cannot be possible that at this stage of our history there is a single subject of our King, and a member of the most glorious Empire the world has ever seen, who can pause and think whether he or she is called upon to do all they can to help to hold it, by saving the lives of the brave men who have given their all for our great cause.
>
> We, who have not been able to give our personal service to our King and country, might do what we can now, and subscribe all we possibly can spare towards an object that will help to defend those who are struggling to hold our great heritage for us and our children.[3]

By May 1915, Baker was starting to develop the theme, central to all subsequent campaigns, of the military importance of aircraft compared with traditional forms of warfare:

> The effectiveness of aeroplanes is now well known to be beyond all question, and it is obvious that aerial bases must in the near future exist in every important part of the Empire. I am convinced that the issue of this war, and our security after the war, depends largely upon an overwhelming superiority in aircraft, both in power and in numbers ....[4]

At this stage, each aircraft cost £1,300, but even though the price soon doubled, funds to cover the cost of eleven had been raised by the end of 1915. Baker's strategy was to persuade the wealthy to give as individuals or in small groups the cost of a full plane that would bear their names, and for others to contribute by region towards an appropriately named aircraft (for example, *The Kinta, The Singapore, The Penang*), through organisations (*The Chamber of Mines, The Civil Service*) or as members of groups (*Ceylon Jaffna Tamils, Malacca Chinese, Women of Malaya*). As a direct consequence of Baker's campaign, the Sultan of Johore gave a squadron of sixteen aircraft to the war effort. All contributions received were acknowledged through the press, thus maintaining public recognition for donors as well as a degree of competition among them. There were literally thousands of individual contributions towards the cost of some aircraft, and a single donor for others. In his publicity, Baker strongly emphasised that the full amount of any donation was credited towards the cost of aircraft: 'All work in connection with this fund is entirely gratuitous. The *full amount* received by the Chartered Bank Ipoh, is paid by them into the Bank of England for credit of the Secretary of the War Office, without any deductions for administrative expenses, stationery printing, postage, or any other cause.'[5]

As 'Honorary Organiser', Baker himself paid all of the administrative costs, amounting to some £7,000 over the four years that the fund operated. In addition, he contributed the cost of four aircraft as sole donor (an Armstrong Whitworth, a British Experimental 2.c., a Fighting Experimental and a De Havilland 5 costing, in all, a further £7,000), started other funds (for example, *The Kinta*) with his own donations, and topped off others. Florence made small contributions, including her bridge winnings, to a number of funds, while Judy gave her pocket money. Total contributions from the family exceeded £15,000. Organising 'The "Baker" Air Fleet Fund', as it was called in the Malayan press, became a full-time occupation as Baker issued a series of appeals, organised fund-raising events, arranged publicity for donors, ensured that major contributors received photographs of 'their' aircraft and liaised with bankers and the Army Council.

The Alma Baker No. 3. **Before techniques of synchronising machine guns with propellers had been developed, the rear-mounted 'pusher' propeller on this 'F.E.' Fighting Experimental aircraft allowed a clear forward field of fire.** SOUVENIR OF THE MALAYAN AND AUSTRALIAN BATTLE PLANES, 1914-1918

Ceremony at the Ipoh Club to mark the anniversary of the declaration of war, August 1915.
MRS ALMA CURTIN

As well as canvassing for contributions, fund-raising events were held. Baker was one of the organisers of the ceremony held at the Ipoh Club early in August 1915 to mark the first anniversary of the declaration of war and, three weeks later, hosted the 'Royal Kinta Circus'. Organised in Judy's name as her contribution to the cause, the circus was held at Baker's small private training track at Batu Gajah with two small grandstands erected especially for the occasion. According to the reporter from the *Times of Malaya*, it was 'a real circus, run along approved lines .... reflecting the greatest credit upon all those associated with it':

> The entertainment comprised equestrian acts by Miss Baker, Miss Hollwey and a Tamil krani, who, though he had never ridden a horse prior to ten days ago, showed both pluck and skill; a cowboy act by Miss Baker, which alike demonstrated the equestrian skill of the young lady and the success which has attended Mr. Baker's horse training; an exhibition of dancing by Miss Hollwey and Mr. Mead; an exhibition of horse training by Mr. Baker, who filled the role of ringmaster with ability; and an interesting turn in which a couple of dogs, a cockatoo, and a toy cart played a prominent part.[6]

In March 1916, leaving Freddie Shepherd, his mining manager, in charge of fund-raising, Baker and his family sailed for Sydney, primarily for health reasons, intending to be

Baker and Toreador perform at the Royal Kinta Circus, August 1915. MRS ALMA CURTIN

away no more than two or three months. They rented Drumeevin, a large house with extensive grounds at Mittagong, a small town about 60 miles south-west of Sydney. Judy, then fourteen, attended Frensham, a prominent girls' school, as a weekday boarder. It was, in fact, the only time that she attended school, otherwise being educated by her mother or a governess. The return to Australia also provided the chance for building closer ties with Florence's brother, Herbert Whitaker, who had retired early from his mill manager's position with the Colonial Sugar Refining Company and was farming a large leasehold property near Grafton in northern New South Wales. Herbert's sons, especially Roderick who was an articled law clerk in Sydney, regularly spent weekends at Mittagong with the family. Another frequent visitor was Sidney (later Sir Sidney) Kidman, Australia's 'Cattle King', who persuaded Baker to join him in investing in a number of cattle stations in the west of the state.[7]

Without the benefit of Baker's immediate presence, and as his return was further delayed, the Malayan fund-raising campaign lost some of its momentum, but with compensating benefits elsewhere for the war effort. As Baker himself later explained it:

> When I went to Australia first, I did not intend to make any appeal. I merely went there on a holiday to recruit my health. Then I found that there was no appeal before the public and I was interviewed by the newspapers there. I told them what I was doing in Malaya, and described the procedure adopted for the

Judy, Floss and Barney, with Colleen, in the temporary seating erected for the Royal Kinta Circus, August 1915. MRS ALMA CURTIN

securing of subscriptions to provide the Government with battleplanes. I thought that would perhaps stimulate some effort. I waited for two or three weeks, but nobody took up the matter and I thought it was up to me to try to help the Empire in Australia ....[8]

In June, Baker approached the Australian Minister for Defence and cabled to London seeking the approval of the War Office for another campaign. That secured, he launched his first Australian appeal early in July. Kidman and his wife each donated aircraft and, in the first year of the appeal, the government of New South Wales gave eight aeroplanes, matching each aircraft donated from within the state. In all, funds sufficient for 41 aircraft had been contributed by the time the war ended.

Baker's son, Pita, still living on the East Coast of the North Island, also made a direct contribution to the war effort. In July 1916, he signed up for the army and joined the Maori Pioneer Battalion. He was single, aged twenty-seven, and had been employed as a shepherd. Starting out as a private, he made lance corporal in a month, having had three-and-a-half years of military training as a cadet at Te Aute College. He was promoted to temporary sergeant for the voyage to Britain on the *Corinthic* in April 1917, and ended his war service as a staff sergeant. He was posted to France early in 1918, saw out the war in the Western European theatre, and remained with the occupation forces in Dusseldorf after the Armistice. Returning to England at the beginning of 1919, he contracted influenza which

**Baker in the uniform of the Batu Gajah Town Guard,
February 1916.** MRS ALMA CURTIN

put him hospital for a few days, but otherwise he seems to have escaped the war without serious illness or injury.[9] There is a remote possibility that Baker may have known of his son's war record, although there is no evidence that this is so. But he would have approved. It was the role of young men to fight; non-combatants like himself and those to whom he appealed, those 'who have not been able to give our personal service to our King and country', should provide the means to carry on the war.

Over time, the tone of the Baker appeals changed to reflect this view, and as public awareness was raised by newspaper reports, the death of loved ones and the return of wounded. The first Australian appeal was timed to draw attention to the second anniversary of the outbreak of war 'when England took her stand for Right against Wrong, for Freedom against Oppression and Tyranny' and asked the question: 'Could any act be more fitting by which to mark this anniversary than to present a fighting aeroplane, or subscribe to the cost of one, which will bear your name, or the name of your town or country, and which will fight in your stead to avenge the unutterable crimes against humanity committed by Germany'.[10]

German atrocities, and the dangers facing Australians, became major themes of the campaign, peaking as crucial battles raged in France in the early months of 1918. Baker had

Pita Heretaunga Baker, about to leave for Europe with the 15th Maori Reinforcements, Pioneer Battalion, 1916. MS KAHUKORE BAKER

no doubts about 'The Kaiser's Dream of World Domination'. Not only would Australia's trade collapse if Germany controlled Europe, but worse would follow:

> The Kaiser's scheme is the fiendishly conceived one that has been zealously carried out in every country Germany has occupied in this war, and in every previous war she has forced on an unsuspecting world – that is, to compel the women of every occupied territory, by shocking atrocities, terror and mutilation, to become the mothers of half-bred Germans – and so fill those territories with a half-bred German population.

For the 'non-combatants of Australia', Baker posed the question:

> Is it not better for you to strain your individual resources to the utmost now to send battle planes to help kill the enemy on the battlefields of France, rather than be faced with the possible awful tragedy of being forced to place your wives and daughters beyond the foul abuses of the German beast.
>
> Our magnificent soldiers have been fighting night and day to save you and yours. Cannot you do something more to help them in their colossal task on the actual field of battle.

For any who were not convinced by the threat of the 'foul abuses of the German beast', there was an appeal to self-interest with a reminder that contributing battle planes to the war effort was the most 'quickly effective' assistance that could be given, and 'by doing so you are helping to safeguard the title deeds to your property in Australia, and ensuring that this land so coveted by the Germans shall remain yours and your children's for ever'.[11]

The role of aircraft during the war had developed dramatically and their growing strategic importance was constantly emphasised. Baker placed particular weight on Lord Kitchener's assessment that a squadron of sixteen aircraft contributed as much to the war effort as an army corps of 2,000 men:

> Since the British and French tore the mastery of the air from the Germans, the Allied casualties have decreased by about 30 per cent. and the German losses in killed and wounded have doubled, and in some cases trebled. Control of the air means the power to direct artillery fire from invisible batteries.
>
> By means of aircraft the British Generals can harry the German communications far behind their fortified lines. Airmen can, and do, soar over the German positions and destroy trainloads of troops, blow up bridges and smash junctions, explode stores of ammunition and harry and worry the German reserves into a state of physical and nervous exhaustion.[12]

Prose of this kind, littered with extravagant illustrations of battle scenes, and frequent references to 'Huns' and 'Hunland', were the essence of the pamphlets prepared for the campaign, most of them being written by Baker himself. The language may now seem extreme, and almost a parody of jingoistic fervour, but it was characteristic of the time, as is shown by even a casual reading of the contemporary newspapers with their reports of the activities of patriotic societies and anti-German organisations.

To Charles Alma Baker, the imperial patriot, any means justified the ends. Moreover, to one who had followed the development of aircraft, and was convinced of their future importance, the war was both a lesson and an opportunity to educate. In 1914, aircraft were small and ill-equipped for combat, their only weapons those carried by the pilots. By the end of the war, they carried machine guns and bombs; the largest aeroplanes had a range of up to 600 miles, could cruise at 100 miles per hour, and some, for example the Handley Page W8, could carry 20 passengers or 2 tons of freight. Aircraft, in both their military and civilian use, were the symbols of progress, and the way of the future. At war's end, Baker looked ahead with confidence:

> In the near future it is conceivable that large bodies of troops with all their *matériel* – as well as foodstuffs and other products – will be carried by Air machines across the widest tracts of sea and land.
>
> Developments in the science of aeronautics, so essential to our economic interests and for our protection, can only be accomplished through widespread public interest in commercial and civil aviation being shown by the Peoples and Governments of all parts of the Empire, and by their whole-hearted co-operation for mutual benefit and protection.

'Bombing Hun Communications'.
SOUVENIR OF THE MALAYAN AND AUSTRALIAN BATTLE PLANES, 1914-1918

If we were in possession of large numbers of commercial and civil flying machines we should be able to rapidly convert such machines into weapons of defence, if necessity arose, and so prevent that sudden attack which so many thinking minds fear may be attempted ....

Perhaps equally important is the provision during peacetime of a chain of strategically situated aerodromes on Imperial soil throughout the world which would provide commercial Air Ports and be available for vital defence work in time of war.[13]

It was from this perspective that as early as February 1917, Baker wrote to the Under-Secretary of State for the Colonies seeking the return of the subscribed aircraft to the colonies at the end of the war:

I ask this, as I think in the near future air power will be even more important than sea power, and that Imperial federation of the air forces of the Empire must come soon; also that aerial bases for the protection of the Pacific will be established in Australia, New Guinea, New Zealand, Fiji, Borneo, Hong Kong, Penang, Singapore, and F.M.S. and if the machines are sent back after the war a large number of the most improved types of aeroplanes, and pilots who have learnt the latest tactics in war, will be at the disposal of the Governments of the different parts of the Empire.[14]

In practice, developments on this scale followed from the growth of civil aviation in the 1930s, rather than from military concerns in the 1920s. Baker did, however, have the satisfaction of seeing the surviving aircraft from his battle squadrons among the planes handed to Australia by Britain at the end of the war, although it is not clear whether this was because of, or despite, his efforts.

There was also satisfaction in the letters of appreciation that had flowed in throughout the war from the offices of British Prime Ministers Harry Asquith and David Lloyd George, as well as Field-Marshal Lord Kitchener, the Secretary of State for War; Bonar Law, the Secretary of State for the Colonies; Lord Montagu, Chairman of the Aviation Board; Winston Churchill, Secretary of State for Air, and many others, including state premiers and governors in Australia and the High Commissioner of the Federated Malay States.[15] In March 1916, when Baker presented funds for *The Alma Baker No. 3*, the *Times of Malaya* could not 'allow the occasion to pass without holding up his generosity and deeply practical patriotism as an example to the whole country':

> 'His conduct has been magnificent .... Mr. Baker has given nearly the whole of his time for almost a year, has presented three aeroplanes, and borne the entire administration expenses of the fund. That is patriotism of the highest character.'[16]

Baker visited Malaya briefly in mid-1919 before returning to Australia en route to the United States and England. He had been away for more than three years but needed only a couple of months to set his affairs in order and again entrust them to Freddie Shepherd and the plantation managers. In any case, his main concern was to gather material for the *Souvenir of the Malayan and Australian Battle Planes* that he was preparing for publication. When it appeared the following year, the *Souvenir* ran to more than 200 pages and included photographs of all the aircraft presented, together with a list of the major donors for each, copies of all of the important correspondence, appeals and reports associated with the venture and a lengthy essay on 'The Presentation Planes, Their Uses and Value' by Lieutenant-Colonel E.A. Ewart. The handsomely produced and bound volume was distributed by Baker to the main donors and subscribers, who were also informed that the King and Queen, Queen Alexandra, the Prince of Wales, the Duke of York and the Duke of Connaught had all 'been graciously pleased' to accept copies of the *Souvenir*.

The fact that Baker produced and distributed the *Souvenir* at his own expense must raise the question of how far it was an acknowledgement of the subscribers and how far a monument to his own achievements. Baker's name appears on almost every page, and several times on some pages, as either a subscriber or, in his role as Honorary Organiser, as the writer or recipient of correspondence, or as the author of an appeal in either Malaya or Australia. On balance, however, such a conclusion cannot be justified; there is no doubt that Baker was proud of his achievements, and derived satisfaction from them and from the public recognition that followed, but there is little evidence to suggest that this was his guiding motivation. Here, elsewhere in his writings and in his contributions to the Second World War effort, there is a consistent belief in King and Empire. Baker's correspondence on the battle plane issue is never self-congratulatory in tone. Then, as now, the public acknowledgment of major donors was integral to fund-raising, and would have been expected by his contemporaries. Throughout the campaign, his own contributions had always been timed to attract the maximum from others – to complete one squadron or to begin fund-raising for another, for example, or to launch a new appeal for a local or sectional fund. Support from politicians and prominent citizens was used in a similar fashion and names were not 'dropped' for private effect. And finally, an accusation of self-aggrandisement is difficult to sustain in the light of Baker's own response to public recognition for his fund-raising.

In a November 1917 telegram on colonial honours to recognise war efforts, Sir Arthur Young, High Commissioner of the Federated Malay States, nominated Charles Alma Baker for a CBE as 'founder of Malayan Aircraft Fund which presented 34 aeroplanes. Has taken leading part in stimulating patriotic efforts.' Baker, by this time in Australia, was asked if he would accept the honour, but he declined. As the Governor of New South Wales reported, 'Mr. Alma Baker is of opinion that if he were now recommended for and given the honour it would adversely affect his campaign in British Malaya and Australia for raising subscriptions'. Baker feared that his motives would be questioned, and he would be accused of working for the glory rather than the war effort, and asked that any award wait 'until victory has been achieved'.[17]

In January 1919, Baker's name was again under consideration for an honour. Sir Arthur Young had renewed his nomination but, drawing attention to the Australian fund-raising as well as that in Malaya, suggested that a knighthood, a KBE, would be more appropriate. The Colonial Office, regarding the matter merely as deferred from 1917 rather than as a new nomination, simply confirmed the original award.[18] There is little doubt that the recognition brought Baker personal satisfaction. He took the family to England, so he could receive his award at Buckingham Palace, and from this time onwards he regularly signed letters and identified himself on photographs as 'C. Alma Baker, C.B.E.'.

But if he was satisfied others were not. Florence thought it 'a pity' that he had not been given a knighthood, an honour that was commensurate with his contribution and would have given him enormous satisfaction. The *Times of Malaya*, ignorant of Baker's earlier refusal of the CBE, expressed surprise that he 'should have been passed over up to the present' and added:

> That Mr. Alma Baker has been honoured will come as no surprise to the
> people of Malaya, Australia, and even India and Ceylon .... But what will

The family in London for the presentation of Baker's CBE **at Buckingham Palace.** MRS ALMA CURTIN

come as a surprise is that the degree of recognition has fallen so short of public expectations. We can conscientiously say that neither Mr. Alma Baker nor any of his friends were particularly anxious for any reward of merit to accrue to him for services that were prompted by a pure spirit of patriotism, but it is impossible to deny that the results he achieved are deserving of something more than a mere Commandership of the Order of the British Empire.

In London, Sir Ernest Birch was similarly unimpressed and wrote directly to the War Office:

> May I as a Civil Servant of 30 years standing suggest to you that the honour conferred on Alma Baker is inadequate in view of his strenuous work in obtaining 41 Australian and 53 Malayan aeroplanes .... I venture to point out that Alma Baker's work compares very brilliantly with that done by others who have received ... higher honours.[19]

If Baker was disappointed at missing out on a knighthood, he kept his feelings to himself; to Birch, he simply commented that the 'Authorities at hand have a better perspective of the value of work done by those who could not go to fight', and let the matter rest.[20] Throughout his life he was always reluctant to discuss his own past, business dealings or achievements. On his wartime patriotism, the final word can be left with Zane Grey, the American author, who had fished with Baker several times in the United States in the early 1920s. On his first arrival in New Zealand in 1926, Grey could only say of Baker that 'He did something big in the war, never told me what it was ....'[21]

THE FINEST OF ALL SEA SPORTS

Baker had effectively retired when he went to Australia at the beginning of 1916. He was nearly sixty years old but still in good health and, with his family, spent most of his later years indulging his enjoyment of world travel. The rubber estates continued to prosper but for nearly two decades he lost interest in their management and development; neither was more than two-thirds planted at the end of the First World War and no more new rubber was established until the 1930s. Although his tin mines were all but exhausted, his income from rubber, which increased steadily as the areas planted in 1915-17 came into full production, meant that he was only marginally affected by the depression of the early 1920s. In any case, his assets were by this time so large, and essentially unencumbered, that the Chartered Bank of India, which had enjoyed his business for thirty years, was more than happy to accommodate him on overdraft. He was in an ideal position to pursue seriously the leisure activities that had recently occupied more of his time. Foremost among these was his love of fishing. Through his own interest, he helped to transform the sport of big game fishing in New Zealand by persuading Zane Grey, the American author, to visit New Zealand and publicise its game-fishing potential.

The visits to Australia had seen the development of closer relationships with some of Florence's Whitaker relations and the beginnings of tentative links back to New Zealand. Business affairs in Malaya could now be left in the capable hands of Walter Vanrenan, who managed the rubber estates, and Freddie Shepherd who divided his time among supervising Baker's few remaining tin mines, developing his own business interests and running the Kinta Club.

One of Baker's assistant rubber estate managers from 1921, and later an estate manager, was Lionel Whitaker, the son of Herbert Whitaker of Broadmeadows with whom the Bakers had often stayed while in Australia. In addition to his management skills, Lionel had a number of qualities that appealed to Baker: he had been a pilot in the First World War, although hostilities had ended in Egypt where he was stationed before he got to fly in combat; he was a jockey who soon became the leading amateur on the Perak circuit, riding many winners for the Sultan; and he enjoyed playing billiards.

As Judy had grown into a young woman, and the family had travelled more, female companions were added to the entourage – first Anna Minnett, Florence's niece, who received £400 a year from Baker, and then Enid Harington, known as 'Poo', who was paid £250. Poo Harington's mother was a lifelong friend of Florence, and her father a surveying contemporary of Baker; the families had been close since they had both lived in Auckland in the 1880s. Poo was employed partly as a travelling secretary to Baker, but primarily as a companion to Florence and to assist in caring for Judy who, despite being taught at home, and 'finished' at Frensham, was not equipped to face the world.

Even as an adult, Judy had an intellectual capacity and pattern of behaviour more akin to that of a twelve- or thirteen-year-old than one of her actual years. Her condition probably had its origin in the circumstances of her birth; she was a first child, born when Florence was forty-two, and the confinement had taken place in Malaya in a difficult climate and with limited medical services. As described by contemporaries, Judy's symptoms suggest mild mental retardation caused by brain damage at birth. Although capable of pursuing all manner of activities with considerable enjoyment and a reasonable level of competence, she was hardly able to maintain an independent lifestyle. It is not surprising, then, that Judy's future was a major preoccupation when Baker revised his will in 1920. He had turned sixty in 1917, and was now forced to face the realities of age. In fact he lived to be eighty-four but he could not predict such longevity and providing care for Judy, and protecting her long-term personal and financial interests became major concerns for the last twenty years of his life and had a decisive effect on the way in which he organised his affairs.

The 1920 will provides valuable insights into both business affairs and family relationships. Baker's first priority was Florence and Judy, for whom he provided the house and estate at Batu Gajah, together with all chattels and personal effects, and an income of £12,000 a year for which, at prevailing interest rates on safe investments, some £250,000 would need to be set aside. After this provision, and before the residue of the estate was divided between his wife and daughter, there were bequests and annuities amounting to a further £85,000.

The beneficiaries in this latter group were divided into three categories. First were those who might be called friends or business associates of Baker himself and included Sir Ernest Birch, the former British Resident of Perak, £5,000 'In remembrance of our long and true friendship'; Sir Arthur Young, High Commissioner of the Federated Malay States and Governor of the Straits Settlements at the time of the battle plane campaign (and the official who had nominated Baker for the CBE), £2,000 'In grateful remembrance'; Walter Vanrenan and Freddie Shepherd, who were to receive £3,000 and £2,000 respectively; John Harwood, a close friend who had been a Baker nominee in the acquisition of rubber leases in 1906 (and was already the recipient of £150 a year) was to receive £3,000; and there was £2,000 for Neville Sievwright, an old friend from Otago days, who was now a stockbroker in London and was for many years Baker's principal agent in Britain.

The second group, Baker's brothers and sisters, were each to receive £3,000 except for Major Valentine Baker, who lived in straitened circumstances in Birmingham; for him an additional £7,000 was provided in a lifetime trust. Of his family, Baker seems to have kept in closest touch with Valentine, to whom he who was already paying £300 a year to supplement a modest military pension. By the late 1920s there is also evidence of continuing, or resumed, contact with his sister Matilda Roxby, who spent time with the family in Auckland and also received a pension.

The third group of beneficiaries was made up of Florence's family and friends and included Anna Minnitt, who was named as guardian for Judy in the event of Florence's death and was to receive a life interest in £8,000; for Poo Harington, there was a life interest in £5,000; and Florence's sister Emily, Lady Walker, who had been widowed and retired to England, was to have a life interest in £6,000. Lesser amounts were provided for Florence's brother, Herbert Whitaker, her brother-in-law, Major Charles Minnitt, and a number of more distant members of the Whitaker family.

The will suggests that by this time Baker had accumulated assets worth at least £340,000 and probably more because, in addition to the specified bequests, the will assumes a significant residue for Florence and Judy. But the amounts themselves are not as important as what the distribution of the funds reveals about Baker's personality and principles. First, there was the emphasis on providing handsomely for Florence and Judy, and securing for them the house at No. 3 Changkat Road, which was as much a symbol of his status and achievements as it was a family home. Second, there was a recognition of family ties, with an interesting difference between his own and Florence's families. To his own family (and to his friends and business associates), Baker made outright gifts and, except for Valentine, equal bequests at a generous level, and even included his eldest brother, William, although 'I am unaware of the whereabouts of this legatee or whether he be actually living or not or whether married or single'. (This comment implies at least some contact with or knowledge of the others.) For Florence's relations, bequests were limited to those with whom the Bakers had kept in close contact and were, in many cases, restricted to a life interest. There is also a considerable emphasis throughout on rewards for long friendship and loyal service. The will was a complicated affair, with different trustees named for Australia and New Zealand, Malaya, and Britain, with the last to receive and administer the residual estates from the other two.[1]

The will was made in London where Baker put the finishing touches to his battle plane *Souvenir*, and saw it through the press. As a bonus, he received his CBE in person from the King rather than from the Governor at Singapore. The honour, which brought the public recognition that was important to Baker and capped three decades of significant achievement, also effectively marked the end of his working life. The rubber estates remained the basis of his income but by the end of the war he had lost interest in their management and had, in effect, retired to pursue other interests.

On the voyage from Sydney to London in 1919, Baker had spent time at the Tuna Fishing Club on Catalina Island off the Californian coast and from that time was a devotee of game fishing, 'the finest of all sea sports',[2] which became the key to his subsequent arrangements for world travel. He had been a keen fisherman for many years. On visits to Britain before the war he had enjoyed the fishing and shooting opportunities on his leased estate at Newton Abbot, where the family spent several months, and he had fished off the

Fishing in the Kinta River, about 1916. MRS ALMA CURTIN

Australian coast. In Malaya, the Kinta River had offered the chance of fish drives behind a temporary weir, spear fishing from a punt, and learning to fish with the *jala*, a circular throwing net used by local Malay fishermen. In 1922 Baker took a 5,000-mile fishing expedition in his small motor yacht along the coast of Malaya, Thailand and Burma, only to reach the conclusion that 'the best sport was not to be had in purely tropical waters for the warm water tended to make the fish lazy'.[3] It was the pursuit of tuna, broadbill and marlin off the Californian coast that really captured his enthusiasm and brought him back to New Zealand, apparently for the first time in twenty-three years.

In April 1923, Baker spent two weeks in the Bay of Islands on a visit that was to help change the sport of game fishing in New Zealand. From his base at Deep Water Cove near Cape Brett he caught two striped marlin, each weighing more than 250 pounds, two modest-sized mako sharks and five kingfish, or yellow tail, despite losing several days of fishing through bad weather. Back in Auckland, he spoke enthusiastically to reporters of the sport he had enjoyed, the tourism potential of New Zealand game fishing and the 'regal sport' it would offer for the Catalina fishermen:

> The sport only requires proper advertising to attract these men, many of whom are millionaires. They would be able to visit New Zealand during your fishing season without running the risk of missing any of the sport at Catalina, and if they could be attracted they would in no sense be disappointed by the fishing which New Zealand has to offer.[4]

Game fishing was then in its infancy in New Zealand, with fewer than half a dozen fishing craft operating in the Bay of Islands. Although the presence of game fish in New Zealand waters was known, and Maori fishermen had caught them for hundreds of years, it was not until 1915 that the first striped marlin was caught on rod and line in the Bay of Islands. The small number of fishermen who made the annual pilgrimage to Russell in the early 1920s generally used British-made salmon-fishing tackle and methods that gave them little chance of fully exploiting the potential of the waters off Cape Brett. Baker was the first to introduce Catalina methods, especially the practice of using the wake of 'tarporinos' (wooden lures) towed behind the launch to attract the fish to the bait, or of using a kite to make the baited hook move about in the water.

Baker not only had the best tackle available but took a keen interest in its design and manufacture. Whereas New Zealand fishermen used their imported British salmon rods, or local rods made from tanekaha (celery pine) with a narrow, large diameter reel mounted below the rod, Baker used a shorter, stiffer American style of rod (though British-made) with a wider, smaller diameter reel mounted above the rod. At Catalina in 1920 he had devised a testing procedure (subsequently adopted by Hardy Brothers, the leading British rod manufacturers) which would match the curve of a rod to the strength of line so that when the line was fully strained it would, in effect, be a continuation of the rod, thus minimising wear and the chance of breakages and lost fish.[5]

While in New Zealand Baker was also experimenting with a radical new reel of his own design. Whereas most reels had only a single gear (usually at a gearing of 2:1 to enable the quick recovery of line), a capstan to control drag and a leather brake, the Alma No. 1 offered two gears (1:1 and 2.5:1), the first commercially available reel to do so, and a neutral point which gave a 'free spool' with an 'instantaneous and extremely simple' switching mechanism between the three. Unique on the market, it was, according to Hardy Brothers, a 'fool-proof' reel. Moreover:

> The immense advantage of the "Alma" over the ordinary fixed multiple reel is that the fish is fought on the direct 1 to 1 gear, which greatly reduces the strain on rod, reel and line. This makes it possible to kill some of the larger fish on tackle lighter than that generally used, as less drag is required. This fact will be appreciated by all anglers who desire to give a fish every sporting chance.[6]

On this visit, Baker's gear attracted a deal of interest among the fishermen who saw it, but occasioned little public comment and no controversy. There was, however, some discussion of the notion that the Bay of Islands could become a mecca for American millionaire fishermen. The Tourist and Publicity Department renewed its efforts to promote the industry with a series of small publications, but more was needed.[7]

At the Catalina Tuna Club, Baker numbered among his friends Tom Mix, the Hollywood actor best known for his role in Westerns, and Zane Grey, the famous dentist-turned-writer who had won an international reputation through the publication of a number of romantic Western novels, including *The Last of the Plainsmen*, and *Riders of the Purple Sage*. Through several well-publicised exploits, and another series of books including *Great Game*

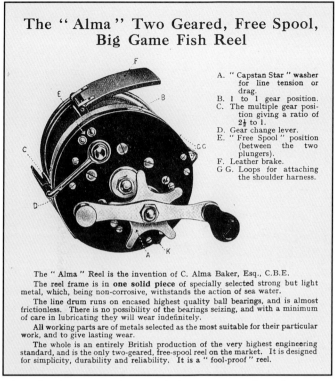

The 'Alma' Two Geared, Free Spool, Big Game Fish Reel.
HARDY'S CATALOGUE OF BIG GAME FISH AND SEA FISHING TACKLE, 1937

Fishing at Catalina, Tales of Fishing Virgin Seas and *The Deer Stalker*, Grey had also generated great popularity for outdoor leisure pursuits and a flattering reputation for himself. One writer has noted that, through his books, Grey

> … sought to establish himself as the greatest fisherman the world had ever known. He lived a life forever chasing that impossible and improbable goal ….
>
> A large part of Zane Grey's life was devoted to manufacturing and maintaining a legend of Zane Grey, with the hope that the myth would outlive the man …. And it was as a fisherman that Grey came closest to living out his dream.[8]

Larger than life in the pages of his own books, Grey could not abide any criticism or threat to his supremacy. Surrounding himself with 'complex veils of arrogance', he was fiercely defensive of his own fishing methods and quick to criticise those of others. But because Grey, alone of the world's sports fishermen, could bestow international recognition on the fishing grounds of New Zealand, he became Baker's main quarry.

When the two next met while fishing for tarpon off Florida in 1924, Baker was ready with his bait of an invitation to Grey from William Massey, New Zealand's Prime Minister, and he hooked the writer with a series of photographs of fish caught in the Bay of Islands. Grey was soon convinced that, with the catch at Catalina declining because of commercial

Autographed photograph for Judy from Tom Mix, late 1920s.
ERIC AND VALERIE GRAY

fishing, New Zealand presented new worlds to conquer and new records to be gained. Only Baker could make it to New Zealand for the 1925 season but a few months later he received a telegram from Grey suggesting that the two meet in the Bay of Islands in January 1926.[9]

Grey duly arrived on the SS *Makura* with three truckloads of fishing, camping and photography gear and an entourage that made Baker's look puny by comparison. The expedition was accompanied by a government cine cameraman, a photographer from the *Weekly News* and officials provided by the Tourist and Publicity Department. Grey's party was organised by Captain Laurie Mitchell, an impecunious Englishman who was Grey's constant fishing companion and who was, one suspects from reading some of the contemporary accounts, a rather better fisherman than Grey himself.

For the next three months Grey's exploits filled the newspapers and illustrated weeklies. Between 29 January and 21 March, he caught no fewer than forty striped marlin, seventeen mako sharks, a 704-pound black marlin, and a 395-pound broadbill swordfish. Records abounded: Grey's broadbill was the first ever caught on rod and line in New Zealand waters; and his 111-pound yellow tail and 450-pound striped marlin were world records for a thirty-six-thread line. Mitchell did almost as well, securing a world record 976-pound black marlin (that was unsporting enough to disgorge seven snapper before it could be weighed), and so bettered the record of 685 pounds that he had set just days before. He also established a New Zealand record for landing five striped marlin in a day.

'Another Trout Succumbs to the Zane Grey Technique', April 1926. *NEW ZEALAND HERALD*

Baker kept a rather lower profile. He stayed at Otehei Bay on Urupukapuka Island, as did Grey, but set up his camp some little distance away, and fished, as he was to do for twenty years, from the *Reliance* with Captain Stan Adamson. He had his most successful season ever at the Bay of Islands, catching a total of eight striped marlin with an average weight of 265 pounds. His best catch, at North Cape, was a 350-pound striped marlin – the first taken on rod and line in the area – landed after Grey's boat had turned back because of rough seas. After leaving the Bay of Islands, Baker accompanied Grey and Mitchell on visits to the Waitomo Caves and to Rotorua before heading south with them for a spell of trout fishing. From camps on the Western Bay of Lake Taupo and at Kowhai Flat (now the Duchess Pool), just south of Turangi on the Tongariro River, the party enjoyed spectacular success fishing the Waihoro and Waihaha Streams, the Tongariro River, and the lake itself. Grey, Mitchell and Baker all caught trout weighing well over 11 pounds, although most they caught were closer to 6-8 pounds; in one day on the Tongariro, Mitchell caught twenty fish and Grey thirteen with Baker, whose catch consistently trailed that of the others, bringing home five.

From Grey's point of view and, indeed, from the perspective of the New Zealand government, the expedition had been a success but Grey left behind feelings of rancour among the local fishermen who resented his arrogance and the way he was lionised by the press, and objected to his swearing in the company of women. They were scornful of the way that he constantly advertised his own success:

> He runs his fishing on circus lines. When he caught a swordfish he announced through a megaphone in grandiloquent tones, "Mr. Zane Grey has caught another swordfish; weight 273 lbs," as the case might be. Then there would be run to the mast head a pennant with "swordfish" printed on it.
>
> One Australian who regarded the procedure as swank, announced, when he caught a swordfish, that it weighed 6000 pounds and in the place of the pennant ran up to the mast head his pajama pants instead.[10]

The New Zealand fishermen also noted that Grey allowed his crew to hook fish for him to land, and the fact that 'his' 704-pound black marlin was actually hooked and played for some time by Mitchell before Grey changed boats to play the fish which he loaded onto his own heavier tackle before landing it. The New Zealanders were prepared to accept all this, but there was a limit to their tolerance. In particular, they resented his use of 'minders' to hold trout pools until he was ready to fish them, and objected to his attempt to buy a large tract of the Tongariro for his own exclusive use.

But all this paled into insignificance alongside their objection to his frequently expressed charge that, when it came to the finer points of game fishing, they were ignorant, unsporting, provincial conservatives. Grey maintained that they did not get the best out of their tackle and nor did they enjoy the best sport because they mounted reel over rod instead of rod over reel, used large triple gang hooks instead of the single hooks favoured by Americans and drifted rather than trolled for their quarry, some of which they then despatched with massive harpoons as soon as they could get their fish close to the boat, instead of playing them to the finish and securing them with a gaff. And as far as trout fishing was concerned, Grey was severely critical of those who gave the fish little chance because, instead of true lightweight fly fishing tackle, they used heavy salmon fishing gear.[11]

The debate over fishing tackle surfaced in Grey's early interviews with the New Zealand press, but sparked no real controversy until articles written by Grey himself were published in the *New Zealand Herald* in February and March 1926. Grey took particular exception to the practice of harpooning mako rather than fighting them to the end; the use of the triple hook which he rejected as unsportsmanlike, likely to result in fish being foul-hooked rather than hooked in the mouth – and thus unlikely to leap and fight in spectacular fashion; and the New Zealand preference for drifting with a deep bait rather than trolling on the surface using small wooden lures or teasers to bring the fish to the surface. Grey advocated the use of 'a short strong rod, one that will bend and spring back, a heavy reel with adequate drag, and powerful line. Reel and Guides must be on top because if they are not the angler cannot brace his feet on the boat and pull with all his might.' To Grey's critical eye:

The New Zealand angler, when he got a bite, merely held his rod up and let the boatman run the boat in the direction the fish wanted to go. He did not strike the fish hard, as we do. He did not bend the rod, or pump the fish hard, as we do. He followed the fish out to sea, and several hours later returned either with or without the fish, mostly without.[12]

As might have been expected, Grey's attack drew a sharp response from local fishermen[13] and a defence from Captain Mitchell (though this showed signs of having been written by Grey himself) and from Baker. As 'he was the chief cause of Mr. Zane Grey's visit to New Zealand', Baker thought it 'incumbent upon him to set right as far as he could the slight irritation caused among fishermen' by their 'misconceptions' of Grey's comments and fishing methods. Baker stressed Grey's wide experience, the reduced wear and tear on rod and line when the strain was spread along the length of the rod by having the reel mounted on top, and that the essence of the sport lay in fighting the fish, rather than merely catching it. Baker added that what Grey advocated as far as hooks and harpoons were concerned was no less than the requirement of game fishing clubs in the United States and elsewhere. But he did acknowledge the undoubted pleasure gained by New Zealand fishermen 'in spite of the rather out-of-date methods' used at the Bay of Islands.[14]

Resentful of the hostile response to his comments, Grey cancelled the remaining articles in his newspaper series, and took his revenge on his critics in *Tales of the Angler's Eldorado*, his account of his New Zealand expedition published later in the year. But despite the critics, Grey was enraptured by the fishing opportunities in New Zealand and returned for several visits over the next few years. In 1927 he brought his 190-foot personal fishing yacht, *The Fisherman*, which had been specially modified for his use; she had a crew of fifteen, could carry three custom-built fishing launches and had no less than 'fourteen staterooms, three bathrooms, two saloons, and such refinements as a photographic darkroom, a special room crammed full with all the fishing tackle that money could buy and ingenuity devise, and a fully equipped forge and carpenter's workshop'.[15]

Baker also returned for the fishing in 1927 but he chose to stay at Rawhiti, along the coast towards Cape Brett from Russell, rather than at the new Zane Grey Fishing Camp designed to cope with the influx of fishermen following the publication of *Tales of the Angler's Eldorado*. He remained loyal to Stan Adamson and the *Reliance*, and developed a long-lasting friendship with E.C. Blomfield, an Auckland lawyer who owned the Rawhiti fishing lodge managed by his daughter and son-in law. There was no obvious parting of the ways with Zane Grey, and the two spent a few days trout fishing together, but from 1927 Baker simply chose to hold himself at a distance. It may have been that he was upset by the controversy of the previous season, or that he did not enjoy the writer's egotistical flamboyance. As one who always preferred to be in charge, he would have had little taste for being a minor player on the Zane Grey stage.[16]

By the fishermen of the Bay of Islands, Baker himself was seen as being quietly spoken, a man who thought before he opened his mouth, a good listener and raconteur who would not try to dominate a conversation. In his later years he did have the reputation of being a

The 504-pound mako shark caught by Baker at the Bay of Islands, February 1929. Record mako for the season. 'Good 3 hour fight . . . leader in gaffer's hands 7 times but would not allow him to be gaffed as I wished to fight the fish to the finish.' MRS ALMA CURTIN

food faddist with a taste for 'Worcestershire sauce and other unlikely condiments' in his tea, and for a health potion called Mate Nog, of which he drank copious quantities.[17]

His knowledge of tackle was recognised, as was his role in developing both Hardy's line of Alma reels and the Adamson hook, which he designed for Hardy Brothers in partnership with the captain of the *Reliance*. Over the years he designed several other items including the Alma Captiva hook for tuna, the Alma Rustless Swivel for trace wire, and the Alma Anti-Kinker spoon for trolling. All of these were manufactured by Hardy Brothers, some still appearing regularly in their catalogues as late as the 1950s. But of all the items the first,

Baker with a rainbow trout caught near Taupo, late 1920s.
BASIL RIKYS

the Alma Reel, was the most significant. It had been used by Baker, Zane Grey and their friends since 1922, and enjoyed a small specialised market until the mid-1930s, when it could no longer match the popularity of the Hardy-Zane Grey Reel (designed for, rather than by, Grey), or Hardy's much more popular Fortuna, for many years the standard for the sport.[18]

In the newspaper reports of 1926, Baker is referred to as a 'Prominent English Sportsman' with 'plantation interests in the East',[19] a misconception that may have begun with Zane Grey's first press conference in New Zealand when he described Baker as an Englishman.[20] There is no evidence that Baker described himself as English, but it is equally clear that he did not advertise his New Zealand origins either. Those who worked for him at this time had no doubt that he *was* an English gentleman on the basis of his 'aristocratic' accent and general demeanour.[21] In *Tales of the Angler's Eldorado*, Mitchell's Englishness is emphasised for American readers with frequent expostulations of 'By Gad!' in his reported speech, whereas for Baker it is 'By Jove!'[22] But this portrayal – or, rather, caricature – of

The 336-pound striped marlin caught by Baker at the Bay of Islands, probably February 1930. Enid 'Poo' Harington on the left. BAY OF ISLANDS SWORDFISH CLUB

Baker, although it might have been accurate as far as appearances went, also reveals the 'hasty writing and careless editing' that was characteristic of Grey's work.[23] Baker is introduced by Grey as 'the English sportsman', and a little later he and Mitchell are described as 'conservative British sportsman'. But Grey had evidently learned more about Baker while they were fishing together around Taupo, for he refers to him later in the book as a New Zealander.[24]

By 1926, Baker had established a regular pattern of world travel that brought him to New Zealand for the big game fishing from January to March, followed by trout fishing in March and April. In Auckland he would take a suite at the Grand, or later a whole floor of the Hotel Cargen, as the family's base for its New Zealand stay. From Auckland he would then travel (always by P & O) to the United States, sometimes to Hawaii for big game fishing but more often to Catalina where he had been made a life member. (Here, he was unlikely to find Zane Grey, for the author had been dumped from membership shortly after his visit to New Zealand for publicly insulting the wife of the club president.)[25] After Catalina, Baker sometimes tried his luck off the coast of Florida before sailing to Britain for the latter part of the summer.

In London he usually stayed at the Langham Hotel with Florence and Judy but spent his evenings in the Devonshire Club. Here, 'Barney' to his friends, he would play billiards or snooker, or 'slosh', a game that combined the other two. He was part of a group that often included Frederick Boyes, a solicitor, and the Sievwright brothers, Neville and George. This triumvirate, as well as being Baker's companions at the snooker table, also handled Baker's affairs in London just as Blomfield, owner of the Rawhiti fishing camp, had become his agent in New Zealand. From England, Baker would sail for Malaya, where he would spend a couple of months before going to Sydney for Christmas, and then on to New Zealand for the fishing. He followed this circuit, with minor variations, from the mid-1920s until he was forced to make changes to his plans because of failing health and the outbreak of the Second World War. On these travels, Baker was almost always accompanied by Florence and Judy, apparently without complaint, although Florence always enjoyed returning to Batu Gajah, which she regarded as home:

> It is good to be in our dear house again, with all my treasured possessions around me, & surrounded by such beauty of hills & greenery, with the wonderful sunshine glorifying everything – our servants were all waiting for us, having incontinently fled from their various billets – much to the indignation & sorrow of the various mems ....[26]

CHAPTER 8

TE KARAKA AND LIMESTONE DOWNS

Through the late 1920s, Baker and his family spent more and more time in New Zealand, but less of it was devoted to fishing as Baker became more involved in the management of new farming investments acquired during the 1926 visit. In particular, he was concerned with two properties near Port Waikato – Te Karaka, which he owned in partnership with his nephew, Eric Baker, and Limestone Downs, which he placed under a manager. But there was little doubt about who held control, and from all points on his world travels Baker would receive regular reports and issue detailed instructions on farm policy through a frequent, almost continuous, exchange of telegrams with Alexander Warnock, a public accountant who, with E.C. Blomfield, held his power of attorney.

Auckland, where Barney and Floss had spent the early years of their marriage, became their base for up to four months each year. Although they sometimes rented an apartment, they were more inclined to take a suite of rooms at the Grand or Cargen to accommodate a party that usually included not only the members of the family, and visitors, but Poo Harington and one or two Asian servants as well. As an acknowledgement of the time that the family was spending in New Zealand, Baker also imported from the United States a 1926 eight-cylinder, seven-passenger Cadillac sedan and hired a chauffeur to take care of it, leaving the car garaged in Auckland between visits. Although Florence and Judy accompanied Baker for part of the 1926 fishing expedition with Zane Grey, and spent short holidays at the farms, they normally remained in Auckland while Baker pursued the fish at the Bay of Islands and, less frequently now, around Lake Taupo. The women were able to resume family relationships and friendships that had been maintained only by correspondence for many years, not only with the Whitakers but also with members of the Baker family, including Barney's sister Matilda Roxby, who now lived in Auckland, and his nephew, Eric Baker, who was a farmer in the Waikato district south of Auckland. It is not clear just how much contact Baker had with his relatives during his visits of 1923 and 1925, but in the latter year Eric and May Baker named their first child Alma Florence after Barney and Floss. In May 1926, the relationship developed further when Eric asked his uncle to invest in Te Karaka, the 2,378-acre property that he farmed south of Port Waikato.

Eric faced serious difficulties on the farm. The foundation of Te Karaka had been laid by his father, Herbert, Charles Alma Baker's youngest brother, who had bought 1,700 acres of bush country just south of the Kaawa Stream, some 40 miles south of Auckland, in 1913. Herbert was no farmer, having worked for the Railway Commissioners after leaving school, where he had risen from clerk to stationmaster by the mid-1890s.[1] In 1913 Herbert was based in Wellington and Eric, then aged seventeen, was working as a clerk for A.S. Paterson & Co. The two travelled to Auckland to buy horses and supplies and then rode south to take possession of the land which was some distance from the nearest road and covered in bush. With the help of the Pairama family, who were close neighbours, Eric built a nikau (palm thatch) hut near the karaka tree that gave the farm its name. Having moved into the hut, which was to be his home for five years, he then set about clearing the land. In 1916 he was rejoined by his father and three years later the farm was expanded by a further 865 acres.[2] At about this point, or perhaps earlier, Herbert acquired further capital from Archibald Peak, an Auckland solicitor, who became a sleeping partner.

After his father's death in 1923, Eric was left owning a quarter of a farm that had been heavily mortgaged to raise capital for development and to survive the depression of the early 1920s. Peak had suffered a nervous breakdown and he, together with all Herbert's legatees except Eric, wanted to quit the business which was encumbered with no fewer than six mortgages to a total value of nearly £12,000, and a further £3,000 in unsecured debt. Interest was in arrears and creditors were pressing for payment. Eric had little hope of raising the funds required to buy out his partners and pay off his creditors, and faced the prospect of losing the product of more than a decade of his own labour.[3] Reluctant to leave the property while any hope of survival remained, and having followed in the newspapers the accounts of the Zane Grey fishing expedition, he decided in May 1926 to go cap in hand to his uncle for a loan. After a meeting in Auckland and a quick inspection by 'The Uncle' (as he was to become known to Eric's family), a deal was struck that involved Charles Alma Baker buying out Eric's partners and assuming responsibility for the debts on the property.

The purchase of Te Karaka was completed in record time. It seems that Eric Baker made his approach when his uncle returned to Auckland after fishing at Taupo with Zane Grey at the end of April. Within three weeks, Alma Baker had agreed to the purchase, reached agreement with Herbert Baker's other beneficiaries and with Peak, finalised management arrangements with Eric and arranged for Blomfield, his erstwhile fishing host, to conduct his legal business in New Zealand and for Warnock to act in financial matters.

At the Te Karaka homestead with Eric, Baker was enthusiastic about the quality of his new property and the potential of the district. Looking across the bush-covered hills towards the sea, he asked about the size and ownership of the adjoining property. Told by Eric that it was 'Bayly's farm' of some 7,111 acres, and that it had been advertised for sale, Baker decided on the spot that he would buy if the price was right. Taking account of the spectacular limestone outcrops that dominated its hill country, he called the property Limestone Downs.[4]

Leaving Warnock and Blomfield to negotiate on details, he raised a bank loan against the security of his investments in the Kidman cattle empire in Australia, and sailed at the end of May for San Francisco and the tuna fishing at Catalina Island. It was all done in a rush, but the area was not unfamiliar to Baker. Although he had not worked in the immediate locality he had conducted at least half a dozen surveys in the Waikato district in the 1880s. Moreover, Arthur Harington, Poo's father and a friend of Baker's from the 1880s, had conducted major surveys around Onewhero, a few miles north-east of the property.

Te Karaka and Limestone Downs had originally been part of the 90,360-acre Te Akau Run that covered a coastal strip 5 miles wide running between Port Waikato and Raglan Harbour. The land had been part of a larger block confiscated by the government after the Waikato wars under the New Zealand Settlements Act of 1863, but had subsequently been returned to Maori ownership, the northern section, including Limestone Downs and Te Karaka, being in the hands of the Ngati Tahinga.[5] In 1866, the Anglican missionary Vicesimus Lush recorded his impressions during a trip south along the coastal path from Port Waikato to the Kaawa, much of it over the country later taken up by Limestone Downs and Te Karaka:

> We got off about 9 o'clock: the country along the west coast (we were seldom out of sight of the sea) is very much broken so we had a series of steep descents and precipitous ascents and our progress was necessarily slow .... at a place called Kawa, a native village, we had stopped for two hours in the middle of the day: here the natives gave us a small hut in which we sat and ate our dinner – bread and butter, peaches and sardines, washed down with wine and water ....
>
> The huts, though looking very picturesque as we winded down the hill on our approach, were on a nearer inspection very old, very dirty and very offensive to the nose ....[6]

In 1868 the entire Te Akau Block was leased by H.C. Young, a visionary who anticipated by a century the steel-making potential of the iron sands of the Waikato coast. Young, his vision denied by the government of the day, sold his lease in 1874 to Thomas Russell, acting in partnership on this occasion not with Frederick Whitaker but with John Studholme.[7]

In 1882, with his grand design bordering on collapse, Russell commissioned Harry Bullock-Webster, an Englishman who had worked for the Hudson Bay Company, to inspect his rural properties. Looking back on his visit to the Te Akau Block, Bullock-Webster noted that Russell and Studholme 'had spent a lot of money on it, but the returns were unsatisfactory, and something had to be done to put it on a paying basis'. He found that 'The run stretched all along the coast, averaging about seven miles broad, running back to dense bush, which formed the boundary. The country was all hills and gullies, fern and flax covered, taking grass well where burnt off and surface-sown, much of it being first class limestone land.' In the area around the Kaawa Stream, Bullock-Webster rode through 'much bush and swamp land with boggy creeks to jump' and later recalled 'that bit of swamp when drained will be useful, I thought'.[8] His inspection complete, Bullock-Webster had to ride to Port Waikato, 'fifteen miles off over an awful track up and down hills and through thick bush', where he spent the night in the stockman's house, formerly a missionary residence, where 'you could see stars through holes in the walls and roof, the rats scampered everywhere, and the fleas!'[9] Harry Bullock-Webster and his wife later settled in Auckland where they became associated with Russell, Whitaker and their associates. In the 1920s, they were still among the close friends of Floss and Barney Baker, a link that raises the intriguing prospect of whether the two men discussed Baker's proposed investment in Te Karaka.

By 1926, the original block had been subdivided and the appearance of Te Karaka, at least, had been altered, by Eric Baker's endeavour, from Bullock-Webster's rather discouraging picture of forty years before. According to Hugh Jones, the stock and station agent commissioned by Baker to value the property, some 1,100 acres, nearly half of the property, had been cleared and grassed and divided into eighteen paddocks using heavy totara posts and kauri battens. Permanent water supplies were available from the streams, there were no noxious weeds to speak of and few rabbits. Eric Baker's 'modern homestead' of six rooms, an office and all conveniences commanded 'an elevated position with pleasant outlook' and, like the ploughman's cottage, shearers' quarters, stockmen's hut, woolshed, barn and implement shed, had been built from heart kauri milled on the property. Jones had no doubt that Te Karaka would provide a good return once development was complete. He

Eric Baker's homestead at Te Karaka, late 1920s. MRS ALMA CURTIN

generally approved of Eric Baker's management, concluding that 'Development throughout is satisfactory, being well planned, the whole of the work showing sound judgement, which will greatly facilitate the bringing under of the rest of the block'.

Jones did suggest, however, that some of the capital investment might have been misdirected; the buildings, yards and equipment were 'sufficient for the handling of a much larger tract of land', whereas the farm itself was substantially understocked. Even so Te Karaka was carrying 1,300 sheep and 200 cattle. Jones estimated that, as it stood and exclusive of timber rights, the property was worth £20,000 and that, fully developed at a further cost of some £5,000, it should generate an income of £4,000 a year. Much of the development cost could be offset by the returns on timber, because the uncleared portion of Te Karaka could produce some 800,000 superficial feet of kauri at 15s per 100 feet, and 1.2 million superficial feet of kahikatea and 35,000 superficial feet of rimu, both at 3s per 100 which, taken together, would add a further £9,000 overall to the value of the property.[10]

Charles Alma Baker paid a little over £21,000 for the property, £6,000 in cash, as well as taking over its debts of £15,000, and it was agreed that the returns on timber would be shared equally between Peak and the new owners. To preserve his quarter share, Eric had to contribute to buying out the other interests, which he did with a loan of £1,500 from his uncle. The purchase completed, the relationship between uncle and nephew was defined in a formal agreement drawn up by Blomfield. Although still entitled to his quarter share of the business, Eric Baker assigned all power over the management of the business to his uncle and agreed to 'act as farm manager for the said Charles Alma Baker and … [to] carry out the directions and instructions of the said Charles Alma Baker … and be subject to the ordinary rules of master and servant and … [to] devote the whole of his time skill and attention to his duties and … [to] receive there for the sum of Three Pounds per week and found as a wage'.[11] There were few signs of 'partnership' in the agreement, but many reminders of Charles Alma Baker's strong preference for independence, and his insistence on always being in full control.

Limestone Downs was a rather different proposition from Te Karaka. Bordered by the Waikawau Stream for much of its northern boundary, and by the Kaawa in the south, it spread from the Tasman Sea on its western boundary, to the Te Akau Line in the east. Although more than two and a half times the size of Te Karaka, Limestone Downs was worth little more than the smaller property in 1926. More than a third of Limestone Downs was still in virgin bush, and the development on the rest of the property had not been particularly well planned or executed. There were nearly 900 acres in natural grassland on the coast but through overstocking and the depredations of rabbits this had mostly been reduced to rat-tail – a poor, spiky grass that survived where little else would grow; another 1,500 acres that had been cleared and grassed had been allowed to revert to weeds and manuka. The only good pasture was to be found in a third area, somewhat smaller than either of the other two, that had recently been cleared and planted.

The balance of the property was made up of some 560 acres of barren ridges and 500 acres of swamp country bordering the Kaawa Stream at the south of the property. Charles Walter, who valued the farm for the mortgagees, noted, in terms reminiscent of Bullock-

Packing in stores from Port Waikato to Limestone Downs, October 1927.
AUCKLAND WEEKLY NEWS, COURTESY AUCKLAND PUBLIC LIBRARY - A12476

Webster's, that 'The swamp will be a splendid piece of country when fully drained and the grass is established'. At this stage, only half of the swamp area had been cleared and drained but the best of it was valued at £15 per acre, compared with £4 per acre for the property overall. Even with this promising area there were drawbacks – the swamp was remote from the other developed areas of the farm and some of the recently drained area was accessible only by using a neighbour's bridge across the Kaawa.

The value of the property was diminished by its remoteness. Approaching by road from Auckland, it was first necessary to travel some distance to the south, and then to take the road through Glen Murray, Waimarama and Waikaretu that had been extended, as a barely formed clay track, to reach Te Karaka and the southern limits of Limestone Downs only in 1925. For Limestone Downs, this meant, in the early days, that all stock had to be moved through this southern road, while the stores coming in, and the wool going out, were laboriously packed over the same 'awful track up and down hills and through thick bush' used by Bullock-Webster more than four decades before.

An even more serious problem was the rabbits, which were everywhere on the cleared country. Despite a poisoning campaign some years before, the rabbits had eaten virtually all the grass off the farm except in the most recently sown areas. The situation had not been improved by the activities of the trappers currently employed on the property who were, Walter found, assiduously 'farming' the rabbits – taking enough to make a good living but stopping well short of eradication as they worked their way around the farm. The farm was more effectively divided by stands of unfelled bush than by fences, making stock movement

Percy Newman's cottage overlooking the Waikawau Stream, October 1927.
AUCKLAND WEEKLY NEWS, COURTESY AUCKLAND PUBLIC LIBRARY - A12477

difficult; most of the fences that did exist were more suitable for cattle than sheep, and all were in bad repair. The farm was fully stocked with 1,400 cattle and 500 sheep. There were two sets of cattleyards but the only building was the manager's cottage, a 'snug little building' occupied by Percy Newman, at the northern end of the farm near the Waikawau Stream.

Overall, Limestone Downs had been allowed to run down over a number of years and clearly required heavy investment and well-planned development if it were to reach its full potential. The purchase was complicated by the fact that only about a third of the property was in freehold title. The balance was leased from its Maori owners and any transactions were subject to ratification by the Native Land Court. Baker first bought out Bayly's freehold and paid for goodwill and improvements on the leases, which meant taking over £21,250 in mortgages and a payment of £4,000 in cash, as well as a further £5,400 for stock and plant.[12] Then, finding the Maori owners willing to sell and prepared to leave much of the purchase price covered with mortgages, Baker set Blomfield to work on the laborious task of buying out the balance of the property.

On his return in January 1927, Baker, impressed with the potential of the swamp area, bought the 800-acre Girdwood Block on the southern boundary of the property and, three years later, expanded Te Karaka with the purchase of a similar area. After an adjustment of boundaries between the two properties to facilitate easier management, Limestone Downs covered some 8,000 acres and Te Karaka 3,600.

Baker's original interest in buying Te Karaka is not difficult to understand. His nephew's approach had come at an opportune moment. Baker's latest plan of bringing New Zealand

Felling a large puriri tree for fence posts at Limestone Downs, October 1927.
AUCKLAND WEEKLY NEWS, COURTESY AUCKLAND PUBLIC LIBRARY - A12478

sports fishing to international attention had been achieved, and rubber prices had recovered after reaching very low levels in 1921-22, leaving him in a position to give financial assistance at a time when he was likely to be receptive to a new interest. And Eric was family. In the regular payments he had made for many years to close relatives and old friends, and in his will of 1920, Baker had shown himself willing to support his relatives. He also had an established interest in rural investment, having put £20,000 with Sir Sidney Kidman for shares in cattle properties during the latter years of the First World War. Te Karaka also offered the prospects of a sound investment, despite the apparent burden of debt and a shortage of working capital.

Limestone Downs also promised to be a good investment, but it meant raising more loans. It was a brave venture for one who had an interest in agriculture but little experience of sheep or cattle. Perhaps Charles Alma Baker, now nearly seventy, felt some resurgence of affinity with the country of his birth. Perhaps, too, his strong pioneering spirit identified with Eric Baker's achievements and would be further satisfied by the development of Limestone Downs. All this might be true, but the evidence suggests that the key to understanding such a major investment at this stage of Baker's life is to be found in his awareness of his own mortality and his concern to provide for Judy who was now aged twenty-three and unmarried. Baker seems to have seen Limestone Downs almost as a dowry for his daughter. The purchase of the property might make it possible for Judy to marry a farmer who would take over Limestone Downs; the pair would be assured of a substantial income and a comfortable lifestyle, living next door to Eric and May Baker who could provide family support and farming advice.

In the press report that heralded the Bakers' arrival at the Grand Hotel in Auckland for the 1927 fishing season, there was little sign of Baker's habitual reticence about his business affairs and unprecedented prominence was given to Judy and her prospects:

YOUNG WOMAN AS FARMER

LARGE TUAKAU PROPERTY

MISS ALMA BAKER'S SCHEME

For a young woman to settle on a big farm of her own, with its attendant duties and responsibilities, is a task for which few women have either the qualification or inclination. However, an arrival by the Marama from Sydney yesterday was Miss J. Alma Baker, daughter of Mr. C. Alma Baker, well-known in New Zealand as the friend and companion of Zane Grey in his recent deep-sea fishing adventures. Miss Baker, who accompanied Mr. Baker from Sydney, will proceed shortly to a 12,000-acre sheep and cattle farm which her father has purchased for her in the Tuakau district.

The property, situated at Limestone Downs, 15 miles out from Tuakau, is partly grass and partly bush, and will provide Mr. Baker and his family with a permanent interest in New Zealand as he expects to spend a good deal of his time in the Dominion in the future. Miss Baker is very fond of riding and she has lived on sheep and cattle stations most of her life.

Mr. Baker intends to stock the farm with Polled Angus cattle and Southdown sheep, but attention will also be paid to the breeding of stock horses and thoroughbreds. On his way to New Zealand from the Federated Malay States, where he has extensive rubber and tin interests, he selected a quantity of purebred stock in Australia for putting on the new farm.[13]

The article contains obvious inaccuracies but it must have been based on an interview with Baker in which he was uncharacteristically open about his plans. Limestone Downs may have been intended as a dowry for Judy, but it became instead a new obsession for Baker himself during the major development phase of the property in the late 1920s and early 1930s.

CHAPTER 9

FARM DEVELOPMENT

By the time that Baker and his family sailed for the United States at the end of May 1926, the purchase of Te Karaka had been completed and negotiations for Limestone Downs had begun. Although it had been agreed that Eric would continue to run Te Karaka, and it was assumed that he would also supervise the manager at Limestone Downs, there had been no opportunity for Baker to decide on either development strategies or management arrangements for his new investments. For the short term, it was sufficient – and obvious – that bush clearing should proceed, rabbits should be eradicated and as much of Limestone Downs as possible placed under freehold title. To achieve even this much meant the beginning of a long series of capital transfers from Malaya to New Zealand as Baker continued to use the profits of existing ventures to finance new enthusiasms. Another important step had been Baker's decision to use E.C. Blomfield and A.E. Warnock, lawyer and accountant respectively, as his attorneys in New Zealand. Given Baker's absence for most of the year, it was their particular interests and talents, as well as Baker's own preferences, that were to shape the developments on both Limestone Downs and Te Karaka over the next few years.

As well as having farming and fishing interests in the Bay of Islands, 'Blomy' Blomfield was a well-connected Auckland solicitor, a prominent member of the Auckland Club and a friend of several Auckland politicians with whom he had both professional and social dealings. Of particular value to Baker was Blomfield's wide experience in dealing with Maori land. At this time, there was an implicit tension between the government's professed desire to protect the interests of Maori landowners, and the settlers' demands for access to the large tracts of land still under Maori control. All transactions involving Maori land required the blessing of the Native Land Court, where judges had to approve in detail the terms of leases and the acquisition of freeholds. The process was often complicated and drawn-out because many blocks had multiple owners, and agreement from all was usually needed before a judge would proceed. The court was supposed to ensure not only that the price was fair but that the long-term interests of owners and their descendants were protected. The value to be placed on improvements to the land, generally in the form of clearing, fencing and sowing, was a further cause of negotiation and delay.

Here, Blomfield was in his element; he first exercised his talents in the purchase of Limestone Downs, which included several areas still under Maori lease or mortgaged through the Native Land Court. Next came the purchase of adjacent leasehold land – Girdwood's Block, mostly south of the Kaawa, which was added to Limestone Downs, and part of the farm adjoining Te Karaka, which came under the management of Eric Baker. The latter had formerly been owned by the Pairama family, the neighbours who had sheltered and worked for Eric Baker when he first took possession of Te Karaka in 1912. Then, because of land legislation limiting the size of private holdings, the titles had to be juggled so that Charles Alma Baker and Florence each owned the maximum of 5,000 acres, and Judy the balance, with a complicated system of cross mortgages, agreements and payments which gave Baker himself control over the whole operation, with sole responsibility for its debts and entitled to any profits.[1]

Warnock, a public accountant, had a long association with Blomfield on whose recommendation he had been employed by Baker. A Scottish immigrant, Warnock ran a predominantly rural accounting practice. Through his connections with stock and station agents, and the city's hardware dealers for whom he acted as secretary, and as President of the Auckland Club, Warnock was well placed to buy and sell for the farms on the best possible terms. Although joint attorney with Blomfield, Warnock effectively assumed responsibility for farm policy and management and soon made clear that he was not merely committed but dedicated to protecting the interests of his principal. Baker set overall policy, approved the budget and established the priorities for stock breeding in particular, but it was Warnock who carried out the policies and controlled expenditure; it was his hand that helped to shape many of the early developments, through his supervision of the farm managers, his regular farm inspections and his determination to eliminate any waste and unnecessary expenditure.

Since neither Eric Baker nor Percy Newman had previously been closely supervised, and neither was fully conversant with formal accounting procedures, there were inevitable tensions. This was less true of Limestone Downs, however, than of Te Karaka. Newman had been Bayly's manager for many years and agreed to stay on for Baker. He was a cautious manager and, because he had always been in a subordinate role, he had little difficulty with the transition. But for Eric Baker, who had done much of the work of breaking in Te Karaka, and who was used to operating independently, it was more difficult.

At first, there seemed to be agreement as to how the financial affairs should be organised: Warnock would handle all major payments from town while Eric ran an imprest account to cover small payments on the farm. Because of the property's extreme isolation, this meant not only the payment of wages but also the provision of household goods from the station store to be charged against the earnings of station workers and of casual employees, mostly local Maori, working on fencing or scrub-cutting contracts. Here, on the necessity of setting credit limits, keeping detailed accounts and having the hands sign for everything they bought, Eric Baker and Warnock were of one mind, the former having already reached the conclusion that 'Maoris are tricky' and had to be watched.[2]

But when Eric Baker sought quotations for fencing wire directly from Auckland

Moving stock on Limestone Downs, late 1920s. ERIC AND VALERIE GRAY

merchants, he soon found that he had trespassed into Warnock's domain:

> The amount in this case is small and relatively unimportant but we feel it better to draw your attention to the matter so as to avoid any misunderstanding in the future …. While we act as attorneys for your Uncle we do not wish you to assume that our duties begin and end in signing cheques.[3]

Within a few weeks, the unauthorised purchase of two horses for Limestone Downs, and some overexpenditure on the clearing of swamp drains, brought another rebuke:

> We don't wish to keep preaching to you the primary economics of business – and farming is business …. An undeveloped bush property requires the utmost care and discrimination on every shilling that is spent in the development stage. Later on when there is an income to give a reasonable return on the capital invested you may be able to relax a little but that time is a long way yet …. [Y]ou are shaking our confidence in your judgement and ability to handle such a large property. Any serious mistakes made now in the capital development and scheme of improvements will be very difficult to retrieve later and is therefore giving us a good deal of anxiety.[4]

With just a hint of sarcasm, Eric Baker wondered if he had taken 'too much liberty in presuming that, as manager appointed by my Uncle, I had power to deal at once with this matter' of the swamp drains, but he was no match for Warnock and after profuse apologies expressed the hope that 'with this explanation I have gone a little way to regain your confidence which you say I have shaken'.[5] He may have done so, but the two were again at odds a month later when Eric Baker was dismissive of some suppliers of grass seed, and tried to play Bucklands off against Wright Stephensons in an attempt to gain a bigger discount. In doing so, he brought down the full wrath of Warnock:

> … the way in which you have dealt with this business is not only in direct opposition to instructions given by Mr. Blomfield and I but it has been done in a way which cannot meet with our approval. Speaking for myself personally I have business relations with all the large firms which I have maintained for many years and I am not prepared to become a party to your methods. Some of the firms you condemn have been in business for many years and still retain their standing and therefore must be given a fair chance of the business.[6]

Warnock then advised all the major stock and station firms that orders in the name of either farm which did not come though his office might be repudiated, so Eric Baker was forced to abandon his methods, which were probably little different than those of any other farmer anyway, and was finally brought to heel. He was made to realise that he was no longer an independent farmer, that 'The Uncle' and his agents had complete control, and that his spending power was limited to items costing less than £20. With that realisation came an easing of the evident tension between Eric Baker and Warnock (it was always Warnock rather than Blomfield who signed the letters) and the emergence of a more comfortable working relationship.

But these were little more than irritations when set against the overall achievements of the first six months of Charles Alma Baker's ownership of the two properties. When Hugh Jones of Bucklands, who had inspected the farms in mid-1926, came back in December, he found that a great deal of progress had been made.[7] On Te Karaka, most of which had already been cleared and fenced, a new cottage had been built for the married couple now employed on the farm, seven new bridges and culverts had been constructed on the Kaawa Stream and some 360 acres of bush had been felled. With the additional funds transferred by Baker, it had been possible to have all trees up to 2 feet 6 inches felled during bush clearance, leaving only the largest standing to be killed in the burn. Jones recommended that, for the next year, efforts be concentrated on clearing and draining some 500 acres of the swamp to create a larger area for finishing off fat stock for the market.

Progress on Limestone Downs had been slower, partly because it had been purchased later in the year, but also because there was less of a foundation to work from. Since its initial clearing twenty years before, there had been a lack of capital for new work and insufficient funds even to sustain the early development. There were few fences to control stock, the swamp drains were largely clogged with debris, limiting the usefulness of the cleared areas and, because of the preponderance of cattle on the property, the previous owners had not even bothered to build a woolshed or a proper set of yards. The quality of the natural grassland had declined, and much of the sown area had reverted to bush or had been abandoned to rabbits. There had been some bush clearance in the spring, with 150 acres being felled on contract at £2 per acre, but most effort had been concentrated on clearing existing swamp drains as a platform for future development. Eric Baker's own estimate was that the potential carrying capacity of the swamp was five times that of the bush-covered hill country, and the development cost per acre was less than one-third. Jones wanted a high priority placed on the development of the swamp, with double fencing of all drains both to reduce maintenance and to protect the stock; a continuing campaign against the rabbits; the clearing of the easy hill country at the head of the swamp; the fencing of the coastal strip where an area of about 1,200 acres was only roughly divided into three paddocks; and a start made on the clearing of about 1,000 acres of dense bush in the north-eastern corner of the property.

Clearly, any significant development would depend on improving access to, and communication with, the properties. Neither Te Karaka nor Limestone Downs was served by electricity or telephone, and the latter, without road access, could best be reached from Port Waikato along the coastal track on horseback, with a return trip taking most of a day. The only alternative was to ride to the southern boundary of the property, cross the Kaawa and pass through Te Karaka to join up with the road that looped eastward through Waikaretu and Waimarama, some 7 miles away, which had the closest post office and school. From Waimarama it was 20 miles north to Tuakau, where stock was bought and sold, and a further 30 miles to Auckland. The linking of Te Karaka and Limestone Downs by telephone to Port Waikato in 1927 made life much easier from a management point of view, but did little to address the basic problem. The completion of the Waikaretu-Port Waikato Road, which would tie both properties into the Port Waikato-Tuakau Road, became a major priority.

On his return to New Zealand in January 1927, Baker lost no time in taking up the cause. The Raglan County Council had already raised a loan of £6,000 for the road and it was to support the county's application for a government subsidy that Baker sought an interview with the Minister of Public Works, K.S. Williams. Pointing out that his properties had already cost him more than £36,000, and that 'access by road for the carrying in of fertilisers and large quantities of fencing material is absolutely essential before much improvement can be undertaken', Baker asked for an interview on either the 17th or 18th of the month when 'I am due in Wellington to meet Zane Grey and his party'.[8] By the time he met the minister, Baker could also report that he had donated £100 to the county to help clear slips and ease bends on the clay road from Waikaretu to Te Karaka. With the promise of a government subsidy, the county was ready to start, and when the Public Works Department subsequently tried to reduce the subsidy it was forced to bow to further pressure applied by Baker through Williams and R.F. Bollard, the longstanding local Member of Parliament, who was also Minister of Internal Affairs (and, like Baker, a keen supporter of racing).[9] A few months later, when it appeared that the available government and county funding would take the road only from Port Waikato to the northern boundary of

Limestone Downs, Baker and Warnock again applied pressure, suggesting that the county might raise a further loan to provide work on the road for the unemployed and, as the final clincher, offered a special donation of £1,000 from Baker so long as the work went ahead without delay.[10]

In trying to formulate policies that took account of the conditions at the farms, Baker drew heavily on the expertise of others, not just by reading the scientific literature but also by employing 'experts'. On soils and grasses, for example, he consulted T.H. Patterson of the Department of Agriculture, as he devised seed mixtures for the varying conditions on the farms. His first attempt in this direction produced mixtures for 'good land', 'light land' and 'swamp land', with as many as sixteen seed varieties per mixture. The total seed order for the autumn of 1927, which ran to some 9 tons of seed at a cost of £528 for 750 acres of recently developed land, indicates the scale of development and explains why the stock firms were so keen to compete for Baker's business. In the following year, nearly three times as much was involved, with fertiliser applications following the same trend as seed. Expenditure on fertiliser rose from £42 in 1927, to £965 in 1928, and to £1,749 in 1929 – Newman's salary, by contrast, was £400 a year – and included superphosphate, basic slag and lime, although expenditure on lime dropped once a tractor-driven crusher was bought for Limestone Downs in 1927. Between 1927 and 1929 some £4,300 was spent on fencing which made for more than 60 miles of new fences over these years. Part of this was for subdivision of existing pasture, but much, too, was for the fencing of drains on the swamp areas and for the fencing of newly cleared land. Bush felling cost about £3,000 in wages over the first three years of Baker's ownership. [11]

Such a development policy was expensive and beyond the reach even of Baker's income from rubber. Much of the development was financed through overdraft, Warnock approaching the Union Bank of Australia for an ever-increasing accommodation. With some £3,000 committed to the purchase of stock in the first few months of 1929, he was forced to write again, but not without assuring the bank that 'I need hardly add that as a result of the progressive policy adopted the prospects of this estate have been entirely altered and it promises to become a valuable and well-known property'.[12]

There was little emphasis on cropping at Limestone Downs except for some turnips for winter feed, or for turnips sown in small quantities with grass seed to provide cover for the young grass. Baker was opposed to any ploughing except for flat land and then, generally, only for establishing a better pasture. Such a policy, though unusual among farmers in New Zealand at the time, was perfectly consistent with Baker's criticism of clean-weeding in his rubber plantations two decades before.

> I have considered the question of ploughing land for turnips and other catch crops ... and have finally made up my mind that no land in this country, especially hilly undulating land, should be ploughed more than once, as at each ploughing a very large proportion of the original humus and bacteria which are essential for plant growth, are washed out of the ploughed areas into drains, swamps, and creeks .... The cost of such ploughing, fertilizing, and

The Samson Sieve-Grip tractor, bought in 1926, now at the Museum of Transport and Technology, Auckland. BARRIE MACDONALD

sowing is not in any way recompensed by the food value of the crops, excepting perhaps for those catering for the early lamb market – a proposition out of my policy. We are Pastoralists growing Stock and Wool – *not Farmers*.[13]

But some ploughing was necessary, especially in laying down pasture in the cleared swamp area. A Samson Sieve-Grip tractor with wide cleated wheels was only the first of many innovative or experimental items bought for the farm. Baker was still a man of 'theories' and could easily be persuaded to buy new ploughs, rush-cutters, fertilisers, seed mixes or castrating tools, many of which were quickly dumped in dark corners of farm sheds as they failed to meet expectations. The Samson, with its enormous weight and narrow front wheel, tended to bury itself in the swamp and was soon banished to a stationary role as a power supply for the saw bench or the lime crusher.

All this development meant a demand for more labour and one of those employed was Fred Rivers, a lad from Russell who had been Baker's boat boy in 1927 and had been forward enough to ask for a permanent job. When Baker left for a spell at the farms Fred was left in the charge of Florence who despatched him to Warnock: 'Will you be so good as to give him an order to some clothier for 2 pairs of strong riding breeches & 2 pairs of leather gaiters, which Barney will pay for .... he is to work under Mr. Newman – Barney says will you kindly tell the boy how he is to get from Tuakau to Port Waikato & arrange with Mr. Newman for him to be met there .... Barney always leaves me numerous strings to tie up & make tidy when he goes away!'[14] Until the new road was completed, and then when it became impassable in the winter of 1928, Fred Rivers was responsible for the almost daily trips to Port Waikato with the packhorses for stores, fertiliser and seed, and subsequently worked on the property as a shepherd for many years.

During his visit in the early months of 1927, Baker's main concern was to check on the progress of the development work and the purchase of stock. He had already decided that his primary object was the production of high-quality wool and beef. In a matter of weeks he had purchased Devon cows in calf from William Mountain in the Bay of Islands and, with an eye to the political future as well as farming, had bought Polled Angus stock from the Matakohe property farmed by Prime Minister Gordon Coates and his brother, Rodney. For Red Polls, he looked to Canterbury and the Otahuna Stud of Sir Heaton Rhodes, a keen fisherman, prominent pastoralist and Minister of Defence from 1920 to 1926. In his desire to find the ideal beef breed, Baker planned to put Polled Angus bulls to Devon and Shorthorn cows. And always, having combed all the available literature, he had an emphatic view on the ideal stock types. Stock buyers were asked to look for Red Poll heifers meeting the Baker criteria:

(a) Body – rectangular, big frame set low
(b) Colour – rich dark red (no white spots)
(c) Head – wide strong and short
(d) Nose – clear flesh colour (no clouds or dark spots)
(e) Muzzle – wide large nostrils
(f) Ears – small and erect. Yellowish tinge inside
(g) Eyes – prominent.[15]

While Warnock was left to deal with the farm managers and the stock agents in their search for Red Poll cattle, Romney rams and the like, Baker motored off in the Cadillac to Wairakei and Taupo, and then to Zane Grey's fishing camp at Tokaanu. Even here, however, he kept in touch with Warnock by telegram with a curious (but economical) mixture of business and pleasure: 'Weather vile fishing poor has Newman been able inspect red polls' or, with reference to a holding paddock at Tuakau he had just purchased for £800, 'get Eric arrange adequate fencing gates right away also cleaning plowing sowing fishing much better rains again on'.[16]

On his travels, Baker spent much of his time, when he was not fishing, visiting well-known stock breeders, and reading any material he could find on stock and farm management. In 1927 he produced for his managers, and for Warnock, a detailed paper on the various methods of establishing and upgrading stud flocks and herds, the relative merits of in-breeding and line breeding, the upgrading of run stock using pure-bred bulls and the importance of progeny testing to maintain the quality of the stud.[17]

With sheep, he showed little interest in breeding for the fat lamb market but was determined to concentrate on wool production: 'My endeavour is to establish a flock of big-framed, good condition sheep, carrying a heavy long fleece of high characteristics and fineness'[18] and he wanted to do so by cross-breeding Corriedale, Romney and Ryeland stock, being tempted towards the latter, then little known in New Zealand, by accounts of a breed that went back to the thirteenth century and was reputed to produce 'a magnificent, dense, fine fleece of high class wool, deep in staple and thickly set on the skin'.[19] He invested heavily in stud stock early in 1927 – Romneys from Featherston and Feilding, Corriedales from New South Wales as well as Christchurch, and Ryelands from England. When the first year's clip had been sold, and Bucklands suggested that it had not been as well classed on the farms as it might have been, Baker employed J.W. Mullon, an experienced woolclasser, both to select his stock and to class the wool at shearing, culling ruthlessly to enhance the quality of both the stud and flock sheep.[20]

It was not only livestock that was imported for the farms. In 1927, for example, as well as purchasing Corriedales from Australia, Baker tried to bring in lucerne plants bedded in soil that had been 'inoculated' with the rhyzobium bacterium in order to enhance their nitrogen-fixing qualities. The idea behind the very detailed planting instructions given to Eric Baker was to establish a bed of high-quality lucerne that could be the basis of subsequent plantings around the properties. In this case, plant quarantine regulations intervened, but the attempt did show that Baker had not only adopted the farms as his current obsession but had also revived his interest in natural soil processes and was determined to keep his properties at the forefront of agricultural knowledge.[21]

Baker's return at the beginning of 1927 also allowed him to review management structures. Despite any reservations that Warnock may have had, Baker's preference was for Eric to take control of the combined properties and he had this in mind when he drew up plans for the new manager's house to be built at Limestone Downs. But Eric's primary loyalty was still to Te Karaka and he refused to move, even for the substantial new homestead planned by Baker. Not used to being thwarted in his designs, especially where the family was concerned, 'The Uncle' thereupon ripped in half the plans for the new house, commenting that a manager who was a hired outsider had no need of such a generous dwelling. The house was later built to this 'revised' plan with a rather strange effect that lasted until it was substantially remodelled and extended in the 1950s. Eric remained to manage Te Karaka, but was relieved of any role at Limestone Downs for which Percy Newman now became manager, responsible directly to Warnock. It made little difference in practice but it was noticeable that from the time the change was made, Baker concentrated his primary stud-breeding programme on Limestone Downs.[22]

The manager's house at Limestone Downs was just one part of a major building programme in the late 1920s. Initially, there were plans for a 'Homestead for Owner', complete with stables and outhouses which reflected Baker's intention to spend long periods at the farm and, perhaps, his hope that Judy would settle there. Even though these plans were subsequently dropped, and the construction of a manager's house was deferred for a couple of years, Baker still proceeded with a head stockman's house, a 'community house' for Newman and the other single men, shearers' quarters and a shepherd's house on the fringe of the swamp. For himself, once it became clear that Florence and Judy would make only occasional visits to the farms, he had a suite of rooms built onto the community house; they were comfortable enough but spartan when compared with the panelled splendour that had been planned for the owner's homestead.[23]

For this work, and for fencing and yards, most of the timber, especially kauri and rimu, was milled from Te Karaka. There was little usable timber left on Limestone Downs except for kahikatea, then used mostly as a box-wood, which was concentrated on the swamp and was milled on a royalty basis by outside contractors. In 1927, it was estimated that some 5 million superficial feet of 'kike', as it was called, was still available for milling on the two properties, a sufficient incentive for the local millers to offer reasonable rates for milling the better timbers required for building purposes. But because most of the remaining timber was in inaccessible areas, there was a continuing need to build and upgrade tracks and roads to wagon standard. Earlier, milling on Limestone Downs had been possible only for timber needed on the farm, while at Te Karaka logs had been dragged by bullock teams to central mill sites and then taken out to the road on specially constructed tramways before being carted out on bullock-drawn wagons. But in the late 1920s, the building programme on the farms and the need for development capital meant a high priority on land clearance and timber milling, just when improved road access made commercial milling viable.[24]

As a first step some 150,000 superficial feet of kauri was felled and pit sawn into flitches on Te Karaka, and then a contract was let for milling and planing the timber needed for construction, and for the felling of the kahikatea on the swamp.[25] Many of the kauri trees were up to 6 feet 6 inches in diameter, but the largest were much bigger. In 1936, a single tree brought down in a storm – with a base diameter of more than 10 feet, and reaching 65 feet from the ground to the first branch – was sold for £200 and milled out at about 40,000 superficial feet of useable timber, which was rather more than had been needed to build the manager's house at Limestone Downs.

Even with Baker's wealth, such a hectic pace of development was difficult to sustain and from mid-1928, after an expenditure over income of some £24,000 in the first half of the year, there was a pause for consolidation. Even by this time, the carrying capacity of the properties had increased dramatically. Cattle numbers had been held at about 1,500 but sheep numbers had been increased from about 1,800 in 1926 to 9,000 by the end of 1928. Stock quality had also been significantly improved with the purchase from the East Coast of 3,500 Romney ewes selected by Mullon.

Although commodity prices for New Zealand farmers had fluctuated through the early 1920s, Baker enjoyed some good seasons before a collapse of wool prices in 1929 heralded the onset of the Depression. This came as a further blow to Baker, who had already been seriously hit by a continuing slump in rubber prices. He had bought the farm properties on the assumption that capital transfers would be possible with rubber prices at about 3s per pound. Over the first six months of 1928 they had dropped to an average of 11d per pound. To make matters worse, prices continued to fall and, at the same time, the British government again imposed production quotas, allowing plantations in Malaya to tap at less than two-thirds of their capacity.[26] By 1928, therefore, Baker's income from his rubber estates was less than one-fifth of what it had been in 1925, and economies were necessary.

At Limestone Downs, expenditure was cut to £215 per month, including all wages, fencing, development work and shearing. Warnock gave Newman a detailed budget and a firm directive: 'kindly keep these figures before you and study them more than you do your Bible'.[27] Eric Baker's expenditure was similarly trimmed and both managers now filed with Warnock monthly reports that covered all purchase and sale of stock, capital works and repairs, and conditions on the farms. At least part of the reason for both the reporting and the retrenchment was Warnock's feeling that Baker did not always get value for his money, and that a message needed to be sent to both local contractors and casual workers. As he

Milling kauri on Te Karaka/Limestone Downs, late 1920s. MRS ALMA CURTIN

complained to Eric: 'Most of the men seem to consider that your Uncle has plenty of money to squander and they want to stand under the golden shower'.[28]

By the time he returned for his annual visit to New Zealand early in 1929, and had the chance to view progress on both properties from the new cottage on the edge of the swamp (from which the married shepherd and his family had been temporarily evicted to make way for him), Baker had reached some basic conclusions as to how future development might proceed:

> After prolonged, personal investigation on the properties and careful consid-
> eration of the various problems confronting us, I have definitely come to the
> conclusion that the only way to make a success of these large undertakings is
> to concentrate for the next year or two on fencing, fertilizing and sowing our
> best carrying areas, leaving fenced-in "Run offs" surrounding the improved
> portions to be broken in by stock.[29]

The major development work of land clearance was called to a halt, apart from the completion of the new woolshed and yards at Limestone Downs, but consolidation continued through 1929 with the purchase of another 2,000 ewes from the East Coast. There was also a 'bold experiment' with autumn lambing, which had only limited success because the ewes seemed disinclined to participate.[30] The year saw the erection of another 6 miles of subdivision fences, and the application of more than 180 tons of superphosphate and 50 tons of basic slag in February and March. This represented the heaviest application of fertiliser for any year until aerial topdressing was introduced after the Second World War. The only consolation was that the road had been sufficiently improved for the sacks to be dumped by truck along the roadside for sledging to the ridges before spreading by hand. But, even then, progress was slow, as Newman gloomily reported: 'Topdressing is going slowly along. About six of the men left after one day at it, they all say they can get a better job on public works. It appears to be hard to get good men.'[31] It was also hard to get honest men; more than one lightened his task by dumping a few sacks of fertiliser down the deep limestone shafts scattered across the farm.

In the late 1920s, as a closer friendship developed between Baker and Warnock, the latter assumed an almost avuncular relationship with Judy, who still accompanied her parents on their travels. For the most part she remained in Auckland at the Cargen Hotel with her mother while her father fished in the north and then spent time at Limestone Downs. She certainly took no role in management of the farm but the hint in the 1927 press report that it might become her dowry did attract some attention. Over the next few months she received a number of enquiries, all from single men, for jobs that might be available, including one from which asked her to 'pardon a stranger's presumption in writing', and offered, among other qualifications for farmwork, that 'I am educated, tall and have a good personality'.[32]

Judy's attentions turned elsewhere, however, to an Irishman the family had met in Ceylon. Gordon Pottinger had been born in Karachi, the son of an officer in the Indian Army. A gentleman, but penniless, he had served in the First World War as a flying officer and had been shot down and seriously injured. He had farmed in Canada for a time and when he arrived in New Zealand in March 1928 Warnock introduced him to stock and station agents who might know of small dairy farms for sale.[33] Later in 1928 Pottinger visited England, hoping for an appointment in colonial Africa after he had been promised, then lost, the position of Secretary to the Resident Commissioner of the Cook Islands.[34] Pottinger and Judy were engaged in February 1929 and, in light of the impending socialising surrounding the wedding, Baker rented a house in the prestigious suburb of Remuera, rather than staying at the Cargen.

In April 1929 Pottinger and Judy were married at St Mark's Church in Remuera, at a service attended by 'a wide circle of friends' including not only Warnock and Blomfield, but Percy Newman and Huntley Connell, his head shepherd from Limestone Downs. Judy wore 'a frock of very old heirloom lace mounted over ivory satin …. Her veil of old Flemish lace was … held in place with a small tiara of diamonds and pearls.' She was attended by Doreen, the daughter of Harry Bullock-Webster, and Eric's daughter, 'little Miss Alma Baker, preceded the bride to the altar, scattering yellow flowers from her small gold basket'. The service was followed by a reception at the Cargen where the champagne flowed.[35]

After the wedding, the newly-weds took up residence at Oranui, the 75-acre dairy and poultry farm that Alma Baker had bought for them near Henderson, just north of Auckland. Ever since Judy had stayed as a teenager with her Whitaker cousins at Broadmeadows in New South Wales, she had been interested in cows and dairying but it was the idea, rather than the practical experience, that attracted her. A large new residence using the very best of materials was built on Oranui for the Pottingers, though it remained empty for months as they travelled to Tahiti for a honeymoon paid for by Baker. Their stay in the

The mouth of the Waikawau Stream, late 1920s. MRS ALMA CURTIN

islands was longer than expected, however, because Gordon first got 'a bad chill on his kidneys', which may have been a euphemism for something worse, and then suffered a serious nervous breakdown that left him 'as thin as a rake'. Judy did her best to feed him up and put some flesh on his bones. It is interesting that she poured out her problems to Warnock, rather than her father, and in their absence it was Warnock who took care of Judy's pet terrier and supervised the last of the construction at Oranui.[36] On their return, with Gordon still in a fragile state, Warnock met them from the boat, invited them out for an occasional meal, kept an eye on their accounts and helped them with the management of the farm.

In effect, Warnock had become Baker's business manager in New Zealand, controlling Limestone Downs, Te Karaka and Oranui, and even minor tasks such as making bookings or shipping the Cadillac to Sydney for Baker to use on a brief visit. To Warnock and those around him, and to Poo Harington, Baker was now 'The Chief', which flattered him when he found out about it. He even relaxed to the point of signing a couple of telegrams 'Chief!', but before long he was tetchily reminding Warnock to address telegrams to 'Alma Baker not Baker'.

Over the next few months, Baker and Warnock kept a close eye on developments at Oranui. The day-to-day running of the farm was in the hands of a manager because even when Gordon Pottinger was at the farm, he could do little. He had never fully recovered from his war injuries and, even at this early stage, was prone to drinking binges to cope with the pain and bouts of depression that were his legacy from the war. Before long, indulgent references in the correspondence between Baker and Warnock to 'the kids' (Gordon was thirty-four and Judy twenty-six) and 'dear old Judy and Gordon' soon gave way to expressions of concern over Gordon's 'health'; within months, the arrangements that had been intended to secure Judy's long-term future were going seriously awry.

As Barney and Floss had left Auckland for England after the wedding, Blomfield arranged a meeting for Baker with Sir James Parr, who had recently been appointed New Zealand's High Commissioner in London and who, before entering politics, had been the senior partner in Blomfield's legal firm:

> As showing what can be done by a man who knows how, I might mention that Mr Baker's estate is now running 10,673 sheep, 36 horses and 1522 head of cattle, and will winter not only these but the natural increase of both cattle and sheep. There is now, I estimate, a total of some 70 miles of most excellent fencing on the estate. Telephones have been installed where necessary, and roads, over which I recently motored for many miles, properly formed and bridged where necessary. One rich valley swamp of over 1000 acres has been thoroughly drained by a proper system of wide and deep ditches, and is now in rich pasture. Experiments are actively being carried on by Mr Baker with "lucerne" and other rich clovers and grasses in different parts of the estate, and he has given and is still giving great attention to the effects of various manures and fertilisers – a subject which he has carefully studied. His tractors, special ploughs and other machinery have enabled him to produce results which would otherwise have been impossible within the short time of his operations. His energy is colossal and his movements in the right direction.[37]

Blomfield was right; the achievements in the first three years of Baker's ownership were impressive, to say the least, but they were not his alone. Eric Baker, Blomfield and Newman had all played a part, but none had contributed as much as Alexander Warnock who had given shape to Baker's ideas, and had imposed his own unique style of management that had not merely kept the books straight, but had guided both Baker and his farm managers along paths which ensured profitable development of the property. The death of Warnock in August 1930, therefore, marks an important milestone in the history of Limestone Downs and Te Karaka under Baker's ownership. Warnock's successor had a different role; as Baker's accountant Esmond Cummane was expected simply to keep the books, and was not given power of attorney. Blomfield, who now had sole responsibility in Baker's absence, was too busy and lacked Warnock's passionate interest in farming; Baker himself was now seventy-two, and starting to develop new interests as the challenge presented by Limestone Downs and Te Karaka took lower priority. As the 1930s advanced, and the Depression began to bite, the momentum of development slowed and Baker was forced to borrow more to protect his properties in Malaya and New Zealand, and to maintain his own expensive lifestyle.

CHAPTER 10

COPING WITH THE DEPRESSION

Given the concentration of Baker's investment in primary commodity production, the Depression of the 1930s had a serious and cumulative impact on his financial situation, an impact exacerbated by his expensive lifestyle, increased borrowing and unwillingness to invest for increased or even sustainable agricultural production. To some extent this unwillingness can be explained by Baker's explorations of biodynamic farming from the middle of the decade, but there were also more fundamental farming and financial problems. In short, Baker's enterprises were like the depleted soils of which he was so critical; in these years, too much was taken out, and too little put back, for them to flourish and produce high yields.

The key to farm development in the early 1930s was the Port Waikato-Waikaretu Road that ran through both Limestone Downs and Te Karaka. The crucial section had been roughly formed in 1927, but still remained impassable for much of the year. The unmetalled clay surface meant that vehicles became bogged and the 'road' was, in fact, little more than a rough track. Even in the winter of 1930 it took Kapi Clarke from Limestone Downs 'all his time to get up [through the farm] with a few Bales of Hay with five horses and a wagon'.[1] It took the county council so long to clear and grade the road, remove the slips and repair the wash-outs after each winter that it was rarely possible to get the wool from November shearing out before Christmas. Baker persuaded E.A. Ransom, the Minister of Lands, to visit his properties and inspect the road in March 1930, so enabling Eric Baker and his neighbours (who put up £50 between them) to persuade the minister to provide £350 and the council a further £100 for improvements. Even so, the road still remained closed to vehicular traffic for much of the year. Baker himself, and Warnock and Blomfield on his behalf, badgered successive Ministers of Public Works, first C.E. Macmillan, then Gordon Coates, for additional funding. Blomfield claimed that Baker was 'probably by far the largest ratepayer in the County' and that he, 'more than anyone, has helped to bring the particular district before the public and give it a good name'.[2]

A partial solution was found in 1932 when Baker built a large storage shed, with both road access and its own loading jetty, near the mouth of the river at Port Waikato, where wool, fertiliser and fencing material in particular could be stored. While stock from the farms was still driven out 'on the hoof' to Baker's holding paddock at Tuakau before being railed to the Auckland market, most bulk supplies still came through the port on coastal ships from Onehunga. Gradually, through the early 1930s, the road was also improved with the application of limestone crushed from roadside rocks and outcrops. But although this improved the road between Port Waikato and Limestone Downs, it did little for the road further south where it ran through the swamplands of both Limestone Downs and Te Karaka. Much of the road was ill-formed and low-lying. Moreover, the county council had sought to economise in construction by bridging only the 'normal' width of the Kaawa and its tributaries and not its adjoining flood plain. In the lowest-lying areas the road embankment was raised slightly, but that was all. As soon as there was any flooding, both road and bridges were likely to be washed away. The problem was compounded by farm drains that were not large enough to carry the volume of water, and by fallen timber that regularly blocked the streams in the uncleared areas of the swamp.

Despite its potential for future development, the swamp area, being flood-prone, was a constant worry, particularly when sheep, rather than cattle, were grazed in the area. After one particularly heavy flood, Eric Baker complained to Warnock:

> I had a very trying time during the week end the weather has been awful with the highest flood I have ever known. Steady rain started on Friday evening on Saturday morning it was still falling steadily so I cleared all the flats but the creek was just a banker. The rain had not stopped on Sunday morning but at 9.30 it looked very black as if it were going to rain harder. The creek was still carrying all the water, ... just as I had caught my horse the skies seemed to open so I lost no time in getting away .... I shall never forget that day out. By the time I had cleared the rams off Pongatiki No 1 flat the creek was just overflowing .... I never experienced rain like it or saw flood water rise so quickly .... the flood was so high at the Port road ... that I couldn't cross the bridge which was about 5 ft under water the whole area was a lake .... I had to go back up the Valley but by now it was a sheet of water. When I got to the bridge on this end of No 4. you can imagine how things looked when I saw the bridge which should have been 3 ft under water, with my end floating. I got off Ginger and climbed on to the high end and it sank with my weight to my waist. Ginger behaved beautifully and followed me over .... a slip came down in front of me and I wasn't game to go on so I went up the fence towards the big kauri. Just as well I did as I had no sooner started to climb the ridge when this slip started off properly right from the top ....
>
> Smaller slips were going everywhere and it seemed as if the whole hill was moving as I climbed it .... I came on home and had a hot drink but as it was still raining very hard I set out for No 1 swamp. It was a sheet of water by this time with just the knobs above water and about 40 ewes clambering on to them. I had a lively time pushing them off and making them swim for the high piece at the top end .... On my way home the rain stopped but I was cut off by

a slip in the big cutting in the track paddock and had to double back over the big hill. Luckily there was a moon so I could see things ....

On Monday morning most of the water had got away from this end so I went to inspect the damage. Needless to say there is not a fence left standing .... Several bridges have gone and have yet to be found. The road is completely blocked in four places ... with dozens of smaller slips as well. I also found three hoggets drowned ....[3]

In 1929, as the Depression worsened and the government introduced new measures to combat unemployment, fresh opportunities for subsidised public works were created and Warnock lost no time in pressing Baker's case; in reply, the minister promised that the project would have 'early and full consideration' by his department and by the end of the year thirty-five unemployed men were working on the road. Rural work was not popular with the unemployed as single, then married, men were forced to leave their families in town and to live rough in camps. At first the men were kept on public works, but from September 1931 Coates, as Minister in Charge of Unemployment (and himself a farmer) tried to get the unemployed 'over the fence' from the roadside onto farms where they might be engaged in the more productive work of clearing and developing new land. The new scheme was intended to adhere to the government's policy of insisting on work before pay rather than simply paying relief, and to avoid the criticism that much of the work provided was soul-destroying, repetitive and non-productive.

Scheme 5, as it was called, was of immediate interest to Baker. He and Blomfield had already explored the possibilities with officials of the Labour and Public Works Departments in 1931 and, at a private meeting at the Cargen, Coates himself had asked Baker whether he would be able to employ any men under the new subsidy scheme. For Baker, the attraction was the chance to accelerate the development of his farm properties while his rubber income was down. There were costs to the farmers – who had to provide accommodation, cooking utensils, transport to and from the job, tools and insurance – but for those who could manage this, there were also definite incentives. In essence, the farmer received an interest-free loan for the *value* rather than the *cost* of the work to be done. As Blomfield explained after a meeting with a senior Labour Department official in Auckland:

> The value of the work is fixed by the employer and the County Council representative assisted, if necessary, by the officer of the Labour Department. The value fixed is not based on wages as heretofore existing as it is realised that such a basis would be prohibitive and more than the farmer could repay. The employer and the Council representative agree upon what they think, having regard to all the circumstances of the case including finance, would be a fair sum as the amount which is to be repaid at the end of the term by the employer.
>
> From Mr. Slaughter's remarks, I gather the amount which of course the employer has to agree would be somewhere about half of what the cost would be with the usual high paid labour.[4]

From the agreed value of the contract, the farmer deducted his costs, enjoyed the full benefit of the improvements for two years, and then repaid the agreed balance in the third to fifth years after the completion of the work.

Baker could see definite advantages in the scheme, but his farm managers were less enthusiastic. Eric Baker thought he could easily find enough work to occupy ten men for eighteen months, but wondered if it was all worthwhile: 'My impression of this class of man is that he only does enough work to say that he is doing a bit and that if we are supplying food etc, a job can work out expensive'. To make sure that he covered himself when preparing his proposal he 'estimated each man doing about $1/3$ of the work a man would do on contract'.[5]

Neither Eric Baker nor Percy Newman was impressed with the scheme in practice. Newman thought the fencing done of such poor quality that 'I think it will be dearer in the long run as the fences will not stand the same as those done under our supervision'.[6] And even though up to thirty men were sometimes employed across the two properties, progress was slow and troublesome:

> The cleaning up and other works under the Unemployment Scheme is going along very slow indeed. In the first place four men were sent out but only stayed one month. Three more were sent out and that is all we have just now. They have been employed at fencing & draining. Their fencing I cannot class as good. At draining they are quite all right.[7]

At Te Karaka, and later at Limestone Downs, the real benefit of the scheme came when recent Dalmatian migrants were employed on draining and clearing work in the swamp. Here, too, there were problems, with a dozen workmen walking off the job in June 1933, but once the operation stabilised under the leadership of Milan (Mick) Hrstich, real progress was made on both properties, and Hrstich's gang was employed on drainage work and scrub-cutting for many years, long after the subsidy scheme had been terminated. As labourers left the farm for other jobs, Hrstich simply recruited new arrivals from the immigrant hostels in Auckland. While working on the swamp, the men lived in the houses of the Pongatiki settlement, just south of the Kaawa, which had been abandoned by the remnants of a Maori community devastated by the Spanish influenza epidemic of November 1918.

For the government, the major attraction of supplying labour for Baker's properties was the prospect he held out of both long-term settlement and short-term development on the farms. In arguing his case to Gordon Coates, now Minister of Finance in the Coalition government, Baker maintained that he proposed to develop large dairy herds – 1,000 milkers on Limestone Downs and 500 on Te Karaka. He also proposed to build a combined butter and cheese factory at Limestone Downs, to serve his own and adjoining properties. He claimed that the whole enterprise could employ some fifteen to twenty families on a permanent basis and would provide benefits for the whole district.[8] The government certainly provided the labour for the development work but there is no evidence of any steps being taken to establish a major dairy venture. It is not clear whether this was yet another enthusiasm that faded quickly, or whether Baker's 'vision' was simply part of a

Scrub-cutters at Te Karaka/Limestone Downs, 1930s. Left to right: Milan (Mick) Hrstich, Tony Yakich, Jack Alach, Steve Hrstich. MRS MARLENE VODANOVICH

strategy to secure development funds. Given Baker's own earlier insistence that he was a pastoralist rather than a farmer, the latter seems the more likely.

Alongside the government work schemes, other development work continued on a commercial basis. In 1933, for example, Woolsey Allen, a Port Waikato timber miller, signed a contract for the removal of 2 million superficial feet of kahikatea from the swamp within two years. Only trees with a girth in excess of 4 feet were to be cut, and Allen was free to construct his own roads and bridges for access to the swamp and to use a team of up to sixteen bullocks to haul logs. For part of the contract, sawmilling camps were established on the station; at other times, however, it was proved simpler to use the Kaawa and its tributaries to float logs to points adjacent to the main road, for loading onto bullock wagons and carting to Port Waikato.[9] Despite the scale of the undertaking, Depression prices for this timber, which was seen as fit only for the manufacture of butter boxes, brought in revenue of less than £1,000 a year. There was a better return when all remaining kauri with a girth over 4 feet on both properties was milled in the late 1930s with Lang Freeth & Co. paying 8s per 100 superficial feet of timber from trees with a girth in excess of 8 feet 6 inches and proportionate royalties for smaller trees. Even so, the kauri generated less than £2,000 in revenue. The removal of the millable timber was the first stage in the development of the final areas of the swamp; all smaller trees and undergrowth were subsequently felled before burning, stumping, draining, ploughing, sowing and fencing.

By the time that most of this work was complete in the mid-1930s, more than 6,500

This kauri at Te Karaka, claimed to be the largest in the district, was felled and milled about 1937-38. From left to right: Eric Baker, Charles Alma Baker and, perhaps, Florence Baker.
MRS ALMA CURTIN

acres had been brought into full production on Limestone Downs; sheep numbers stood at more than 12,000 by 1933. Some 80 miles of seven-wire fences had been erected, and 30 miles of ditches, all 5 feet wide and 5 feet deep, had been carved through the swamp. Even so, the development of the swamp continued to pose difficulties and to demand heavy expenditure, much of it to repeat work already done. In April 1935, for example, Newman reported 'one of the worst floods that I have known' on Limestone Downs: 'the swamp fences are all down & some of them washed across the paddock & means new fences as in places strainers have been washed out and wires broken …. in slips the new burns suffered a good deal … the two year old burns suffered rather badly quite a lot of it has slipped'. And this was just the start. It then rained on twenty-eight days in June, and nineteen days in July with the result that 'All heavy land and swamp land is full of water and very wet for the stock'. Newman had 'not seen the swamp paddocks so wet and soft since they were drained as they are this winter …. all roads, tracks, etc are in very bad repair'.[10]

By the mid-1930s, the properties had cost Baker a total of £140,000, about half of it covered by mortgages and overdraft, and half by capital transfers from Malaya.[11] By 1934, the burden of maintaining an overdraft of £40,000 was beginning to affect Baker's finances and, faced with the continuing slump in rubber prices, he was forced to seek the consolidation of his debts in a single mortgage covering both properties.

In his private life, too, he had been forced to make adjustments. In 1932 he and Florence had returned to Batu Gajah, buoyed by 'a very happy letter from Judy', now living at Oranui – 'you would not think she had a care in the world'. Florence, too, was delighted to hear from Judy's housekeeper that 'Gordon was on the water wagon where I hope he will have strength to stay' but, as she confided to Blomfield, 'you know my opinion of his character, & I fear it is too good to last long'. Florence herself, as always, was '*very* glad to be back in my dear home, & rejoicing in the garden, which is looking so beautiful, with heaps of flowers out so that I can keep the house filled with joys'.[12]

Superficially, all was happiness, but there were real concerns. On the financial side, Florence told Blomfield that 'Everything out here is as bad as ever, & everyone cutting down expenses'. Everyone, that is, except Charles Alma Baker. On the farms and plantations he economised like everyone else, reducing wages and cutting back on maintenance and other expenditure, but for Baker himself it made little difference. Throughout the Depression he continued to draw £700 per month, £8,400 a year, to cover his own household, travelling and living expenses – a drain that was to have a significant, and cumulative, impact on his overall financial situation in a time of declining income.[13]

And despite the apparent cheerfulness, Florence was not well. On the boat from New Zealand she had 'just escaped peritonitis'— and it turned out that she had incurable cancer of the bowel. Despite her illness, she and Barney sailed for the Antipodes as usual late in 1933, and took their customary suite at the Cargen where she was treated by Dr E.B. Gunson, an old friend. As Florence had feared, Gordon had fallen off the water wagon and was still suffering from severe depression. He committed suicide at Oranui in February 1934. A coroner's hearing, carefully stage-managed by Baker, found that he had committed suicide 'whilst depressed by illness'.[14]

Just three months later Florence died in Auckland, but if Baker felt grief at the loss of his companion of nearly forty-eight years, he did not share it with others. Even with those closest to him, he showed no emotion and did not discuss his wife's illness or her death. He remained, as he had always been, private, self-contained, slightly aloof and undemonstrative.[15] But he was again faced with the need to provide for Judy, as well as to adjust to the death of her mother. The financial side he covered with a new will, with generous provision for Judy, his own family, Florence's relatives, their old friends and acquaintances. He took

Judy back to England where Dr Gunson, who had travelled with them as a family friend, introduced them to Madame Clara Novello Davis, founder of the Royal Welsh Ladies Choir and the mother of Ivor Novello, the popular playwright and composer. Judy took music lessons with Madame Novello and toured on the continent with the choir. She formed a close friendship with Emily Mules, a soloist with the choir, and her daughter, Betty. Not wishing to return to Malaya or New Zealand, Judy remained with them in England, in effect becoming a member of the family.[16]

For his part, Charles Alma Baker continued to travel the world, visiting in turn New Zealand, the United States, Britain and Malaya, fishing where he could, and managing his commercial empire at long distance through a stream of detailed telegrams dictated to Poo Harington, who travelled with him as secretary, and developing a new enthusiasm, this time for Rudolph Steiner's philosophy and his theories of biodynamic farming.

CHAPTER 11

COMPOST AND COSMIC FORCES

It was inevitable, perhaps, that in old age Charles Alma Baker should ponder the meaning of the lessons learned through his various enterprises, and what gave unity and purpose to it all. Typically, he did not seek the answers in conventional religion but, after a period of searching, found them through the philosophy of Rudolph Steiner; typically, too, Baker pursued this new discovery with his usual energy. Moreover, he did not accept even Steiner's views in their entirety, but made them his own. Baker's enthusiasm for biodynamic farming, as it is now called, is not difficult to understand in the light of his long interest in agricultural methods, his willingness to experiment and his growing conviction that much of the natural world had yet to be satisfactorily explained.

The intellectual journey that led Baker eventually to his adoption, and then modification, of the Steiner philosophy in the late 1930s, had begun in the early 1900s with his purchase of the Kinta Valley Estate. Much earlier than other rubber planters or, indeed, the government's agricultural 'experts', Baker had perceived flaws in the then orthodox 'clean-weeding' policy, maintaining that it deprived the soil of humus and made it vulnerable to erosion. Baker developed the practice of digging the weeds into the soil for humus and, at the same time, using their roots to bind the soil against erosion. He was also a pioneer of using groundcover planting in rubber plantations.

Even at this stage, Baker read widely on agricultural matters; his library items contained such titles as *Practical Forestry and its Bearing on the Improvement of Estates*, *A Fertile Soil Means a Prosperous People*, and *Livestock on Every Farm*.[1] But he was also interested in wider issues, and in trying to explain the processes of natural science. This led him to reading on 'genetic philosophy', which sought to apply the principles of scientific investigation to the study of philosophy, seeking to discover 'truth' through investigation and the determination of relativities, rather than by the application of logic to principles assumed to be true. Following on from the nineteenth-century debates between creationists and evolutionists, one of Baker's favoured writers claimed that science did not destroy the hope of a future life but, rather, suggested that 'reality extends beyond the penetration of a finite mind', and argued (with Baker's approval) that 'Our most recent science has opened to us the reality of an invisible world'.[2] The notion that a guiding intelligence had shaped the evolution of the world and all living things remained fundamental to Baker's personal philosophy for the rest of his life.

There is little evidence, however, that Baker pursued the philosophical and religious issues with any enthusiasm at this stage. Like his father, he was outwardly an Anglican, an occasional rather than a regular churchgoer, but a supporter of the church cause. Just as Andrew Baker had offered the Assembly Room at the Northern Hotel in Oamaru for a fund-raising concert for the local Anglican church, so his son donated a new carved altar screen to the small 'English' church at Batu Gajah. He also supported Zionism, showing occasional interest in the activities of the British Israel World Federation. As he got older, however, he moved away from orthodox Anglicanism towards a belief that 'cosmic forces' had a direct bearing on the lives and fortunes of humankind.

This came much later, in the mid-1930s. In the years during and immediately after the First World War, Baker concentrated his attention on the recent discoveries in technology, particularly those affecting aircraft and imperial defence. Still from an 'imperial' perspective, he also explored the impact that recent scientific discoveries might have on food production (and therefore on trade and imperial security), and was particularly taken with the recent progress in research into the nature of vitamins and vitamin-deficiency diseases. Although scientists had become familiar with the role of carbohydrates, fats and proteins in diet by the end of the nineteenth century, it was not until 1911 that Casimir Funk, a Polish biochemist, had coined the term 'vitamines' to describe a group of nutritional components essential to maintain life; by the end of the First World War the term 'vitamin' was coming into common use with research focusing on the nutritional role of Vitamins A, B and C (the only groups identified to that point), and the diseases apparently caused by vitamin deficiency.

Baker's window into this new world was *Vitamines: Essential Food Factors* by Benjamin Harrow, a physiological chemist at Columbia University. Harrow's work was first published in 1922 and Baker's underlined and annotated copy records his initial interest in the subject, while his endpaper jottings and attached notes trace the growth of his interest in vitamin-deficiency diseases and the progress of his own researches into the recent literature. The product of this work, published in a small pamphlet of about thirty pages in 1923, was rather grandly entitled *De-Vitaminised and De-Mineralised Foods: Setting Forth the Wonderful New Discoveries of Vitamins and their Direct Bearing on Life, Growth and Health* and was published by Baker at his own expense. In the pamphlet, Baker acknowledged half a dozen authors whose works he listed (and whose works are all listed by Harrow) but made no reference to Harrow's own work, which was clearly the major source for his study. Baker not only borrowed heavily from Harrow, but seems to have taken literally his injunction that 'if we can tell the people, take such and such foods because they contain such and such proteins, which in turn are rich in such and such amino-acids essential to life, then we have contributed very definitely to the welfare of mankind'.[3]

This is what Baker set out to do in his own work, a pamphlet for private circulation: 'It is merely intended as a rough summary of data for my friends and others who have not had the advantage of access to the more recent literature on this subject. My earnest hope [is] that it may enable them to avoid the numerous de-natured foods at present on the market; they are injurious to health.'[4]

Although Baker's imperial concerns are still evident in the claim that 'recent startling scientific discoveries and revelations …. show that the stamina of the human material on which we must rely for the maintenance of the Empire is steadily being undermined through the consumption of faulty foods',[5] there is, again, a feeling that Baker is ahead of his time (certainly in terms of public awareness) in his urging readers to avoid what would now be called junk foods and to eat wholemeal instead of white bread, not to overcook vegetables, to cook potatoes in their skins, to avoid polished rice and to eat a few dates or raisins after a meal. Overall, there is a plea for balanced diet, and for imperial governments to publish 'a simple and clear table, giving the true values of all food' together with 'exhaustive lists of balanced dietaries suitable to the means of all classes'.[6] In part, Baker was responding to recent government reports on avoidable deficiency diseases, but there was a continuity with his own earlier views on the relationship between the soil and the production of food.

During the First World War, Baker had adopted a high profile as a public-spirited fund-raiser; he had corresponded with ministers and senior officials, and had hovered on the fringes of power. He enjoyed, and cultivated, his relationship with public figures. He was also an inveterate scribbler, and had on various occasions issued private publications on rubber planting, the training of horses for circus and polo and, on an early trip to England, in support of a Conservative candidate for parliament.[7] His largest project in this line had been his battle plane *Souvenir*, published in 1920.

All of this raises the question of whether he had some wider purpose in writing on vitamins, because the main body of his pamphlet concludes with the suggestion that 'the physical fitness of our people is of such importance that it might well be made a subject for discussion at the next Imperial Conference'.[8] No sooner had the pamphlet appeared than Baker wrote to Stanley Baldwin, the British Prime Minister, and to the Dominion Prime Ministers, urging action on an imperial front. In later years, he was to claim that he did succeed in getting the issue onto the agenda of the Imperial Conference, although there is no record of any such discussion in the official record. He also claimed that discussion at the Imperial Conference led directly to the Pure Food Acts of the late 1920s, which does not seem to be the case.[9] But even if he overestimated his own influence, the imperial agenda was still there – some of his published work was grandly dedicated to 'the Empire and to Mankind' – and Baker seemed to pursue a cause rather than mere publicity for himself. His interest then waned for a time, as he became engrossed in his farm properties, but did not disappear completely. Towards the end of the decade, he bemused, perhaps bewildered, his farm managers when he presented them with a lengthy paper he had written on amino acids and their importance in livestock management.[10]

In the late 1920s, Baker was more concerned with the development and management of his farm properties than with 'life-giving foods', as he called them, although his reputation as a food faddist among the fishermen of the Bay of Islands suggests that he did not entirely lose interest in the subject. But in the 1930s new experiments on the fertility of soils again caught his attention and eventually led him towards the work of Dr Rudolph Steiner, which was then becoming better known in the English-speaking world.

Baker started with the widely reported work that had been carried out in England since the turn of the century at the Rothamsted Experimental Station under the leadership of Sir Daniel Hall and Sir John Russell. Then, consistent with his early interest in composting on his rubber estates, he focused on the role of humus in soil formation and fertility.[11] Here, because of its tropical background, the work of Sir Albert Howard was particularly important. Howard, a British agriculturalist, was, for many years, Director of the Institute of Plant Industry at Indore, India, where he became famous for his work on using agricultural waste products as humus. The resulting 'Indore Process' of compost manufacture by individual farmers depended on a continuous supply of mixed vegetable wastes and the use of cattle dung to convert it into humus suitable for application to the soil.[12]

Following his exploration of this advancing knowledge of soil fertility, Baker re-examined his own views and was quick to acknowledge that, in his 1923 pamphlet, he had concentrated primarily on food that had been 'de-natured' through its treatment and preparation after harvest and that he had 'failed to realise that it is the actual condition of the soil in the first instance that governs the health of plant, animal and man'.[13] As a consequence, Baker published in 1938 *The Soil and its Products*, a pamphlet which laid great stress on the historical importance of humus in 'Nature's balanced soil' with the claim that 'It was the foods from these living soils that put into the blood-stream of our progenitors those vital forces which enabled them to build the stalwart British stock'.[14]

Leaving the details to one side, four main themes dominated this pamphlet. The first was that the natural balance of the soil, and the agricultural methods which had preserved it, had been lost in the late nineteenth century with the development of artificial chemical fertilisers, especially superphosphate. The second was that the production of deficient food from deficient soils had caused an increase in disease, especially cancer. Writing in the shadow of Munich, Baker was concerned with the broader implications of unhealthy food for human and national character: 'Is it impossible for us to imagine that the present ruthless policies of so-called civilised Nations, where men have been trained and armed for the deliberate purpose of aggression, murder and theft, have been caused in some part by the continuous consumption of faulty foodstuffs grown on impaired soils, thus producing impaired mentality?' His strident claim that 'Nature has no disease! Who has blundered? Not Nature!' presupposed that in an ideal state, in which man was fully in harmony with nature, cultivating its soil properly and eating 'life-giving foods', there would be neither disease nor war.[15]

As his third theme, Baker argued that existing difficulties with maintaining a living soil could be overcome either through Howard's Indore process, or through the biodynamic farming methods of Dr Rudolph Steiner. In this regard, the latter was given a slight edge as complying 'more with Nature's requirement for the production of food adequate to human and animal needs than any other system now practised'.[16]

The fourth theme showed that Baker was moving firmly towards an acceptance of the Steiner view of the world. There was, as the foundation, a clear commitment to the idea of a deity with man as a conditional trustee for nature: 'Can any deny that the Earth and all that it comprises were made by an All-seeing Creator, and given to Man in trust for his legitimate use for the production of life-giving foods from generation to generation, and that the Creator is still its real owner?'[17] After his own 'search after fundamental facts concerning the activities of life as far as I am allowed to know them', Baker had come to accept the basic principles of Anthroposophy, as Steiner called his system of belief. As defined by Steiner, Anthroposophy was 'a path of knowledge to guide the Spiritual in the human being to the Spiritual in the universe'.[18] In Baker's explanation, neither Steiner nor Anthroposophy are explicitly mentioned in this context but, as he saw it:

> In man two worlds meet, one is open to our senses, one is unseen. The world which is open to our senses is the realm of matter permeated with life, the unseen world is life itself. In the true sense a human being is only he who strives for consciousness of both these worlds. We have to do so all the more as we in every moment of our life meet in the world open to our senses the effect of the unseen world.[19]

Although his pamphlet was not specifically published as a Steiner tract, Baker certainly arranged for distribution of free copies – he claimed that he was paying to have some 50,000 copies printed in all – through such Steiner agencies as the Sunfield Agricultural Centre at Stourbridge in England.

Baker had apparently first discovered Steiner through the work of Ehrenfried Pfeiffer, whose *Short Practical Instructions in the Biological-Dynamic Methods of Agriculture* was first published in English in 1935. Baker bought a copy in London in September 1937 and, from his annotations, it would seem that he was immediately drawn by the emphasis on composting and the concept of 'a living soil'.[20] Pfeiffer later became the great populariser of Steiner's theories of agriculture in the English-speaking world, and especially in the United States, and in these early works he tended to concentrate on practical issues, such as the making of compost and the application of special preparations, rather than on the philosophy underlying the Steiner method. For this latter dimension, Baker almost certainly relied on Steiner's famous 'Agricultural Course' of eight lectures given at Koberwitz Castle in Germany in 1924.[21] The lectures first appeared in English in 1938, and were available from Sunfield, where Baker was a visitor, but given out only sparingly to believers by devotees who were mainly refugees from Nazi persecution and were, moreover, fearful of ridicule for what their critics called a 'muck and magic' approach to agriculture. Baker also seems to have been familiar with Guenther Wachsmuth's writing on *The Etheric Formative Forces in Cosmos, Earth and Man*, which had been available in English since 1932, but Baker's own views on the philosophical and spiritual issues were not discussed at any length in any of his publications.[22]

Baker was a reformer rather than a philosopher and, emboldened by the success of this first pamphlet, he prepared another, *Peace with the Soil*, in 1939. In many ways this repeated the message of *The Soil and Its Products* although, written on the eve of war, it made a more strident appeal for governments to act in the imperial interest – '*No living agriculture. No*

Empire'.[23] There was also a more emphatic endorsement of the Steiner method of agriculture and evidence of some dependence on Wachsmuth in the claims for the importance of cosmic forces in shaping the lives of humankind: 'it is essential that the manifold cosmic forces, which operate on the soil and on plant growth, be recognized and considered before the great Mother-Earth can recover her fecundity …. *Forces* more than *Substances* govern plant growth'.

With this, Steiner would have readily agreed, but Baker went much further in his attempt to understand how it was that plants might contain substances, such as trace elements, that could not readily be found either in the soil where they grew or in any nutrients they had been given. It was the complex relationship between soil, plants and animals, and the effect of one on the growth and health of another, that most intrigued Baker. Now, even though these processes are still not fully understood, modern scientific wisdom would presuppose that any differences between the composition of the plant, and the soil and nutrients in which it grew, could be accounted for either by chemical transformations taking place within the plant itself or by the plant accumulating from the soil substances that were present only in minuscule quantities. In the 1930s, however, these issues were much less well understood, and research of this kind was in its infancy. But it was no mere theoretical interest; rather, it was a long-standing attempt to understand process so that the productivity of agriculture might be improved. As early as 1928 Baker had grappled with the problem in a long letter to Warnock:

> it has always appeared to me that to produce the highest grade of beef, mutton and wool, these pasture grasses must contain, in an organic form, the mineral salts necessary for building up of their skeletons and flesh.
>
> The pasture mixtures that have been put down in every part of the world have been more or less blind mixtures …. The grasses have been chosen simply because they grow well, and are consequently more or less a blind filling only. The grasses that contain the mineral salts similar to the make up of bone, flesh, milk and wool, must enable stock to do a good deal better than if they were pastured entirely on grasses that grew well, but which perhaps contain in each class only a small proportion of the necessary salts, omitting to a serious degree other necessary elements contained in other grasses.[24]

A decade later, now convinced of the importance of 'cosmic forces' in shaping the natural world, Baker sought to solve the dilemma in a different way. His own solution, tentatively put forward in *Peace with the Soil*, was that the explanation lay in the deposit of minute quantities of cosmic dust which gave effect to nature's grand design:

> The question must arise in many minds as to the exact constituents of the 250 million tons of matter that are said to fall on the earth every minute the sun shines. Approximately one ten-thousandth of an ounce falls on every square mile of land directly under the sun's rays. This matter falls with the speed of light.

Mingled with our light waves there must indeed be a universal presence of
cosmic dust surrounding the earth; if this is not so, where do plants get their
hereditary and pre-ordained percentage of mineral salts, when such salts are
not in the earth, or in the water in which they grow?[25]

Here, Baker moved beyond established scientific knowledge and agricultural common
sense – and even beyond Anthroposophy – to a philosophy that was distinctly personal. He
seemed to recognise it as such and tempered his views in published statements.

As well as seeking to publicise his theories of agriculture, Baker applied them in
practical experiments on his rubber plantations and at Limestone Downs, although not
with a great degree of success. He quickly found that there were difficulties in the way of
putting theory into practice. Through the 1930s, he had faced serious financial difficulties
on his rubber plantations while he was trying to develop Limestone Downs and Te Karaka.
Not only had the price of rubber fallen disastrously – from an all-time low of 7d per pound
in 1930, to less than half of that by 1932 and without a recovery beyond 8d per pound
before the outbreak of war – but, in an attempt to eliminate a world glut, British Empire
planters had also been restricted in their output. The fact that from 1934 Baker's plantations were permitted only to produce between two-thirds and three-quarters of their full
potential obscured the reality that more trees were needed to meet the permissible quota,
because the Depression coincided with the natural decline in production from trees that
had been planted in the early years of the century. After some experimentation, the
industry had learned to overcome this latter difficulty either by replacing old trees with new
varieties, or by removing most of the branches from a tree and grafting new high-yielding
buds onto the old root stock. Baker did neither. He refused to replace his old trees or to
plant new ones, and he had no faith in bud grafting.

To some extent these difficulties or, rather, the failure to address them, reflected the fact
that Baker had ceased to take any active interest in the management of the plantations and,
according to his general manager, 'the maximum had been taken out ... and the minimum
ploughed back in since long before the War (1927 in fact)'.[26] In 1926, the purchase of Te
Karaka and Limestone Downs had drawn his attention further away. With his conversion
to the principles of biodynamic farming, however, Baker's attention again turned to the
rubber estates, and from about 1938 he tried to rejuvenate his rubber trees with generous
applications of compost. Estate labourers were put to work constructing compost heaps
each up to 30 feet long, 12 feet wide and 6 feet high, and yielding some 8 tons of compost.
He also had a tractor especially adapted for applying compost to the trees, although it did
not work particularly well, and always gave problems. Despite Baker's claims for the efficacy
of his methods, those more closely concerned with the management of the plantations were
not impressed with the results.

In 1940, Baker tried to initiate experiments at the Kinta Valley Estate, planting some
170 acres of new trees, half cultivated according to the principles of biodynamic agriculture
and half by government agriculturalists according to conventional methods. To carry on
this work, Baker pleaded with Peter Fraser, the Prime Minister of New Zealand, to waive

Making compost at the Kinta Valley Estate, April 1939. ROBIN BOYES

wartime restrictions and release from government employment L. Courtenay Hall, an agricultural journalist and radio announcer who was one of the leaders of the fledgling biodynamic movement in New Zealand:

> I am carrying out intricate research work regarding the improvement and yield of my present rubber with exhaustive experiments with compost materials .... the result of this research work will probably be of the greatest value to the Empire for the indispensable key product rubber. Now and in the future, its indispensability to the Empire both commercially and financially is almost beyond imagination .... this is the last big Empire work I shall be able to undertake.[27]

Hall was not given permission to work for Malaya, however, and the experiment had made little progress before the outbreak of war; with peace, the new planting was absorbed into the main body of the plantation.

For properties like Limestone Downs, Baker had already acknowledged that eliminating artificial fertilisers would prove difficult and take a long time. Neither the nature nor the scale of the operation suited the intensive composting that Baker favoured; that system was, after all, essentially designed for and suited to small-scale and peasant farming. Even so, he did have two 5-acre trial plots put into grass in 1938. One was treated with Fantastex, a proprietary fertiliser, and the other, sown in the afternoon two days before the full moon, was supposedly cultivated according to the Steiner method and treated with cow horn spray made according to Steiner's directions.[28] Given that both areas had been cleared and topdressed with an equal mixture of lime and superphosphate just months before the experiment, and that the 'Steiner' area was again topdressed with superphosphate, guano and potash after planting and immediately before the cow horn manure was applied, the scientific value of the experiments must be questioned. Percy Newman seems to have accepted Baker's detailed directions happily enough. He reported that 'Every detail in connection with this ploughed area was carefully carried out', including using stock to tread the seed into the ground; he did suggest, however, that 'perhaps the wool of the sheep may suffer on account of the dust'.[29] In 1940 there were further experiments with small plots of potatoes and turnips. To supervise this work, Baker employed B.G. 'Winky' Winkfield of Auckland, another prominent member of the biodynamic movement who supplied all of the Steiner treatments.

Despite a constant flurry of telegrams concerning the experiments, there were few other signs of these ideas being carried through into farm management. During the main development period in the late 1920s and early 1930s, there had been heavy applications of superphosphate, basic slag and other fertilisers at Limestone Downs to encourage pasture growth. Later, Baker was to argue against the sustained use of chemical fertilisers, although he accepted their use as an expedient on properties like Limestone Downs. In practice, however, the decline in the use of fertiliser on the station from about 1933, and the fluctuations in its use later in the decade, seem to have been linked to the price of rubber, and the availability of development capital, rather than based on any decision of principle.

In the late 1930s, there was little literature in English on the Steiner movement, let alone on the agricultural theories that were but a small part of the overall philosophy; indeed, the movement was better known for its educational theories and for its work in caring for handicapped children. There had therefore been a ready market for the Baker pamphlets, and enough enquiring and congratulatory correspondence to persuade him to persist. But by 1938 Baker was eighty-one years old, suffering from a liver complaint and having trouble with his eyes – others had to write all his letters for him. Nor could he rely on those who had earlier helped with his publishing ventures. Poo Harington, who had retired to England in 1939, and Lionel Whitaker, who had largely composed some of the earlier publications from Baker's rough notes, did not have the knowledge of the specialist literature.

So, in 1939, Baker turned to Samuel Levy Bensusan, a novelist and journalist who had many qualifications for the work. A former literary adviser to the Theosophical Publishing House and editor of the *Theosophical Review*, Bensusan was a close friend of Sir Donald Hall and had published extensively on English agriculture, most notably in *Latter-Day Rural England* (1928). After several conversations and a protracted correspondence, Baker was convinced that Bensusan shared his own conviction 'that a living soil is an indispensable pre-requisite for plant, animal, and human health'. After declaring that it was 'necessary to state the facts and indicate the remedy as clearly and precisely as possible', and that he did not wish to 'side-step any issue however difficult or involved', Baker nonetheless felt that, 'after mature consideration', some restraints might be necessary. As he neither wanted to upset the establishment, nor to be controversial, Bensusan was instructed not to make 'any statement which could be construed as an attack upon existing Social, Financial, or Business interests'. And even while Baker wanted it to be 'clearly stated that Steiner envisaged Cosmic Forces as part of nature's life cycle, of which no unit may be disregarded', he was again cautious: 'I cannot admit that a free and frank statement of the position either calls for or warrants, in such a work as projected, any excursion into religious or philosophical controversy and I expressly wish to avoid anything of that nature'. A practical reformer, Baker was to some extent torn between his conviction that change was necessary, and his desire to be seen as an establishment figure. He wanted 'his' work to be seen as a tract for agriculturalists, not as a statement of religious philosophy.

It was, perhaps, with his own dilemma at Limestone Downs in mind that he briefed Bensusan on the issue of superphosphate and other 'artificial fertilisers':

> The necessity to recognise the need to proceed piecemeal with organic manuring is a concession to practical difficulties and is not a departure from principle. It cannot be too strongly stressed that our ultimate objective is complete organic fertilisation: artificials are named as harmful, contrary to natural Biological laws and they must go. Artificials can however only be abandoned when organics are available to every farmer in sufficient quantities and at economic prices: no stone may be left unturned to achieve that position.[30]

At this distance, it is difficult to know just how much of *The Labouring Earth* is Baker and how much is Bensusan. Certainly the book was written by Bensusan (who also arranged for a foreword from Lord Addison, a former Minister of Agriculture who had published his own *Policy for British Agriculture* in 1939), even though it was published under Baker's name and he owned the copyright under the publishing agreement. Bensusan's fulfilled his brief to expand *Peace with the Soil*, and Baker's ideas ring through, especially in the discussions on the importance of the cosmic forces and the role of cosmic dust in agricultural production. The statements of the Steiner philosophy and methods have an obvious origin in the works of Steiner, Pfeiffer and Wachsmuth. Baker read the first two-thirds of the draft in mid-1940 but, given the exigencies of war, it is not clear whether he saw the rest of the manuscript before the book appeared in London a few months later.[31] He did occasionally correspond by cable with Bensusan on such details as including references to the work of Dr L. Kolisko, whom he knew, about the moon's influence on plant growth. In general, however, after Baker had sailed for New Zealand late in 1939 he left Dr E.B. Gunson, his doctor and a close friend, to handle the details.

Under the circumstances, it is not surprising that *The Labouring Earth* contains little new material; rather, Baker's views are reworked somewhat repetitively and supplemented by information from government and League of Nations reports about the current state of agriculture and recent improvements in plant and animal husbandry. As with Baker's earlier work, there is a constant call for government investigation of the validity of alternative approaches to agriculture, and a concern that official research was not addressing the important issues. Bensusan was critical of scientists' failure to cure the ills of

Turning a compost heap at the Kinta Valley Estate, April 1939. Those supervising, from left to right: H.F. (Hutch) Hutchinson, Lionel Whitaker, Charles Alma Baker, Roderick Whitaker. ROBIN BOYES

agriculture and, like Baker, he cited recent outbreaks of facial eczema for which there then seemed to be no known cure.[32] Here, certainly, Bensusan was in tune with Baker's briefing which, reflecting the Steiner view on the importance of spiritual over material considerations, had declared that: 'The failure of Science to go to the root of the problem represents Science's inability to think and act biologically and one cannot accept its present "a priori" hypothesis, based in frank materialism, as being adequate'.[33]

As a ghost-writer, Bensusan served Baker well, concluding in his name with an apocalyptic declaration that tied Baker's current views and his vision of a war-torn world to themes he had first explored in 1923:

> If my theories are correct – and here is their significance in a sentence – what I have called de-natured foods are the cause of the spread of such plagues as cancer, influenza, rickets, pneumonia, dental troubles and a host of others; they are the origin of the worst happenings of the intestinal region. On the other side of life they attack the nervous system and are responsible for the violence and hysteria that run riot through the world today, perpetuating hatreds, causing wars, and threatening the fabric of civilization. Food that lacks the full flow of cosmic forces must bring about deterioration of physical and mental health.
>
> .... It is nothing to me that I may not see the general acceptance of the views I have set out, since acceptance must follow as surely as light follows darkness in the visible world, and what greater reward can come to any worker than the knowledge that he has thrown a beam of light before those who work in darkness?[34]

CHAPTER 12

IN THE TWILIGHT OF A LONG AND FULL LIFE

In what he called 'the twilight of a long and full life', Baker was concerned primarily with his theories of agriculture, and with the making of wills that would assure the future for Judy and minimise death duties. The outbreak of war, and especially the Battle of Britain, also brought a resurgence of patriotic fervour, and a determination to help the war effort, but Baker had few resources available because of problems on the rubber plantations and at Limestone Downs. Low prices for rubber, declining production and Baker's refusal to countenance bud grafting or replanting meant declining returns and little money to spare for farm development in New Zealand. Nor was Limestone Downs meeting expectations. Because of financial difficulties, the pace of development had been slowed and, in particular, the amount of fertiliser applied had been cut back, causing pasture deterioration. Stock performance soon fell.

There were a number of problems with the stock. Most serious had been the effects on the sheep of facial eczema in 1938 when the Waikato had suffered its first major outbreak of the disease, and even experienced farmers had little idea of how to cope. Facial eczema, caused by spores generated by rapid autumn grass growth, affects the liver in a way that makes unprotected skin susceptible to burning in the sun; in many cases, permanent liver damage affects fertility and mortality. Only much later, and then largely by accident, was it found that the disease could be controlled to some extent by zinc treatments. In 1938, that knowledge was not available.

On Limestone Downs, Newman drenched the sheep with Epsom Salts and sulphur, and painted the head of any visibly affected animals with 'a mixture of Grease, Stockholm Tar, Te Trol Sulphur and lamp black'.[1] At Te Karaka, Eric Baker gave his sheep a drench of Epsom Salts one morning, a calomel tablet the next and then another dose of salts; he painted their faces with a mixture of limewater, linseed oil and carbolic acid.[2] Neither was sure that the treatment was working, but it was all that was available and they felt helpless if they did nothing. Altogether, hundreds of sheep were lost, either immediately from the disease or later during lambing, or from becoming lost in the bush where they had sought protection from the sun. Lambing percentages and wool production were also affected.

Newman had also begun to question whether Limestone Downs had the most suitable stock for the local conditions. Baker's obsession with fine wool production had led him eventually to a Corriedale-Romney cross, but the Corriedales, which thrived on the South Island high country, did not do so well in the wetter Waikato climate. Moreover, once Mullon had been employed to improve the quality of the wool, he culled and bought sheep on wool quality alone, a policy doubted by Newman:

> I think to[o] much attention is paid to wool & both constitution & general make up is not given enough consideration. I find Corriedales are hard enough to keep right both in their feet & Health in this wet climate and unless we are going to breed from strong good condition rams we are doomed to failure with this breed of sheep. Being manager I think it is my place to draw Mr Bakers attention to these facts & I hope in the near future to be able to cull any Corriedale & its crosses that show any defects at all from the flock. I feel sure there are on the market a more compact good body & shorter legged type of Corriedale than what we are getting at Limestone Downs if there is not then it does not say much for the breed.[3]

By the end of the decade the farms faced a number of difficulties. As well as problems with the stock, the carrying capacity of the farms was declining, and Limestone Downs was still bearing the burden of Baker's livestock breeding experiments. The initial fertility that followed the burning of felled bush on newly cleared land had worn off, and the reluctance to apply superphosphate to established pastures was soon reflected in decreased pasture quality.

From mid-1939, the farm managers were constantly drawing the attention of first Blomfield, then Baker himself, to the difficulties they faced. Newman found that he had insufficient winter feed for his cattle and that most were in 'rather low condition'. Both farms had difficulties in keeping hoggets in good condition. As Newman reported:

> it is my considered opinion that to rear this class of sheep we will have to either topdress several paddocks & keep them for these sheep alone or else grow some root crop to see them through the months of May & June. These sheep have had all the attention that it is possible to give them this year & the results are very disheartening indeed to me. I drenched them since weaning every three weeks & moved them every six days to fresh pastures with no beneficial results. If we wish to carry hoggets we must provide something better than what we are doing for the months of May & June.[4]

Six months later, Eric Baker complained that 'the pastures have not the bottom in them that they should have' and went on:

> The Pastures are not carrying the amount of feed they should for this time of year. Even when a paddock is shut up it is very slow in coming away. I feel

quite sure that the better grasses and clovers are running out and poorer grasses are taking charge of quite a lot of the country which used to do the stock so well.[5]

By early 1940, Cummane, who had previously kept the books rather than advising on farm policy, felt constrained to warn Baker of the seriousness of the problems he faced. The farms were carrying a combined overdraft of £60,000, on which interest was accumulating, and production was falling. Running costs were high, with a total of fifteen permanent employees on the properties and, much of the time, a similar number employed on fencing, drain clearance, bush clearing and rabbit eradication. As well as running three trucks, the two farms also engaged outside carriers for carting stock, fertiliser, fencing material and stores. Moreover, and on Baker's instructions, a considerable acreage had been put into sunflower seeds, which could not be sold at a profit and cost the farm good pasture land. To Cummane, 'Such a state of affairs, does to any man with business acumen, seem a most extraordinary position'. Over the previous few years, the woolshed and shearers' quarters had been extensively rebuilt, accommodation had been provided for an increased workforce and there had been a considerable investment in farm machinery. Cummane concluded that 'much of the moneys continually being spent on more Buildings and Plant and Machinery should be spent *directly* in increasing Production – to carry more Sheep – to produce more Wool, to provide more Revenue and to ultimately reduce the heavy liability to the Bank'. Between 1938 and 1940, the number of sheep being carried had fallen from 11,500 to 8,500 – a drop of 25 per cent; the number of lambs being shorn had fallen by 30 per cent; the overall numbers of stock being sold had fallen by 47 per cent.[6] In response to Cummane's report, Baker cut capital expenditure and approved a much heavier application of fertiliser than the farms had seen for many years. But these measures were palliatives only; the farms needed a considerable injection of funds if their productive capacity was to be improved.

Baker had little enthusiasm left for the farms, however. He maintained the rituals of earlier times, travelling the world each year, but his heart was no longer in it. It was now more than six years since Florence had died; he saw Judy only on his visits to England, and these had been curtailed by the outbreak of war. Poo Harington had retired to England meaning that he now had to make all his own travel arrangements and get hotel secretaries to type his letters. He was eighty-three years old, suffering from 'a congested liver', and having great difficulty with his eyesight. Even the fishing had lost much of its attraction.

From the late 1920s, Baker had continued to visit the Bay of Islands each year, with the usual mixed success. There were other highpoints, such as fighting a large striped marlin in January 1935, with the Duke of Gloucester and the Governor-General of New Zealand among the audience on the other launches. Despite his regular visits to the Bay of Islands, however, Baker had never caught the really big fish of which fishermen dream. Yet he persisted, and in February 1937, just a month after his eightieth birthday, he finally landed a huge 850-pound black marlin, the largest for the season and then the third heaviest black marlin ever caught at the Bay of Islands. From the *Reliance*, with Stan Adamson at the

The 850-pound black marlin caught by Baker at the Bay of Islands, January 1937.
PHOTOGRAPH BY NOEL HARRIS, COURTESY ERIC AND VALERIE GRAY

helm, Baker fought the fish which jumped no less than twenty-five times during a battle lasting two and a half hours before Noel Harris, the gaff-hand, could secure it and, later, photograph Baker with his prize. Emboldened by this success, Baker wrote a 'Rough Guide to New Zealand Big Game Fishing' which Hardy Brothers incorporated into their 1937 catalogue. With thousands of copies issued worldwide, and with the author and his black marlin adorning the cover, Baker's achievements, and his theories on methods of fishing and fishing tackle, were brought to the attention of an international audience. This publication, and the events that it recorded, marked the culmination of Baker's fishing career.[7] Almost as a farewell gesture, Baker then updated the piece to take account of the 1938 season and republished it privately as 'a rough guide for the uninitiated to these renowned fishing waters'.

Baker's last season was in 1940 when his eyesight was failing, his health was generally poor, he was feeling the cold and the weather was consistently bad. When he did manage a couple of days' fishing, the best he could do was to foul-hook a 330-pound striped marlin, which promptly took more than 630 yards of line as it dived to the ocean floor where it died and presented Baker with a dead weight that was too heavy for him to lift. After two hours, assisted by Stan Adamson and Noel Harris, he hand-lined his catch to the surface, only to find that it had been mauled by sharks or barracuda which had stripped off most of the flesh, leaving him with little more than half a fish.[8] Feeling sorry for himself, he returned to Limestone Downs to finalise the farm budget with Cummane and Blomfield, and then sailed for Malaya in May 1940. Baker took no further part in the management of either Limestone Downs or Te Karaka.

As Baker's health deteriorated rapidly, he put what energy remained into his telegraphed correspondence with Bensusan over *The Labouring Earth*, and into efforts to generate imperial interest in fund-raising for the war effort. Not content with being the largest private donor to the Malayan War Fund, Baker made additional, direct payments to the British government in August 1940 and February 1941. This £30,000 (all in borrowed funds) was to be for the purchase of six aircraft for the RAF, the first four of which were to be called *The Alma Baker*, *The Alma Baker Malaya*, *The Alma Baker Australia* and *The Alma Baker New Zealand*.[9] On accepting the first gift, Lord Beaverbrook, the Minister for Aircraft Production, assured Baker that 'The magnificent gift which you have sent us will be applied at once to adding four fighter aircraft to a squadron which guards the citadel of freedom'.[10] In the Malayan press, Baker denied the 'magnificence' of his gift, and reminded readers of the generosity that they had shown towards his battle plane fund during the First World War. It was vintage Baker:

> This is the last World War any of us will experience; its end will mean either the continuation of happiness and prosperity for ourselves and others; or tyranny, beggary, and slavery.
>
> If the monetary assistance we can now spare is deliberately and selfishly withheld from the Empire now by all non-combatants, we will be greatly helping the defeat of the world's greatest Empire, and all that it means to the world today. Each self-sacrifice, each donation, will help towards crushing the enemy. We must all give now to the limit and keep on giving to the end.[11]

Given the state of his finances, this was a bold, if desperate, move that he justified by the precarious situation faced by Britain and its empire. Neville Sievwright, on the other hand, thought he was 'mad to encumber his interests to such a large extent particularly at his age and his bad state of health'.[12] In his last days, Baker returned to the concerns that had governed many of his actions, and almost all his public life, since the First World War.

After his return to Malaya towards the end of 1940, Baker's health continued to decline though he was reluctant to admit it and refused to discuss it. He still smoked heavily (always Craven A) and each evening expected either Lionel Whitaker or his brother Roderick to play billiards. Baker had, apparently, known that he had cancer before he left New Zealand

The Alma Baker Malaya, a Hurricane, under service in the Desert Campaign. IMPERIAL WAR MUSEUM

because he arranged for Dr Gunson, who had treated Florence and was an old family friend, to accompany him to Malaya. Early in 1941, as he weakened further, he rented a spacious bungalow overlooking the ocean at Batu Feringgi on Penang Island, where he was nursed by Gunson and Frances Whitaker. As always, though, he tried to maintain his independence. As Lionel Whitaker reported to Poo Harington: 'He took a lorry load of furniture down for his own room and when the Chinese Towkay who owned the house came round to visit he was very much amused at the way all his new and very modern furniture was dispensed with and Uncle Barney's old but comfortable stuff in its place'.[13] His condition continued to worsen and he suffered a stroke at the end of March. He could no longer eat and, according to those with him, he 'simply faded away' on 8 April 1941.

Even in death Baker ended up in a bureaucratic wrangle with the colonial authorities. Penang and Perak were different states with a customs border between them. Penang, as a major port, was a focus of smuggling activity that made customs officials particularly vigilant. Concerned that Baker's coffin might be packed with drugs or contraband, they insisted that it be opened for inspection. Baker's death rated only very few lines in the local newspapers which, twenty years before, had been full of his fund-raising activities for the war effort. His funeral at the Anglican church at Batu Gajah was a 'peaceful and impressive ceremony' but a small affair; one local resident who had known Baker for forty years lamented that it was 'a very small attendance, the older one gets ... the fewer at ones funeral'.[14]

The burial was arranged by Gunson and Florence's nephews, the Whitaker brothers – Lionel, who had worked for Baker since 1921 and shared his house since Florence died in 1934, and Roderick, who had worked on, then managed, Pondok Tanjong since 1929. Their family had been close to Barney and Florence Baker at least since the early years of the century. Yet Baker had been such a private man, and so reticent about his own affairs, that neither Lionel nor Roderick knew the date or year of his birth. In correspondence with the Sievwrights and Poo Harington, they speculated on his age, all suspecting that he was older than the eighty-four years to which he had admitted. Poo Harington recalled that 'Barney told me many times that he was born six months after the battle of Alma – the news taking that time to reach N.Z. and that was how he received the name .... I believe this would make his age 86 or 87. Judy, too, always agreed that he was older than he thought.'[15] In fact, Baker was right about his age but less sure, or deliberately misleading, on family history. And he did celebrate his birthday, at least in earlier years, because there is the evidence of books given to him as gifts, inscribed and dated 6th January, even if his nephews-in-law were unaware of this. In preparing the headstone for his grave, they had no hesitation in declaring that 'He served God, King and Empire' but they then consulted history books rather than the official record on the other details. In the end they could only give his date of birth as 14 September 1854, the date of the British landing at Alma in the Crimea.

Baker with Lionel Whitaker and his daughter, Iona, Batu Gajah, 1938. ANTHONY AND IONA GREEN

CHAPTER 13

A KIND-HEARTED GENEROUS MAN

As Charles Alma Baker's life stretched beyond eighty years, and his health deteriorated, he became increasingly concerned with ordering his affairs, especially as far as his daughter was concerned. Through the 1920s and 1930s he had made and remade wills as his circumstances changed but in the late 1930s the concern became obsession. Since Baker died in the midst of war, the situation was further complicated, not just by the difficulty of communication among the various executors, but because his contribution of £30,000 towards the war effort just months before his death had deprived his estate of any liquid assets it might have had. The situation was exacerbated when any chance there might have been of covering the payments, at least in the short term, was denied by the Japanese occupation of Malaya. Baker's final act of patriotism seriously jeopardised not only the arrangements that he had made for Judy's protection, but also a wide range of bequests to those who had earned his friendship or gratitude, or both, in the course of a long and varied life.

Baker's first concern, however, was always Judy. He was sharply aware that she was in her late thirties, widowed and unlikely to remarry. She could be independent in day-to-day matters but was incapable of running her own affairs and, being naive in financial matters, certainly could not be trusted to manage Baker's estate. Through her singing, Judy had become friendly with Emily Mules and her family, and especially with Betty, Emily's daughter, who had married Joe Niemann just before the war. From 1938, Judy had lived on the Timbercroft estate in Ewell on the southern outskirts of London in a house that she owned in partnership with Emily Mules, although with her share paid by a mortgage taken out by Baker and managed on his behalf by the Sievwright brothers. In 1939, Judy moved in with Joe and Betty Niemann and remained with them, almost as a member of the family, until her death thirty-seven years later. Always convinced that Judy's unworldliness would leave her prey to adventurers, Baker tried to ensure that she was comfortable but that she had no control over major assets or large sums of money.

In making his will, Baker sought advice from those who had helped to manage his affairs for decades, especially Blomfield in New Zealand and, in London, his friends from the Devonshire Club, the Sievwright brothers and Frederick Boyes, the last being a solicitor

The Devonshire Club, London. ROBIN BOYES

who divided his legal practice between the Temple and the town of Huntingdon, near Cambridge. Baker's first instinct was to stay with the advice of Blomfield who urged him to make four wills, one each to cover the assets in Malaya, Australia, New Zealand and Britain, an arrangement that would have given a large measure of autonomy to the various groups of executors and was supposed to have minimised the possibility of any single government claiming control over, and death duties on, the combined assets.

Boyes pointed out that with the four wills there would be no overall guiding hand to replace Baker's. He argued for a single will that would have restricted the power of executors in Malaya, Australia and New Zealand and would have ensured that, as Baker intended, overriding power remained in the hands of the English executors. Baker accepted this latter provision because Judy lived in England, but it was also in keeping with his imperial view of the world and his own commercial empire. He also accepted the idea of a single will, but then dithered endlessly over the question of whether to enhance his English executors' control by having all of his assets sold – something he could not bring himself to do – and the proceeds remitted to England for investment, or whether all assets should be retained with the idea of generating a larger income for the future. With the outbreak of war, rubber prices had risen dramatically, giving the prospect of long-term returns that would far exceed simple interest on investments.

Baker soon realised that to sell his farms and plantations would not only mean abandoning cherished projects but also that, if his estate were to cover the proposed bequests and annuities, the income from Malaya and eventually from Limestone Downs would be needed. But if Baker would not make a new will, he took Boyes' advice at least to the point of authorising the preparation of a codicil that gave his English executors power over the whole estate. The decision taken, and the draft approved after much further consultation, Baker declared himself ready to sign in September 1939, just days before leaving England, much to the relief of George Sievwright who had been badgered constantly by Baker and was beginning to show signs of some exasperation as he wrote to Boyes: 'I am afraid you will have to engage the Town Hall in which we can suitably be housed to discuss the terms of an event of historic importance viz his will as he now insists that Neville should also be present .... We should arrive at about 10.30. I don't think Town Band or Guard of Honour will be necessary.'[1]

On what proved to be his final trip to New Zealand early in 1940, Baker was again pressed by Blomfield, and again changed his mind, with the result that upon his return to Batu Gajah he made four new wills, although specifying that, as the assets in each country were realised and the appropriate bequests paid, any residue was to be forwarded to the English executors, who were to have ultimate control. Frederick Boyes wrote to Baker maintaining his original view, but adding: 'when the time comes – and I hope it is many years distant – all those to whom you have entrusted the carrying out of your wishes will loyally do so'.[2] In England, those executors were the Sievwright brothers, Poo Harington and Norman Boyes, Frederick's son, who had qualified as a solicitor in 1929 and was a partner in the family firm. Also a member of the Devonshire Club, Norman Boyes had known Baker for some years and his appointment was intended to protect Judy's interests by providing for the administration of the estate in the longer term.

Baker's wills, finalised just three months before his death, represented a summary of his life and achievements and, at the same time, provided a commentary on aspects of his life that he had tended to keep private. Quite remarkable, for example, was the list of his own relatives, his wife's family and their friends who had been the recipients of his largesse during his lifetime and were to have their living standards protected with his death. Baker's major assets, the Kinta Valley Estate and Pondong Tanjong Estate in Perak, were to be retained and managed for the estate by Lionel and Roderick Whitaker; Limestone Downs was to be controlled by Blomfield and Eric Baker. Eric still owned a quarter of Te Karaka and was to inherit the property outright after five years. Also to be expected were the generous payments to Blomfield, the Sievwrights, Poo Harington, Dr Gunson, Lionel and Roderick Whitaker, and Barney Baker, Valentine's son, all of whom received more than £1,000. Most of the beneficiaries were relatives of either Barney or Floss and received a few hundred pounds, but there was also £50 each for 'my native clerk Shanmoghoun' and 'my faithful Chinese cook Ee Heng' and £200 for 'my loyal and attentive chauffeur R.N.

Bayers'. Stan Adamson, 'my loyal and attentive deep sea fishing Captain', received £250 and shared Baker's fishing gear with Blomfield and Poo Harington. Among those listed was Carrie Kennedy, Baker's niece, who had not expected to receive anything at all, and told Blomfield that she was 'deeply touched by my dear old uncle's kindness', adding that he had 'always been a kind-hearted generous man'.[3]

In all, some sixty beneficiaries received either outright bequests or annuities under one or more of the wills, but there were two noteworthy absentees. The first was Frances Whitaker, Lionel's wife, who had managed Baker's Malayan household for the best part of a decade and had nursed him through his final illness. Either Baker had taken her for granted, or considered that he had already been sufficiently generous to Lionel.

The second omission was Pita Heretaunga Baker, Charles Alma Baker's son, who was farming in the Opotiki district and serving as an officer in the local Home Guard at the time of his father's death. In the 1930s, he had helped bring Sir Apirana Ngata's policies for the

Pita Heretaunga Baker, mid-1960s. MS KAHUKORE BAKER

development of Maori land to the Bay of Plenty, and for twenty-five years after the Second World War, he was to serve as Chairman of the Whakatohea Maori Trust Board. One of Pita Baker's sons worked in the pulp and paper industry; the other, Heretaunga Pat Baker, became well known as an author in the 1970s through the publication of his controversial novels, *Behind the Tattooed Face* and *The Strongest God*, both of which dealt with the history of his mother's Whakatohea people. It is interesting to observe that when Pita Baker married Florence Penny at Rakaia in 1920, he recorded his father's name as 'Alma Baker', and his occupation as surveyor. On Pita Baker's death certificate in 1984, his father's occupation was now given as 'rubber planter', which shows that the son at least knew about the father. This brings us no closer, however, to knowing whether the two ever met, or whether the father even knew about the son.[4]

Apart from the farms and plantations, Baker's assets were to be sold. There were a few remaining shares in some of the Kidman leasehold cattle properties in Australia, although Macartney Abbott, Baker's Sydney solicitor, suspected that these companies had been managed as part of the Kidman empire in a way that ensured minimal profit for outsiders. To his surprise they realised £4,250 when the leases expired at a time of high stock prices. Abbott also found that 'Mr Baker held a long list of shares in various valueless mining ventures in this State. We had these investigated by members of the Stock Exchange of high standing and found that they were so valueless that we did not show them as an asset in the application for probate.'[5]

In New Zealand, Limestone Downs, with stock, was valued at £64,000 and Te Karaka at £23,000, but once mortgages and overdrafts had been taken into account, their net worth was only a little over £40,000 and the farms were still not profitable. In England, there was Judy's house and a large overdraft at the Chartered Bank of India, Australia and China, and a few personal effects, including clothes held by a Savile Row tailor, furniture at Newton Abbott and portraits of Baker and his wife that had been insured for £500 each but were now valued at £25 for the pair.[6] The most important assets were the rubber plantations that were valued at £160,000 after death duties of about £70,000 had been allowed for.

Even without Baker's final patriotic gift, the estate would have been struggling to pay the specified bequests, including the £200 per month for Judy that was the first charge on the estate. To guard against this possibility, Baker had given a second, reduced schedule of payments (though, ever the optimist, he had also attached a codicil authorising the purchase of further aircraft from his estate at the discretion of his executors). When Baker died, the English executors looked to Malaya for the funds to meet their obligations. Lionel Whitaker was confident that with wartime prices 'a very considerable profit will be made', although he was quick to assume that he and Roderick would be allowed to get on with the job and that the English executors 'will not require long monthly reports on the Estates, or all the detailed forms evolved by Mr. Alma Baker'.[7] Over the next few months, the estates were highly profitable, allowing the executors to clear overdrafts and, once minor assets had been realised, to hold about £2,000 in England. The situation changed dramatically as soon as Japanese forces invaded Malaya in December 1941.

With the Japanese occupation, Lionel Whitaker, now general manager of Baker's estates in Malaya, and H.F. (Hutch) Hutcheson, manager of the Kinta Valley Estate, were both called up as officers in the Volunteer Reserve. Frances, Lionel's wife, was evacuated through Singapore. Roderick Whitaker, manager at Pondok Tanjong, came south to Batu Gajah to check on the Kinta Valley Estate, but then found his return to Taiping cut off by the advancing Japanese Army. He joined the Volunteer Reserve at Ipoh aerodrome, where he was given rifle and uniform and helped to dig trenches across the runway to prevent Japanese aircraft from landing. Batu Gajah, to the west of the main line of the Japanese advance, missed the worst of the invasion, but by the end of January it, too, had been abandoned. In line with official scorched earth policy, Roderick burned the Kinta Valley Estate's rubber factory to the ground and then made his own way south to Singapore. He joined up with the British Army with a commission as second lieutenant, acting captain, because of his familiarity with local languages and because, unlike most of the British officers, he could distinguish between Malay, Chinese and Japanese. But before he had so much as fired a shot, Singapore fell and Roderick soon found himself in Changi, where he was reunited with Lionel and Hutch. Despite conditions that were harsh in prison, and much worse on the Burma railway, both the Whitaker brothers survived the war, as did Hutcheson, who had been kept in Singapore the whole time.[8]

Once the Malayan remittances stopped, the executors were forced to withhold all payments except those to Judy. This left only Limestone Downs as a possible source of income and it, too, was hardly in a healthy position. Still making a loss before the war, Limestone Downs was barely profitable even when prices rose in response to wartime demand. The government had recently increased death duties by a third, making the estate liable for a payment of £15,000. Moreover, the heavy capital expenditure in the 1930s and the failure to maintain pasture quality had created long-term difficulties. As Blomfield explained:

> Mr Baker's expenditure was largely incurred in continuous experiments in stock breeding and in agricultural work, all of which was exceedingly costly and unprofitable. A large total was also spent by him in purchasing, without conferring with his managers or myself, unnecessary and impracticable plant and machinery each year he came to New Zealand. Much of this was constructed to carry out his own ideas and is unsaleable.[9]

In recent times, Baker's main sheep experiments had seen Corriedale rams crossed with Romney ewes, and the resulting progeny crossed with the Leicester in an attempt to increase sheep size and wool weight. Instead, the flock lost all consistency, and performance was poor. As Eric Baker noted:

> This unevenness in wool, frame and constitution reflected in many ways. More lambs had to be sold as culls than should have been the case, the Corriedale cross ewe when sold at 4 and 5 years was not in demand and returned a very low price. Mortality during the Hogget stage was far too high, and those that did come through were small and weedy as two-tooth ewes which reflected in the lambing percentage.[10]

As a consequence, Eric Baker as executor and Percy Newman as manager embarked on a major culling campaign immediately after Baker's death. No further Corriedale rams were used and, irrespective of age and condition, all Corriedales were culled and sold in 1942 and 1943, a policy that brought some improvement in overall stock quality but increased the farm's dependence on aging Romney ewes and led to a reduction of breeding ewes on the property from 6,200 to 5,450. A similar policy was adopted regarding the cattle, with the removal of Baker's Angus, Devon and Shorthorn crosses, which were 'weedy and small with no constitution and frame', and a move back to pure Aberdeen Angus stock. The heavy culling, although laying the basis for future development, reduced profits in the shorter term.

Faced with reduced stock, outstanding death duties and income tax liabilities, the New Zealand executors were in no position to pay bequests or annuities and, in any case, tended to view the New Zealand properties in isolation from the overall estate. Under Baker's will, the New Zealand executors were empowered to postpone the realisation of assets without reference to the English executors, which meant that little could be done from London, despite a strong inclination to sell Limestone Downs and invest the proceeds. Eric Baker, who believed that more would be raised if the farm were subdivided and its more accessible easy country sold for dairying, was reluctant to agree.[11] Poo Harington, in particular, wanted to see the bequests paid despite the express wish in Baker's will that the farms be retained.

> ... so what is the use of the Stations? As none of us here are experienced in sheep and cattle farming, we are absolutely in the hands of people who are not even well known to us, and, if I may say so, never enjoyed the same confidence as the Whitakers in Malaya when "the Chief" was running things.[12]

But 'the Chief' had gone, and the position of those left behind was made more difficult when he was followed by others: in March 1942 Blomfield died and, shortly afterwards, Newman was forced to resign through ill-health. In England, Frederick Boyes died in 1943, Neville Sievwright in 1945 and George in 1947, leaving Norman Boyes and Poo Harington to guide the Baker estate as the only surviving English executors. Given immediate post-war conditions, there was little that could be done.

To Poo Harington, at least, it seemed as if those at the New Zealand end were simply delaying matters. She was unimpressed with stories of bureaucratic delay, the need for birth dates to establish succession dates for the estate, and the necessity of investing even more capital in the farm if its development potential were to be realised. The situation anticipated by Frederick Boyes had, in fact, come to pass – the various groups of executors were each controlling a share of the assets without any having effective overall control or being in a position to set policy. The New Zealand lawyers, who had advised the making of four separate wills, were the object of continuing suspicion. As she confided in Boyes:

> The New Zealand situation is simply deplorable .... The tragic part of it is that I know for a fact (Mr Baker having constantly discussed his affairs in detail with me), that he particularly wished the English Executors to have full

powers in all the countries concerned, and that the last thing he would have desired was for New Zealand to have a "free hand" .... there appears to be nothing to do but stand by and see all the possibilities of the extensive New Zealand possessions lost to the Estate.[13]

In New Zealand, Eric Baker and Trevor Sparling, Blomfield's partner of more than twenty years who succeeded him as executor, set about developing Limestone Downs. With Alf Catherwood as manager after Newman, they concentrated on carrying out deferred maintenance and improving the quality of the stock. With these policies, and continuing high prices during the war, they were able to pay some death duties but were still awaiting a final assessment. Until it was received, and the indebtedness of the estate firmly established, they were reluctant to put the income to any other purpose and for some time the Commissioner of Stamp Duties, who handled the matter, would not give them approval to remit any money to England. Poo Harington became ever more impatient, unwilling to share the view of the New Zealand executors, or even of Baker himself, that Limestone Downs might one day be the estate's most valuable asset:

> Speaking entirely for myself, I wish that the whole N.Z. Estate could be disposed of as soon as everything is in order. It will never be of any use and is unlikely to be of the smallest financial benefit to Mrs Pottinger. I realise, however, that endless trouble would be placed in the way of such an arrangement by those on the spot.[14]

There were further delays as the war dragged on; death duties, outstanding taxes and penalties were not finally paid until 1951, by which stage the executors were able to pay all bequests through the profitability of Limestone Downs, which had been boosted in 1950-51 by the effect of the Korean War on wool prices, and the restoration of the rubber estates in Malaya.

When the Whitaker brothers returned to the Baker estates after the war, they found that although the plantations had been ransacked by the Japanese forces, little rubber had been tapped during their absence. When Lionel called at Batu Gajah briefly en route from Rangoon to Australia after being released, he was appalled at what he found. Baker's old house at Changkat Road was being used as an orphanage for Tamil boys. The garage, servants' quarters and engine shed had been removed; all the furniture and fittings were gone except for a carved screen and the billiard table which was without cloth, cushions or pockets. The house itself was in a 'disgustingly filthy condition'. The manager's house next door, now an orphanage for girls, was in a similar condition.

At the Kinta Valley Estate, Whitaker found that most of the buildings that had been left standing were in such a state of disrepair that they would need replacement, and the rubber itself was so overgrown that it would take months to clear and bring back into production. As a plantation, Pondok Tanjong was in a slightly better condition if only because there had been no opportunity to destroy the processing facilities before the Japanese advance.

Basic reconstruction work on both estates was begun under the direction of the British

Military Administration in October 1945 but it was not until April 1946 that the Whitakers were back in Malaya trying to get production going again. Labour was scarce; some of the former labourers had remained on or near the plantations during the war, although many were weak and ill. Tools were expensive. So much rehabilitation work was necessary that the estates were only slowly brought back into full production, although Lionel Whitaker was soon noting with satisfaction that, after being forcibly rested for nearly four and a half years, the 'trees already show signs of yielding like bore drains'.[15]

Because of the state of the processing plant, all rubber was initially sold as latex direct to the manufacturers, thus creating immediate returns and, at the Kinta Valley Estate, saving the £1,000 that it would cost to build a smoke-house when there were so many demands on funds. In order to get the plantations back into full production, and to restore plant and machinery, the Malayan estates borrowed more than £40,000 from the Rehabilitation Board,[16] and the servicing of these loans, together with the outstanding demand for death duties, placed the Malayan executors under enormous pressure. Moreover, rubber prices began to slide during 1948 and for some years production was threatened by the communist insurgency that reached serious proportions from mid-1948 and was not finally brought under control for almost a decade. Gangs of marauding Chinese constantly harassed plantation workers and attacked Europeans as part of a widespread guerilla campaign. In July 1948, Lionel Whitaker complained that he had to take a police corporal and three constables with him when paying out wages and a few months later had further problems:

Roderick Whitaker inspecting young rubber trees at the Kinta Valley Estate, 1960s. ANTHONY AND IONA GREEN

Land cleared and contoured for planting rubber, Kinta Valley Estate, 1950s. ANTHONY AND IONA GREEN

'It was unfortunate that the ambush of the police truck in which 8 were killed and 4 wounded happened only 5 miles beyond Pondok Tanjong, as it may affect the prospects of obtaining a man to accept the position of Resident Manager.'[17]

Despite the difficulties, a new manager was hired to take the place of Roderick Whitaker, who moved to the Kinta Valley Estate, replacing Hutcheson. Pondok Tanjong, in particular, remained vulnerable to attack – a tin prospector working on the estate had to shoot his way out of an ambush late in 1949 – but it was for other reasons that the executors tried to sell the estate in mid-1949.[18]

Between them, Limestone Downs and the Malayan estates had paid basic bequests and annuities but not the full amounts specified by Baker and there was little prospect of meeting the loan repayments and death duties for which the executors were now being pressed. In addition, outstanding maintenance on the rubber plantations was causing increasing difficulties. So the decision was taken to put Pondok Tanjong on the market, but potential buyers were hardly enthusiastic about the prospect. As one broker put it to Lionel Whitaker: 'we fear that owing to the large percentage of old rubber and poor condition of the buildings, we regret we cannot put the proposition up to any of our Companies'.[19]

The executors were now reaping the consequences of Baker's policy of deferring maintenance and his refusal to contemplate bud grafting or replanting. The war itself, and post-war difficulties, including indebtedness, had exacerbated the problems, but were not their fundamental cause. To a buyer prepared to inject capital, the estate was still valuable, with about 2,500 acres planted in rubber. When rubber prices moved upwards sharply in 1949 in response to the demands of the Korean War, Pondok Tanjong was sold for £52,500,

Guards and fortifications at the Kinta Valley Estate, 1950s.
ANTHONY AND IONA GREEN

which enabled the executors finally to pay off all outstanding duties and taxes, and to pay Judy Pottinger and other beneficiaries the full amount of their inheritance.

Wartime shortages, the need to complete deferred maintenance and the government's financial controls had all inhibited development at Limestone Downs and Te Karaka in the decade after Baker's death. To some extent, however, these difficulties were offset by good prices during the Second World War and the even higher returns in the early 1950s during the Korean War. By the mid-1940s, stock numbers had almost recovered from the culling that had followed Baker's death, and Limestone Downs was carrying more than 9,000 sheep, mostly Romneys, and 1,375 cattle, mostly Aberdeen Angus and Hereford. The property was generally in good shape, with more than 6,000 acres in good grass, 60 acres for cropping, 250 acres in rough grass and only 800 acres remaining in bush. The 800 acres of former swamp land was partly grassed and partly still under development, with many logs and stumps showing through the surface as the swamp settled over time. With land, buildings, plant and stock, the property was valued at £82,500 in June 1944.[20] Te Karaka had been managed by Eric Baker since the death of 'The Uncle' in 1941. Less had been spent on its development so that about 1,300 acres remained in bush and scrub or was still being cleared. Te Karaka had some 300 acres of rolling country or drained swamp, and cropped about 85 acres, leaving some 2,000 acres in grass. The property ran a small Romney stud of about 500 sheep, together with 4,300 flock Romneys and 700 cattle. Valuers for the Union Bank put the property's worth at £32,500.[21]

In terms of Baker's will, Te Karaka could have been passed to Eric Baker in 1946, but the transfer was delayed by wartime difficulties and by the government's plans for post-war soldier settlement and by its control on prices and sales of farm land. By 1946, the Department of Lands and Survey was developing a scheme for the amalgamation then subdivision of properties around Limestone Downs as part of its rehabilitation policies. The English executors welcomed the move as a means of realising assets and paying debts, but Eric Baker resisted all initiatives, even going to Wellington to plead the case before the Commissioner of Lands in the hope of buying time until after a forthcoming general election.[22] Despondent on his return, he concluded that 'If this Socialistic Government is returned again we will have no hope of holding the Estate but will have a good chance of doing so if the National Party get in and it looks as though there will be a change of government.'[23] Well known to National Party politicians through his work in local government and as a long-standing member of local and national committees for rabbit control, Eric Baker sought protection for Limestone Downs if, as he expected, National won the 1949 election.

By early 1951, the New Zealand executors were in a buoyant mood. National was in office, and the threat of compulsory purchase by the Crown seemed to have been averted; high wool prices had enabled the executors to pay all outstanding duties and taxes, and the sale of Oranui, the Pottinger farm near Henderson, had contributed to the payment of Judy Pottinger's inheritance. Feeling optimistic, Eric Baker pushed on with the development of both farms. He was one of the first in the district to experiment with aerial topdressing, an innovation that did away with the laborious spreading of fertiliser by hand on the hill country, and opened the way to a significant improvement of productivity, particularly on marginal land.

With debts cleared and the future looking bright, the next step was to transfer ownership of Te Karaka from the estate to Eric Baker. It was not a simple process, because the exact relationship between Eric Baker and his uncle was not legally clear. In one sense they were partners, Eric Baker owning a one-quarter share in the original property, even though he had not contributed any further capital for land purchase, mortgage clearance or farm development. On the other hand, the 1926 contract between the two clearly established that Eric Baker was to work as farm manager for Charles Alma Baker who had the right to use or sell the farm as he chose; Eric Baker could not share in the profits, nor was he liable for the losses. It was, in short, a master and servant relationship, with 'The Uncle' in complete control. But with Alma Baker's death, Eric received his reward for managing the property during his uncle's lifetime, for managing both farms for a further ten years, and for continuing to guide the affairs of the Alma Baker estate in New Zealand. To secure his inheritance, Eric had to accept responsibility for outstanding mortgages of £8,000 but that was a modest price to pay in the heady days of the wool boom.[24]

With the basic legal formalities now complete, Pondok Tanjong sold and Te Karaka transferred to Eric Baker, the role of the executors in England, Malaya and New Zealand underwent a fundamental change. Rather than being preoccupied with crisis management, they were now able to plan for the longer term development of Limestone Downs and the Kinta Valley Estate to provide for Judy Pottinger and to consider the future of the assets if she died childless, as she seemed destined to do.

CHAPTER 14

A DREAM COME TRUE

In the early 1950s, a number of factors came together to give the policy-making for the C. Alma Baker estate a new certainty and to provide a foundation for major developments over the next twenty-five years. Most important, perhaps, was the advent of a wool boom and a rubber boom, both prompted largely by the demands of the Korean War. The Malayan executors were able to sell Pondok Tanjong, to clear death duties in Malaya and to release funds for the payment of legacies and annuities. In New Zealand, the wool boom saw all the death duties, tax arrears and interest paid by 1954. Eric Baker assumed full personal ownership of Te Karaka leaving the New Zealand executors – by this stage Eric Baker and Trevor Sparling – to concentrate on Limestone Downs. The threat that Limestone Downs might be seized by the government for the rehabilitation of returned soldiers had also receded, although a number of properties around the Baker farms had been subdivided for closer settlement. With the tolerance of the tax authorities in Malaya and New Zealand, the executors had been able to implement Baker's final instruction that his farms and estates were to be maintained to generate the returns necessary to pay legacies and annuities and to produce future income for Judy Pottinger. But although the properties were able to provide an income in the short term, both Limestone Downs and the Kinta Valley Estate needed substantial investment if the value of the assets were to be maintained, and they were to provide continuing protection for Judy.[1]

The Kinta Valley Estate was in a particularly bad way. Not only had it been abandoned for the war years, but it had been running down for decades. In the 1930s, the profits of his rubber plantations had been transferred to New Zealand for investment in Limestone Downs and Te Karaka, or had been consumed by Baker himself in supporting his travels and lifestyle. Baker had turned his back on replanting or bud grafting as a way of replenishing production and had not bothered even to plant all the available land for the first time. The wartime 'rest' given the trees during the Japanese occupation gave a brief, renewed burst of productivity after 1945, but that was all. For a decade after the war, all available income had been used for essential reconstruction work and to support Judy Pottinger. Maintenance had been deferred and there had been no new investment. Lionel and Roderick Whitaker planned to embark on a major replanting programme that would see most of the estate replanted within ten years, but would cause a severe drop in income over the intervening period. Although the early part of the programme could be financed from revenue, the Malayan executors soon found themselves under financial pressure and looked to their New Zealand counterparts to provide Judy Pottinger with both her basic annuity of £1,200 and further income, paid at the discretion of the English executors, of up to £3,600 a year.[2]

By the mid-1950s, Limestone Downs was well able to stand the additional burden. Although cleared and sown in the 1920s and early 1930s, Limestone Downs had remained, in many ways, a pioneering venture, also starved of capital from the mid-1930s, and managed conservatively by Eric Baker and Percy Newman. Eric Baker had cleared the property of his uncle's more bizarre cross-bred stock during the war, and had concentrated on building up a Romney flock, but it was not until Alf Catherwood was appointed manager in 1942 that there had been a serious attempt to develop quality lines of cattle. From 1938 there was no capital for investment and, for more than a decade, little or no fertiliser had been applied. In the immediate post-war years, the demands of the tax collectors had taken precedence over the needs of the farm. But by 1950, wool prices were increasing and more funds were available for development. Eric Baker had aerial topdressing strips built on both Te Karaka and Limestone Downs. For weeks on end, three Tiger Moth aircraft were based on the farms, spreading superphosphate. With a pay load of only 550

Aerial topdressing at Te Karaka, 1950. MRS ALMA CURTIN

pounds a trip, it was slow work, and loading the hopper by hand meant heavy labour, but for all concerned it was far preferable to spreading by hand. Stock capacity soon increased by 20 per cent, allowing the property to carry some 12,600 sheep and 1,500 cattle by 1954. But all this was essentially remedial work; it was not until 1957 that the carrying capacity of the farm was restored to its 1938 level. There were fewer rabbits on the property – in no small measure a tribute to the work of Eric Baker, who had been instrumental in founding the Te Akau Rabbit Board on which he served for more than thirty years. But little else had changed, and the swamp area in particular was badly in need of redevelopment to deepen drains and to remove the stumps and roots that littered the paddocks. Basic development policies were still set by Eric Baker, but it was Dan O'Connell, appointed manager in 1950 who was, at least in his own estimation, to be the saviour of the property:

> Before taking position as Manager, I inspected property with Mr. E. Baker. I could see it was in a completely run down condition and suffering from about 25 years of neglect.
>
> On riding over the property I found there wasn't a decent fence or gate on the place and the pasture showed signs of gross mismanagement. I realised it would take 10 years to get it in anything like order. Mr. Baker agreed and said he wanted a manager who would take hold of it and pull it together. As a start it took over a week with 3 men to clean up around the buildings.
>
> SHEEP: Found the quality extremely poor. To buy ewe lambs each year for replacement would have been too drastic so adopted a patient policy of culling as much as possible each year and buying good rams ....
>
> CATTLE: When I took over they were running 3 and 4 year bullocks and 378 breeding cows. As this policy was unprofitable, I changed to all cows and selling yearling steers.
>
> There was so much pasture to clean up that I was obliged to build up the cow tallies to 1000. Although this punished them the place was eventually cleaned up ....
>
> STUD CATTLE: On taking over in 1950 I found there had been an attempt at breeding replacement Bulls but they were in a sorry state. Discussed this with Mr. Baker and agreed we would have to buy a good stud Bull and a few heifers.[3]

Dan O'Connell, known as 'Necktie' to the men because he often wore a tie and jacket when he was working on the farm, was a hard, driving manager, which meant that relations were not always good on the station and staff turnover was high. The driver of the rural mail delivery van, who also provided a taxi service to Tuakau, used to unnerve newcomers by speculating on how long it would be before he was taking them back to town, their days (rather than weeks or months) of employment at Limestone Downs brought to an end by resignation or dismissal. As George Marshall, one of the stockmen recalled, 'You could hardly say "Good morning" to them, they were gone the next day'. Remote from the station hands, O'Connell did not encourage familiarity, instructing the men on their day's work with a meeting at the yards at 7 o'clock each morning. O'Connell, later joined by his wife,

Elsie, remained at Limestone Downs for twenty-five years. He had a vision of what the property could be and, in his first ten or fifteen years as manager, the station went through a transformation unmatched in its history, except for the first five years under the ownership of Charles Alma Baker, when most of the accessible land was cleared and fenced.

In this period, Limestone Downs provided a comfortable income for Judy Pottinger. Although remaining a major concern for the executors of the Baker estate, to O'Connell, at least, this imperative was largely irrelevant. For him, the property was being developed for its own sake, 'because it was there', to meet its full potential. At first there was a period of consolidation and catching up on maintenance, and a concentration on stock improvement. In O'Connell's first few years new Romney rams were bought in and the flock culled hard. When he arrived at Limestone Downs, there were only about twenty stud cows on the property and, as an early step towards improvement, the estate purchased an Embassy line Polled Angus stud bull for 600 guineas from Wallace (Denny) Johnstone's Puketutu Stud at Te Kuiti. Then, through the 1960s, a number of stud heifers were bought, building to about 100 the stud herd, which was used to produce bulls for the run cattle and for sale.

By the late 1950s, most of the second-growth bush and scrub had been cut, fences renewed and pastures improved by topdressing and further sowing. But it was all expensive, and the situation was not helped by fluctuating commodity prices and a severe drought in the mid-1950s. The caterpillar tractor bought second-hand before the war was due for replacement, the farm trucks (both bought in 1932) were falling apart and aging farm machinery needed constant repair. The main sheepyards could not hold stock and were like a quagmire when it rained; the shepherds had to tie a dog in the worst of the muddy patches to keep the sheep clean on their way to shearing. In 1959, Limestone Downs was still carrying a mortgage of £8,600 and an overdraft of £23,000. Eric Baker could not see how the farm could service this debt, cover Judy Pottinger's income and make a serious commitment to the redevelopment of the swamp area to provide an increased fattening capacity for the stock, especially beef, raised on the hills.

But he complained a little too soon, for the policies of a decade were about to bear fruit. At 30 June 1960, Limestone Downs carried 15,813 sheep and 2,432 cattle, an increase of more than 50 per cent over stock numbers a decade before. Sales of wool for the year exceeded 450 bales (each of about 350 pounds) for the first time and the farm sold 7,200 sheep and 626 cattle to give a profit before tax of just under £28,000. Even allowing for income tax, which absorbed some 60 per cent of gross profits, the station was able to halve its overdraft. It had now made the critical breakthrough, to a point where it could finance major development from revenue. Profit before taxes averaged more than £23,000 throughout the 1960s.

In terms of the landscape, the greatest change had been wrought in the swamp area which, although still subject to occasional flooding, was redrained and renamed 'the flats'. A new large drain was excavated around the base of the surrounding hills to remove run-off direct to the mouth of the Kaawa, which was straightened to improve the flow to its mouth. With the help of army engineers on an exercise, the bar across the stream mouth was

Preparing to muster cattle at Limestone Downs, 1951. Left to right: Dan O'Connell, Neil Davies, George Johnson, Gerald Leeming, David Daunton, Henry Marshall. C. ALMA BAKER TRUST

blasted to improve the clearance of floodwaters. All the drains were cleared and lowered, this time using McRobbie's dragline from Pokeno rather than the shovels that Mick Hrstich and his gang had used in the 1930s.

The most time-consuming task of all was the reshaping of the swamp land itself into a series of hills and hollows that would facilitate drainage and yet provide protection from floods. First, however, stumps and old timber that had been exposed as the swamp land dried and settled, and now clogged the drains and littered the paddocks, had to be cleared. At a rate of about 100 acres a year, the flats were put under giant discs and the 'sticks', which could include everything from twigs to stumps, gathered by machine or by hand and burned. Then the discing and clearing was repeated, endlessly it seemed, until the ground was clear. The clearing provided abundant employment for station hands, their families and locals who could stand the back-breaking work and the monotony; at least one young man declared himself too intelligent to spend a lifetime picking up sticks, and walked off the job. The final task of shaping the paddocks fell to Alex Lumsden, who farmed in the district and also worked at Limestone Downs as an agricultural contractor throughout the O'Connell years. Superbly competent at both maintaining and using heavy machinery, Lumsden was able to establish the required levels and gradients 'by eye', with only minimal assistance from surveyed levels.

As the transformation of the swamp progressed, all the fences were replaced and new fenced roads, which facilitated the movement of stock and machines, were constructed.

A mob of 160 bullocks en route to the Tuakau sale, 1951. Dan O'Connell at near left.
C. ALMA BAKER TRUST

Bridges and culverts were replaced. Finally, the paddocks were cropped for a season, then sown in grass. Elsewhere on the station, a similar pattern and pace of development was maintained, clearing second growth, adding roads, improving pasture. The station employed a full-time fencer all year round as part of a staff of about ten, excluding casuals and shearers and, in the course of twenty years, virtually all the fences, some 80 miles in all, were replaced.

At the Kinta Valley Estate, some 1,200 acres had been replanted by 1962, but not without difficulty. Lying several miles out of Batu Gajah, the estate was vulnerable to attack from the few remaining bands of Chinese guerillas who killed an overseer on one occasion, and robbed labour gangs of food and other supplies. In the mid-1950s, European staff still went about armed, and took care to vary their routes through the estate. A blockhouse was built behind the security fences now surrounding the estate and a regular force of thirty special constables stationed on the property.[4] The Whitakers took advantage of the estate's long road frontage to concentrate planting in this area where security could be more easily organised. Completing the replanting would take a further six years, and the Whitaker brothers, as the Malayan executors, were anxious to finish the process and for the New Zealand estate to bear the costs of Judy Pottinger's income during that time.

Eric Baker was reluctant to agree, taking the view that development of Limestone Downs was also being delayed by a lack of capital. In 1956, when there had been a similar concern over priorities, Norman Boyes, representing the English executors, had visited Malaya and had been joined in New Zealand by Lionel Whitaker, so that the executors from all three countries (the Australian estate having effectively been wound up) could inspect the various properties and establish priorities. This time, it was Eric Baker who travelled to Malaya, and he came away convinced that the immediate needs of the Kinta Valley Estate outweighed those of Limestone Downs which would, therefore, continue the payments as before. Here, both Eric Baker and the Whitakers were at odds with the English executors, who were becoming increasingly nervous about the future of the Malaysian assets and favoured immediate realisation before the value of the plantation was further affected by political instability.

Eric Baker had planned a further trip to consult the English executors in mid-1963, but died suddenly, in May. Te Karaka he left in trust for his wife, and then absolutely to his daughters, Alma and Valerie. In response to pressure from his wife and daughters, and in recognition of his own advancing years, Eric had 'moved to town', building for his family a fine home at Papatoetoe with kauri, totara, and rimu felled on Limestone Downs and Te Karaka. In the forty-eight years he had owned or managed Te Karaka, he had seen it transformed from dense bush to productive farm. For Limestone Downs, too, it was the end of an era in that it was Eric Baker who had effectively drawn Charles Alma Baker to the location and, after 'The Uncle's' death, had managed the estate for a further twenty years, supervising Limestone Downs through a phase of consolidation and major redevelopment.

The only outstanding problem of any substance at Limestone Downs was a dispute over the estate's performance as lessee on a block of 933 acres, the major part of which had never been freeholded but was useful because of its carrying capacity and crucial to the operation of the station because it could facilitate the handling of stock. It was owned by several local Maori in the name of Mrs Te Ata Kirkwood, who was reluctant to sell. After the owners had initiated legal action over the state of fencing and pasture on the block, the executors, who had been reluctant to spend while their tenure was uncertain, resolved the issue by purchasing the block for £15,000. This was rather more than they had hoped to pay but, even so, it was a good price. Dan O'Connell thought that, once fully developed, the block would be worth at least £24,000.

The purchase of the Kirkwood Block diverted some funds from farm improvement but hardly slowed the overall pace of development. In the late 1950s and early 1960s, Dan O'Connell had built new cattleyards and extensions to the woolshed which, excluding yards, covered some 10,000 square feet; some repairs, at least, had been necessary after a tornado had ripped the roof of the woolshed during crutching. The new seven stand shed, which was regularly worked by Bill Meech's gang from Hawke's Bay, could handle some 1,600 sheep in a good day. The manager's house, originally built to Baker's truncated plan of 1928, was finally completed in a way that fitted well with the original plan for the homestead. The lower floor of the extension was given over to a billiard room, of which Baker would have approved, where Dan O'Connell played his shepherds for their wages. But O'Connell's pride and joy were the circular sheepyards, built to his own design, which were unique in the district. The yards were built to hold a mob of 4,000 sheep in eight segments each holding 500 sheep. All timber for the project was milled from trees felled on the property.

Eric Baker's death brought some uncertainty, but not for long because the direction of change had been set under Dan O'Connell's management, and most of the implementation had been carried out. The farm was clearly viable, providing sufficient revenue to cover maintenance, new investment and Judy Pottinger's income.

From the point of view of the English executors, the problems of Limestone Downs had largely been resolved, and the interests of the estate were secure. The Kinta Valley Estate, on the other hand, presented only continuing uncertainty. Although the Whitaker brothers had embarked on a replanting scheme, its completion and future were by no means assured. The removal of the old trees, however poorly they were producing, reduced income; the continuing Malaysian Emergency not only made planting and weeding difficult, but also cast a shadow over the future. Despite being relieved of meeting Judy Pottinger's income, the estate was still making a loss. There was also uncertainty over management. Roderick Whitaker had retired in 1961 and Lionel, although still riding the occasional winner after forty years and 300 victories on the Malayan turf, was sixty-eight in 1964.

With control held in the family, as it were, management on the estate had not kept pace with developments elsewhere, and there was tension between Lionel Whitaker and D.B. Gardner, Roderick's successor. The labour was restive, and much of the plant was antiquated. Since 1959, the English executors had favoured selling, despite depressed prices, to prevent future losses. To Poo Harington, it seemed that Lionel was making excuses; to Gardner, Lionel was an old-fashioned amateur planter. For his part, Lionel was convinced that, given a little time, the estate could be returned to profitability, but the English executors took alternative advice, and decided to push for a sale.[5] Although there was little demand for large estates because of the political climate, Kinta Valley was a good prospect for speculative 'fragmentation' – subdivision into owner-occupied small holdings.[6] With the estate's value dropping almost by the month, the matter became urgent. Some advised waiting through the political crisis but when an offer of £268,000 was received early in 1965, it was accepted. All outstanding debts and mortgages were paid, and the proceeds remitted to the English executors, who promptly lent £26,100 to the New Zealand estate so that all outside borrowing on Limestone Downs could be cleared and the station could operate free from bank and stock firm pressure through a period of government-imposed financial restraint and bureaucratic controls. So the assets of the Malayan estate, which had made a significant portion of Charles Alma Baker's fortune, and engaged much of his life, were finally realised.

Norman Boyes was in Malaysia for the sale of the Kinta Valley Estate in 1965 when he learned that Trevor Sparling had died suddenly in Auckland, leaving the New Zealand estate without an executor. He therefore flew on to Auckland where he organised the appointment as trustees of Dan O'Connell and John Sparling, Trevor's son and a partner in his firm. To assist O'Connell, and in effect to succeed Eric Baker, the trustees appointed Denny Johnstone as farm adviser and, later, as trustee.

Lionel Whitaker and Eric Baker at Limestone Downs, 1956. ERIC AND VALERIE GRAY

Change was also taking place among the trustees in England, with the appointment of Robin Boyes, Norman's son, who was continuing in the traditions of the family law firm which, increasingly since the war, had shifted the emphasis of its business from London to Huntingdon. A few months later Poo Harington, with a younger trustee now learning the ropes, began to suggest that she should retire. At the end of 1967, she wrote to Norman Boyes: 'I am sad about giving up, but I am sure that the time has come for me to do so .... I am sure that my dear old Barney would not wish me to become a bother to the other trustees, and my dotage is rather overdue.'[7] Despite the self-deprecation – she was seventy-six at the time – and a subsequent claim that 'I have just had my 84th birthday and am only fit for pottering', Poo continued to serve as a trustee and to take a sharp interest in the affairs of her dear old Barney's estate until 1979.[8] Her place as trustee was then taken by Roger Moore, who had farming interests and was chairman and managing director of Woodhouse Hume, one of Britain's largest wholesale butchers active in both domestic and international markets.

Despite these changes in the overall management of the estate, policies at Limestone Downs continued fairly much as before. With the completion of the redevelopment of the flats, the normal carrying capacity of the station rose to about 30,000 stock units by the end of the 1960s with some 20,000 sheep and 2,000 cattle, and exceeding 35,000 stock units in a few good years. To maintain such high numbers of stock through the winter, some 12,000 bales of hay were taken off the farm and stored each year. In 1969, a record 30,887 sheep were shorn at Limestone Downs, but numbers soon began to fall as beef prices improved strongly in the early 1970s, making a shift of emphasis desirable. In anticipation of Dan O'Connell's retirement, Ray McCraw was appointed as stock manager, in effect assistant manager, in 1965. McCraw held this position until 1971 when he left for a promotion, and because of differences with O'Connell.

As O'Connell's health deteriorated, his oversight of the farm was increasingly carried out from inside, or on top of, his distinctive white Landrover – called 'Danny's Rest' by the men – and with the aid of binoculars which he used to monitor the progress of work on the station. A particular target of his attention was Claude Cartier, yarn-spinner, fencer and prankster, who was not always where he should have been but, when he could be found, was not afraid to take time out from his work to stare back at his manager. Staff turnover remained high. Even Elsie, Dan O'Connell's wife, thought that Dan was 'tough' on the men, and intolerant with the less experienced workers: 'I think a lot left who needn't have done … if he was … a bit more tolerant we'd have kept more staff, especially the younger ones'. But Dan was not given to discussing farm policies with Elsie, and he discouraged her from mixing with the wives of station hands, preferring that they keep their distance.

There was, however, always a core of long-serving faithfuls, many of them from local Maori families: Henry Marshall, who worked at Limestone Downs from 1951 until he retired in 1965 aged seventy-eight and his son, George, who was employed at the station from 1957 to the mid-1980s. A grandson also worked there for a time in the 1960s. The Marshalls were originally from the Kaawa village and had been among the original owners of the Girdwood Block bought by Charles Alma Baker in 1928. Kapi Clarke, packman, axeman and fencer, worked at Limestone Downs for more than fifty years. There was also Ben Hoete, whose father had worked on the limestone crusher for Baker, who built more than 20 miles of fences on Limestone Downs and who talked Dan O'Connell into building the system of lanes for moving stock around the farm. Dana Hoete has spent most of his working life at Limestone Downs.

Between 1950 and the early 1970s, Limestone Downs was transformed, largely at the hands of Dan O'Connell. From the outset, O'Connell had a vision for the station and, unlike his predecessors, was inhibited neither by the interference of Charles Alma Baker with his theories and impractical schemes, nor by the restraints imposed by debts and heavy mortgages. The groundwork had largely been done by Eric Baker and his predecessors, and O'Connell had the determination to override opposition. He also had the good fortune to benefit from the wool boom in the early 1950s, and then the increasing returns from the property itself. For him, as Elsie said, it was like 'a dream come true'; in her view Dan ran Limestone Downs 'as though it was his own farm, but he had no financial worries …. it was a wonderful way to live'.[9] O'Connell died on the farm in 1973 and was succeeded by his assistant manager, Neil Dempster.

In the early 1970s, farming at Limestone Downs reflected trends in New Zealand's rural industries in general. Britain's entry into the Common Market subjected New Zealand's primary exports to a new degree of competition. Domestic inflation, exacerbated by the oil

Redevelopment work on the swamp, 1963. ROBIN BOYES

Redeveloped paddocks on the flats ready for planting, 1963. ROBIN BOYES

Romneys on the redeveloped flats, 1963. ROBIN BOYES

View from the Kaawa Stream boundary, looking north. C. ALMA BAKER TRUST

Shearing at Limestone Downs, late 1960s. RAY McCRAW

The circular yards, woolshed and shearers' quarters at Limestone Downs. C. ALMA BAKER TRUST

Working sheep in the circular yards, late 1960s. Capacity 4,000 sheep, 500 for each segment.
RAY McCRAW

shocks of 1973-74, brought a dramatic increase in farm costs. Successive governments, hoping for an export-led economic recovery, poured subsidies and incentives into the rural economy. Accordingly, policies at Limestone Downs, which had largely been set according to the needs of the Baker estate, or of the farm itself, were increasingly being driven by, or in response to, government approaches. In 1971, additional stock were held to earn $9,000 in incentives under the government's sheep retention scheme, and this marked the first in a series of responses to such policies.[10] Two years later, after making a profit before tax of more than $100,000 in 1973, Limestone Downs deferred planned developments and placed $50,000 in a farm income stabilisation scheme that would bring a substantial tax advantage. Limestone Downs, like many other farms, was then hit by outbreaks of facial eczema in 1970 and 1971, by three years of drought in the early 1970s and a sharp fall in beef prices in 1974-75. The government's response to these market problems was to guarantee minimum prices for farm commodities, which had the effect of increasing farm income by 20 per cent in 1975-76.

The English executors continued to take a close interest in Limestone Downs, with Norman Boyes visiting the farm in 1965, and Robin Boyes in 1972. This latter visit was particularly important, because it marked the beginning of a process of deciding the future of Limestone Downs after the death of Judy Pottinger, who was then sixty-nine and in declining health. Although Baker's original instructions had urged his executors to maintain his properties at least for a time so that the fruits of his investments might be harvested, it had not been envisaged that either Limestone Downs or the rubber estates would be held indefinitely. They had clearly met their primary purpose, to maintain Judy Pottinger in a comfortable if not luxurious lifestyle. She had, in fact, been well sheltered from outside pressures and secure among friends, through a combination of the income from the estate and the dedication, friendship and tolerance of the Niemann family. Now, Judy Pottinger's advancing age raised the question of whether Limestone Downs should be kept or sold, and the purposes to which the resulting income should be applied.

Dan O'Connell supervising the workers. This work of an anonymous artist appeared on the wall of the single men's quarters.
RAY McCRAW

CHAPTER 15

THE C. ALMA BAKER TRUST

When Judy Pottinger died in February 1976, Charles Alma Baker's will had fulfilled its fundamental purpose of protecting his daughter during her lifetime. For his English executors, the immediate task was to implement the provision that, should Judy die childless, then all those who had received bequests under the four original wills should receive a second payment the same as the first. Although this presented practical difficulties in locating the original beneficiaries or their heirs, it was, in a sense, a finite task. More problematic was the task of interpreting the clauses governing the use of the residual estate. Baker's instruction that the major assets should be maintained for a time rather than sold had been followed to the extent that the Australian assets and the Malayan plantations had been sold, and Te Karaka had passed to Eric Baker. These developments, particularly as they had been shaped by unforeseen political events in Malaya, had necessitated a modification of the provision that the Australian estate would be realised first with the proceeds passing to New Zealand; that the New Zealand assets would be realised next, with the proceeds passing to Malaya; and that when the Malayan assets were realised the total estate would have been finally transmitted to Britain. In this way, the English executors were placed in ultimate control.

The fundamental issues of whether to retain Limestone Downs, and the purpose to which the income from the estate would be put, had now to be resolved according to the terms of the English will. Here, Baker had specified that if Judy should die childless, the residue of his estate should be used for 'the furtherance of the science of agriculture in all its aspects but more particularly in those branches with which I have been connected in my lifetime as evidenced by my work and my writings or to or for any bodies or institutions of an educational or charitable nature as my trustees may think fit'.[1]

The various executors had given thought to this matter from time to time over the years, but by the early 1970s the matter had become more pressing and the whole matter was explored in depth during Robin Boyes' 1972 visit to New Zealand. Although the form of future developments was by no means clear at this stage, there was agreement among all concerned that Limestone Downs should be retained if at all possible, with both the farm and its income being used for agricultural science and education. Everyone concerned,

The trustees and New Zealand Committee of the C. Alma Baker Trust. **Left to right, back row: David Frith, Christopher Horton, Warwick Deighton (Farm Manager), Norman Boyes, Hon. Leslie Gandar, Dr Lindsay Wallace, Sir Alan Stewart; front row: Professor Alan Frampton, Roger Moore, Robin Boyes, Kevin Lowe.** THORPE STUDIO, PUKEKOHE

both in New Zealand and Britain, saw the New Zealand focus as appropriate, given that it was the country of Baker's birth, and Limestone Downs, Baker's last major investment project, as an appropriate memorial to his life and achievements.

But the path ahead was by no means clear. First, it was necessary to resolve whether the residual clause, to use the estate for agricultural, charitable or educational purposes as defined in the will, did create valid charitable trusts in terms of the law. Although legal opinion in both Britain and New Zealand suggested that they could be, there was always the possibility that this interpretation might be challenged in court. There were ambiguities in the wording of the original will, and a question as to whether English law should or could apply to the assets owned by Baker in Malaya and New Zealand at the time of his death. Should such a challenge succeed, Baker would be regarded as intestate at the point of Judy Pottinger's death and the residue of his estate would pass to the beneficiaries of her personal estate.[2] These legal and procedural difficulties in the will would take five years to resolve.

The trustees sought detailed advice from John Whittaker, a Lincoln's Inn barrister specialising in Chancery matters, and further advice from Lewis & Co. in Ipoh (successor to the firm that had prepared the Baker's wills in 1941) and John Sparling and Charles P. Hutchinson, QC, regarding New Zealand law. Negotiations were also entered into with Betty Niemann as executrix of Judy's estate; she accepted that agricultural science as covered by the will was a charitable activity and agreed not to challenge the will. An approach by summons was then made by the trustees to the Chancery Division of the English High Court for an order to confirm the legal position. The other parties to the action were Mrs Niemann as Judy's executrix, and the Attorney-General, who had overall responsibility for charities in England and Wales. John Sparling was a co-defendant on behalf of the legatees under Baker's New Zealand and Australian wills over technical matters concerning exchange rates and currency issues regarding the payment of bequests.

With the consent of all parties, a court order was obtained in November 1978. After confirming the details of respective exchange rates for the repeat payment of the original bequests in the Australian and New Zealand wills, the court confirmed that the residuary clause in the English will created valid charitable trusts.[3] With this hurdle cleared, the trustees next had to propose a scheme for the implementation of the will that met with the approval of the Charity Commissioners for England and Wales.

For some time, the English trustees had been canvassing the options with their New Zealand associates. The trustees wanted to keep Limestone Downs if at all possible, but beyond that a range of options was considered. At an early stage, for example, the trustees envisaged developing Limestone Downs as an agricultural teaching and research institution connected with similar research stations in Britain. It soon became clear, however, that establishing such an institution would be difficult because of the high cost of salaries for researchers and technicians and providing facilities for students. The whole matter was complicated by the remoteness of Limestone Downs. Other schemes, which would have involved using the income from the property for a range of local and regional educational and charitable purposes, including the building of a hostel at Tuakau High School, were also considered. The alternative, of selling the farm and using the consequent income for agricultural research and education, would have meant that once the New Zealand assets were realised, the funds would have to be transferred to the English trustees.

With these difficulties in mind, Denny Johnstone, representing the trustees, approached the Hon. L.W. Gandar, a farmer who was then Minister of Education and Minister of Science and Energy in the New Zealand government. Gandar was also Chancellor of Massey University which had a strong faculty of agricultural and horticultural sciences.[4] On Gandar's advice, Johnstone and Sparling approached the university to seek help with their predicament.

All the difficulties were canvassed at a meeting at Massey University in May 1979 attended by Denny Johnstone and John Sparling representing the Baker estate and, for the university, Gandar, Dr Arthur Ward, Gandar's successor as Chancellor and formerly general manager of the New Zealand Dairy Board, and the Vice-Chancellor, Sir Alan Stewart. In discussion, a plan evolved of using the farm for research to some extent, but also of building a close relationship between Limestone Downs and the university in terms of shaping farm development, and applying the farm surplus to agricultural research and education. Sparling came away convinced that the university had 'splendid facilities for research in all aspects of agriculture' but concluded: 'we shall have to convince the English Trustees that even though the concept of a research station at Limestone Downs is a laudable one, the practical difficulties of isolation and the expense of paying trained staff would be so great that although it may survive for a time ultimately the Government would have to step in'.[5]

In fact, the English trustees quickly warmed to the proposal, especially after they had discussed the proposal in September 1979 with Gandar, who had then taken up his new position of New Zealand High Commissioner to Britain, and Alan Frampton, Dean of Agricultural and Horticultural Sciences at Massey University. Gandar and Frampton's enthusiastic advocacy of using Limestone Downs for research purposes, and the property's potential to contribute to New Zealand farming, convinced the trustees to proceed. Through Gandar, they asked the university to come forward with a proposal for

> a scheme which would, in essence, contain the retention of Limestone Downs
> .... [T]he farming operations would include some longterm projects of an ancillary nature complementary to the activities of the University in the scientific and development fields, and the University would be likely to provide a scientific officer to oversee such studies and functions. The income produced by Limestone Downs ... would then, subject to normal reserves being retained on a commercial basis for the running and development of the property, be available to be utilized by the University for certain specific research and educational projects.[6]

With broad agreement reached, the English trustees approached the Charity Commissioners with a draft scheme, forwarding at the same time a letter from Gandar who argued that the sale of Limestone Downs 'would be a great loss to potential agricultural research' and that the property 'would be an extremely valuable component of an integrated research and development effort' for research, teaching and extension work.[7] For his part, the Treasury Solicitor, representing the Attorney-General, thought it 'a most unusual case' but complimented the English trustees on maintaining the goodwill of all parties, and said that his department had no objection in principle to the draft plan.[8]

The Charity Commissioners did, however, note the problems posed by the will, and the practical difficulties of an English trust conducting a significant portion of its activity in New Zealand. Accordingly, they suggested that the trustees consider operating not under the first part of the residual clause – 'the furtherance of the science of agriculture' – but the second – 'any bodies or institutions of an educational or charitable nature':

> ... it seems to the Commissioners that the simplest course would be for a new charity to be set up having objects similar to those in the draft "Scheme", to which the trustees could hand over the New Zealand sheep station and the other assets pursuant to the terms of the Will, which empowers them to pay or apply the balance of the residuary estate "to or for any bodies or institutions of an educational or charitable nature" as they think fit.[9]

If the new charity had a more straightforward definition of both the agricultural and charitable purposes of the trust, the intention of Baker's original will could be preserved without its complications.[10] The trustees accepted the commissioners' suggestion and proceeded to establish the C. Alma Baker Trust, transferring to it the residue of Baker's estate, including Limestone Downs. The new trust's aims were 'the furtherance of the science of agriculture; the advancement of education; and such other charitable purposes as the Trustees shall from time to time think fit'.[11] The priorities of this new trust, an independent charitable organisation, would be set by its own trustees and not by any assumptions as to what Baker's views might have been.

Over the next year or so, the details of a proposal were hammered out in negotiations among the English trustees, the Treasury Solicitor, the New Zealand trustees and Massey University. The trust would be controlled by the trustees in England and administration of the farm and policies for its development and management determined by a 'New Zealand Committee' appointed by the English trustees, although three of its members would normally be chosen from nominees put forward by the university. A significant appointment would be the chairperson of this committee who would also be appointed by the trustees. Although it was originally envisaged that farm surpluses would be channelled to research at Massey University, they were now to be available 'for or towards the furtherance of the science of agriculture in such charitable manner as the New Zealand Committee shall think fit'. The terms were, therefore, narrower than those of the parent trust where the trustees had the additional power of utilising income for the advancement of education and for other charitable purposes.

While all these discussions and negotiations had been proceeding, Limestone Downs had continued under existing managerial arrangements. Neil Dempster, Dan O'Connell's successor, remained in charge of the farm, with John Sparling and Denny Johnstone as the New Zealand trustees of the Baker estate. There were few significant changes in policy except to ensure that Limestone Downs received the maximum benefit from the government's livestock incentive scheme and the new supplementary minimum prices which, in response to a dramatic fall in the country's terms of trade, guaranteed returns on farm commodities. Since his arrival, Dempster had been keen to build a Polled Angus stud and had made some progress using stock on the farm and new blood bought in from Johnstone's Puketutu Stud. In many ways, however, the farm was in limbo while its future was determined, making for a certain reluctance to commit funds to development work with either the farm or its stock. Even so, fuelled by artificially high prices for primary produce, and rising domestic inflation, land values rose dramatically in the late 1970s; the value of Limestone Downs doubled within the decade. In October 1980, the farm was valued at $2.4 million and carried stock worth $500,000.

Before finally proceeding with the scheme, two of the English trustees , Robin Boyes and Roger Moore, visited New Zealand for discussions with the New Zealand trustees and representatives of Massey University. As part of the visit they were shown over a number of the university's agricultural research units and farms and, impressed with what they saw, reported back to Norman Boyes. The English trustees then obtained the necessary approval

Warwick Deighton, manager of Limestone Downs since 1981, with Jess and Tip. WARWICK DEIGHTON

of the Attorney-General and the Charity Commissioners to the final form of the trust deed which would come into effect from July 1981 with Johnstone as chairman of the New Zealand Committee.

Despite all the planning, the new venture had a troubled birth. If they were to be responsible for managing the farm in accordance with predetermined development policies, university representatives wanted to deal directly with the resident manager and were reluctant to work through a committee chaired by Johnstone. Moreover, they felt that Johnstone, as trustee, chairman of the New Zealand Committee, supervisor of farm policy and supplier of stud stock to the farm, would have a serious conflict of interest. This could affect the development and implementation of new policies that, in some aspects, needed to differ significantly from those followed in the past if the maximum potential of Limestone Downs was to be realised. Rather than a smooth transition, there was something of a stand-off with Kevin Lowe, the university's nominee as farm adviser, unwilling to work through a structure dominated by Johnstone, and the situation further complicated by the latter's plans to live in Queensland for six months of each year. After considerable acrimony, Johnstone was forced to step aside. Dempster, loyal to Johnstone, and finding his own policies criticised, resigned rather than work under the new arrangements. Remote from developments, the English trustees feared that the whole venture was about to collapse: Johnstone had been pushed aside, the manager at Limestone Downs had resigned and the man nominated to replace him was employed on a farm administered by the university. It all looked rather like a Massey takeover.

A way through the impasse was negotiated with Christopher Horton, who had been chosen to chair the proposed New Zealand Committee in place of Johnstone, taking a crucial role. Horton, who had owned a farm property near Limestone Downs and was a partner in the stockbroking firm of Hendry, Hay, Smythe & Horton, had been appointed because of the financial expertise he could bring to the committee. As well as having these qualifications, he was a long-standing friend of the Boyes family. He was ideally placed to reassure the English trustees, and recommended the changes for approval. With some apprehension, they agreed.

These upheavals, coming when the establishment of the new C. Alma Baker Trust was imminent, forced changes in appointments within the New Zealand Committee. As planned, Massey University nominated its new Chancellor, Dr Lindsay Wallace, a former Director of the Research Division of the Ministry of Agriculture and Fisheries, Alan Frampton, Professor of Agricultural Economics and Dean of the Faculty of Agricultural and Horticultural Sciences, and Sir Alan Stewart, the Vice-Chancellor. The trustees also appointed Horton, John Sparling and, in place of Johnstone, David Frith, President of the Auckland branch of Federated Farmers and later Chairman of the New Zealand Meat Board. Kevin Lowe was to be farm supervisor and David Bateman, an accountant at Massey University, secretary of the committee. The position of manager was offered to Warwick Deighton, who had been responsible for a major redevelopment of Riverside, a Wairarapa farm administered by Massey University.

Since 1981, Norman and Robin Boyes and Roger Moore have remained as English trustees (Norman Boyes completing fifty years as a trustee of the Baker estate in April 1991) and there have been few changes to the New Zealand Committee. Frampton resigned from the committee in 1982 when he left Massey University, and his place was taken by Kevin Lowe. Frampton returned less than a year later, however, when John Sparling, 'the sole survivor of the old guard' as he called himself, stepped aside for business and personal reasons, although remaining involved as a legal adviser to the trust and a nominee owner of Limestone Downs. From the beginning of 1983, the Hon. Les Gandar, who had completed his term as New Zealand High Commissioner to London, joined the committee as chairman, an arrangement that had been foreshadowed in 1981.

CHAPTER 16

A VALUABLE AND WELL-KNOWN PROPERTY

Once the structural issues of management had been resolved, the New Zealand Committee immediately embarked on an evaluation of the farm and its potential with Kevin Lowe, Warwick Deighton and a range of specialists from Massey University taking leading roles. From a philosophical point of view, Lowe proposed a radical change – from running Limestone Downs along the principles of 'extensive farming' usually associated with station management in New Zealand to a much more intensive system of land use. The difference, he argued, was one of scale, not of kind, and the full potential of Limestone Downs would be realised only under such an approach. He and Deighton proposed the subdivision of existing paddocks, smaller mobs and herds, improved stock quality, tightly managed rotational grazing and a close monitoring of the performance of both stock and pasture. The emphasis was to be on improved performance rather than an increase in stock numbers although that, too, would follow from the change. The committee accepted the proposed thrust of development and, under the chairmanship first of Chris Horton, and then of Les Gandar, provided strong backing for Lowe and Deighton.

Although this approach would be new for Limestone Downs, and unprecedented in the district, it was by no means unknown to the new management team. At Riverside Farm, a property of some 670 hectares near Mount Bruce in the Wairarapa, Lowe as supervisor and Deighton as manager had already redeveloped a farm in this way. Since 1978, Massey University had been responsible for managing Riverside under the will of the late Sydney Campbell whose family had bought the original homestead block in 1856. Under the will, the university holds a long-term lease on the farm which supports research for the study and development of agricultural and pastoral farming.[1] Although the venture had only been operating for about three years when Deighton moved to Limestone Downs, the results even by that time had convinced him and Lowe that the same management philosophy could be applied to much larger properties. But that had yet to be proved, and an initial evaluation by Lowe in April 1981 suggested that stock, infrastructure and management would all have to be transformed if the new policy were to be a success. An initial development plan was accepted by the New Zealand Committee in July 1981, with the main emphasis for capital expenditure on stock improvement, paddock subdivision and water reticulation.[2]

The first step was to conduct a full assessment of all stock. The figures for July 1981 showed 3,096 cattle and 19,622 sheep, with a total of some 33,000 stock units, or 12 stock units per hectare of available land. In reality, however, these figures were artificially inflated because the government's livestock incentive scheme was based on 1 July figures, and large numbers of stock had customarily been held for this date, and then sold as soon as possible afterwards. The wintering capacity of the property was, in fact, much lower than the figures suggested; in practice, seldom more than 12,000-13,000 sheep and 1,200 breeding cows, or about seven to eight stock units per hectare, were carried right through the winter. Such distortions were common on New Zealand farms at the time when, in effect, successive governments encouraged farmers to farm for the subsidies and the associated capital gain rather than in the best interests of their farms and stock. For Limestone Downs, returns from the scheme had been in the region of $100,000 a year, which had been incentive enough.

The property also carried a considerable number of horses and goats. The latter had been regarded as a pest in the early days, and managers from Dan O'Connell's time had been encouraged to keep the goat numbers down by being allowed to keep the profits from sales as a manager's perk, sometimes used, at least in part, to provide amenities for the staff. But with the high prices paid for mohair in the late 1970s, the goats were tolerated and fine-haired bucks were introduced to improve the quality of the stock. But although the goats could keep down weeds and brush on rough country, they could also eat large quantities of good feed. One of the first decisions taken was to sell or slaughter as many of the goats as possible within three months. The proceeds were put towards the construction of a new swimming pool for use by the staff and their families.

But broad policy was only part of the problem. Inspections showed that overall stock performance was poor. The lambing percentage had fallen well below 70 per cent partly because of the quality of the rams and also because of recent severe outbreaks of facial eczema. Over the years, the Romney flock, with locally bred ewes and rams from Johnstone's Puketutu Stud had developed woolly 'closed face' characteristics, which meant bringing the sheep into the shearing shed for 'wigging' every two months. The absence of records and monitoring meant that dry ewes, many of which might not have produced a lamb for two or more seasons, had not been culled. Over the latter part of 1981, a ruthless culling operation was undertaken on the farm, with some 10,000 sheep being sold. All rams on the farm were killed or sold. In the first year, nearly 200 new rams were bought in, together with more than 7,000 ewe hoggets. Sheep bought in over the next year or two to boost performance were, on average, 5-7 kilograms heavier than their counterparts at Limestone Downs. In particular, the New Zealand Committee sought permission, through the Ministers of Agriculture and Lands, to buy in Romney ewes and rams from the government's Waihora Stud in the Bay of Plenty, where stock were monitored, bred and culled on performance rather than appearance. By agreeing to participate in continuing monitoring and trials, Limestone Downs acquired proven stock but, and as important, it issued a clear signal to staff, and to the district's farmers who were watching developments with a keen interest, that, above all else, future farm management was to be performance driven.

There was a similar policy towards the cattle. The Angus stud, which had been the focus of much attention, was also found wanting. Although pedigree had been recorded, performance had not. Asked to validate and evaluate the stud herd, stock agents found that marks were indistinct, foot problems were prevalent and a quarter of the cows had not calved for two years. As with the run cattle, calving was haphazard and spread over a long period. Only one-third of the stock was still regarded as acceptable for stud purposes by the breed classifiers of the New Zealand Angus Association. As a consequence, and because of the intensive demands on labour and pasture to maintain a stud, the decision was taken to sell the best of the stud stock and to incorporate the rest into the commercial herd.[3] All cows and heifers that did not become pregnant in the 1981 breeding season were culled, and surplus bulls sold.

For the future, the committee decided to establish a rotational breeding system that involved introducing Hereford bulls to mate with Angus cows for the advantages of 'hybrid vigour of first-cross steer progeny, improved growth and lactation of first-cross heifer progeny and a premium paid at market for white-faced-black beef cattle'.[4] Of the resulting calves, steers were to be raised for sale to the works or as stores, while heifers were to be mated with Friesian bulls. Again, of the progeny, steers would be raised and sold, while heifers would be mated with Angus bulls, and so the cycle would go on. Past practice at Limestone Downs, and indeed generally at the time, had been to mate heifers at the age of twenty-six months. On the basis of experimental work at the Whatawhata Hill Country Research Station and elsewhere, it was decided to experiment with mating heifers at fifteen months. The goal was to mate heifers that had reached a target weight of 250 kilograms, although in the first few years the condition of the stock meant that a minimum of only 225-230 kilograms could be achieved.[5]

In this first year, the emphasis was on culling poorly performing stock, buying in replacements and planning for longer term change. There was also a heavy commitment to clearing deferred maintenance, and some capital development, including the construction of an additional staff house and Baker Cottage, which was provided for visitors to the farm. Farm motorcycles were introduced, although most of the shepherds still used horses.

For the existing staff, the new policies represented a radical change from the past. Some accepted the thrust of new developments but others were resistant to change either through loyalty to the old regime or because they questioned the wisdom of what was proposed. In the latter regard, at least, they were in good company. Many of the district's farmers who attended the first Limestone Downs Open Day early in 1982 were sceptical, and even openly scornful, of the idea that a property the size of Limestone Downs could be farmed intensively. Many dismissed the plan to introduce closely managed rotational grazing and paddock subdivision using three-wire electric fencing to contain sheep and run cattle. At that time, electric fencing was becoming increasingly popular on dairy farms, but was used only occasionally with commercial cattle, and very rarely with sheep.

From a distance, Denny Johnstone was strongly critical of the new management team, warning the trustees that he was 'quite alarmed at some of the changes Kevin Lowe is bringing in, in a new area where he has no experience' and, with regard to Deighton, suggesting that it was 'just ludicrous' to appoint someone from a smaller property and from outside the district. He argued that to bring in Hereford bulls to cover 'the beautiful Limestone herd' was 'nothing less than sacrilege'.[6] Personalities aside, Johnstone's opinion none the less represented the traditional view of how a station should be run – as an extensive operation with paddocks of 100 hectares or more, with stockmen on horseback using large teams of dogs to muster stock and move them between paddocks or to centralised yards.

Under the circumstances, it was a brave move for the trustees not only to approve a management structure that placed Limestone Downs policy in the hands of a committee in which university-trained 'experts' rather than practical farmers had strong influence, but also to accept a broad policy option that went against the prevailing wisdom and would dramatically change the direction of development on the property. But once the basic concept was accepted, the 'Massey team' knew that its approach could be vindicated only by results, and wasted little time in embarking on its restructuring programme. Inevitably, there were tensions on the farm and some discomfort in the New Zealand Committee where both old and new regimes were represented. But there was little compromise on the basic principles, which made for high staff turnover on Limestone Downs in the early years. As the benefits and profitability of the new policies became evident, however, morale improved, together with staff commitment and loyalty.

After the improvement of stock quality, the next priority was to investigate water supplies, because paddock subdivision could not proceed until reliable reticulation could be provided. The task was undertaken by Robin Clarke of the Department of Agricultural Engineering at Massey University. He found himself facing a complex arrangement of tanks, dams and springs that were used to supply houses and stock through a dual system of 'clean' and 'dirty' water, which depended on a single network of pipes for distribution to tanks and troughs. The system, which had evolved over decades, was largely unrecorded and provided only an unreliable supply to parts of the farm. Much of it was in need of repair but there were no isolating valves to facilitate maintenance. Some of the dams, to which stock had direct access, were leaking and were little more than 'paddock puddles', where heavy cattle use in winter caused serious pugging.

Over the next few years, a new reticulation system, costing nearly $100,000 in the first year and twice that over a decade, was developed, with a new 225,000-litre reservoir near the woolshed that was supplied from a spring-fed weir within a 29-hectare securely fenced catchment area next to the airfield. From this point, much of the farm could be supplied with reticulated water by gravity feed. Smaller dams, also fenced off from stock use, were used to supply troughs. An alternative scheme, using artesian wells rather than a central dam, was abandoned because of unsatisfactory flow rates from a number of bores drilled on various parts of the farm.[7] Domestic supply was based on rainwater tanks at each house, supplemented by large catchment tanks at the woolshed and covered yards.

Mustering at Limestone Downs, early 1980s. C. ALMA BAKER TRUST

By the latter part of 1982, a development team headed by Peter Grant was responsible for carrying out this work, as well as extending the system of lanes to facilitate stock movement, the consequent track development for vehicle access and the subdivision of existing paddocks into smaller, more easily managed areas of 15-20 hectares. Lanes and boundary fences continued to use the conventional structure of posts, battens and wire, but all subdivision was carried out with electric fences that a two-person gang could install at a rate of more than a kilometre per day. At the change in management in 1981, the farm was subdivided into 60 paddocks but this figure is misleading because of the number of very small paddocks near the manager's house that had been used for the Angus stud and for horses. Many paddocks were larger than 100 hectares, with one close to 600 hectares. By mid-1983 an area of some 800 hectares covering the north-west of the property had been subdivided and fenced. In addition, new covered yards with an area of 1,000 square metres had been built, the woolshed had undergone major repairs, a further house had been built and existing dwellings had been substantially upgraded. Progress with the improvement of stock quality was much slower. The farm continued to buy and breed replacement stock and to improve stock performance with closer pasture management. As a symbol of the change, Limestone Downs sold its hay-baler in 1983. Previously, up to 12,000 bales a year had been made and stored but now closer control ensured sufficient pasture without the need for supplementary feed.

Aerial view of Limestone Downs, early 1980s. C. ALMA BAKER TRUST

The cumulative benefits of the new policies soon began to show. The lambing perform-ance for 1982 rose to 72 per cent, the highest for many years, but with Waihora ewes achieving as high as 95 per cent and station-bred ewes, even after heavy culling, achieving only 60 per cent. In 1983, the overall performance reached 85 per cent. Similar success was achieved with the cattle, with calving returns climbing from 50 to 83 per cent. By the end of 1983, ewe numbers had reached 21,500 and 1,200 cows had been mated that year. Farm profits of about $150,000 a year had been absorbed by new developments, as had a loan of $250,000 from the parent trust. But with this major expenditure out of the way the committee anticipated rising farm income, and so could begin to contemplate the distribu-tion of profits in accordance with the terms of the trust. With some satisfaction, the New Zealand Committee noted that at the Open Day for the district's farmers in February 1983, 'there appeared to be a greater level of sympathy and understanding of what is being undertaken on the farm'.[8] Some had even paid the new team the ultimate compliment of adopting aspects of the Limestone Downs strategy on their own properties.

The same pace of development continued for the next two years. By mid-1985 water reticulation for all areas between the main road and the coast had been completed and had been followed by further fencing and subdivision. Nineteen eighty-four alone brought the completion of more than 14 kilometres of reticulated water supplies, 5 kilometres of permanent fencing and more than 20 kilometres of electric fencing. Throughout this process, about twenty new paddocks were created each year (bringing the total to 130 by 1984), thus facilitating tighter stock control.

The Kaawa flats, 1993. BARRIE MACDONALD

By 1984, stock carried over the winter had stabilised at about 22,000 ewes with a further 7,500 ewe hoggets available as replacements. There were also about 1,100 cows and 500 heifers to be used as replacements, or sold. In all, stock on Limestone Downs represented some 36,500 stock units, which did not fully utilise the enhanced carrying capacity of the farm in a good season. For both sheep and cattle, the farm could now to provide its own replacement breeding stock, so freeing up the funds that had been used to buy ewe hoggets. The management team was reluctant to increase sheep numbers further without expanding handling facilities and chose, instead, to develop a bull beef operation on the Kaawa flats. The performance of about 120 Friesian yearling bulls purchased as an experiment late in 1982 suggested good profits and led to the purchase of 250 weaners in 1984 and twice that number in 1985. Purchased at weights of about 85-100 kilograms (at an average of $137) , the bulls were sold after twelve to fifteen months (for an average of $582) as they reached live weights of 440 kilograms (and a carcase weight of 230 kilograms) and as feed supplies on the farm diminished in the autumn. Nineteen eighty-four was a particularly good year as far as weather, farm conditions and animal health were concerned, leading to record performance and profits in the 1984-85 year. An overall 98 per cent lambing percentage was recorded, alongside 86 per cent calving for the run cattle. More than 140,000 kilograms of wool were sold at an average price of $3.30 per kilogram. A systematic and pre-planned system of rotational grazing was introduced and monitored for the first time. The purchase of a set of portable yards greatly reduced the time taken over tasks such as docking and drenching, and meant that sheep were saved from the stress of movement to and from

Docking lambs, 1993. Left to right: Alf Harwood, Richard Skinner, Judy Taylor, Julie Day, Monique Croon, Bruce Campbell, Warwick Deighton. BARRIE MACDONALD

central yards. In the 1984-85 year, gross farm income topped $1 million for the first time, leaving a profit of $482,000 after farm expenses had been met.

To some extent, this performance reflected the development of the previous five years, but the application of new technology and research findings was also significant. In taking any steps towards funding research, the New Zealand Committee was particularly concerned with ventures that would assist (and profit) Limestone Downs, but would also apply to farming in the Raglan district. Given the heavy losses suffered through facial eczema, and the difficulties caused by the fact that much of the damage that affected fertility and mortality was sub-clinical and not easily detected, the committee joined with the Ruakura Research Station and animal scientists at Massey University for a major programme investigating facial eczema on the farm, with a view to developing a line of rams resistant to the disease.

Led by Professor J.K. Syers, there was a similar investigation of the fertiliser requirements of the varied soil types found on the farm. The committee invested heavily in the development of a new Fertiliser and Lime Research Centre at Massey University. At a time when the reduction of subsidies was causing fertiliser prices to increase sharply and leading farmers to seek cheaper alternatives to applying single superphosphate on a uniform basis, the Syers team overturned much of the conventional wisdom. Experiments with the application of rock phosphate at Limestone Downs helped to set a trend for hill country farms and made a significant contribution to growing interest in 'low-input' agriculture.

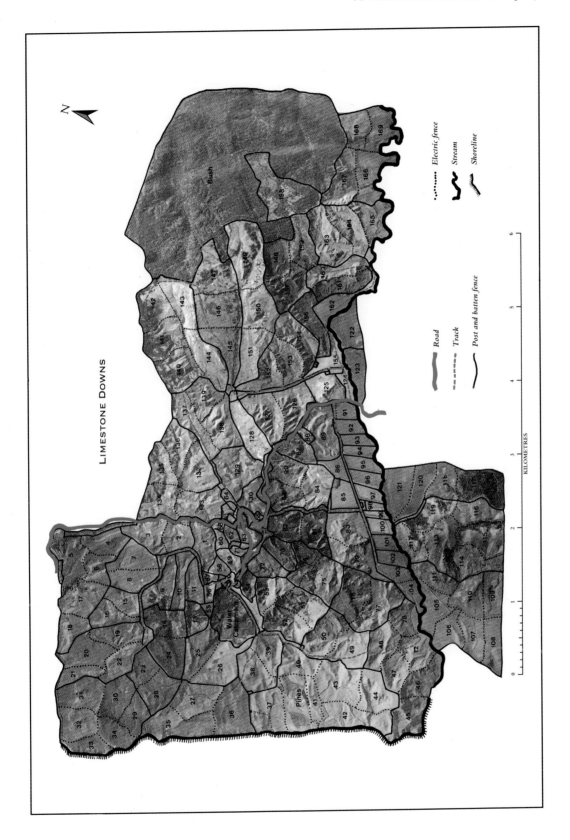

LIMESTONE DOWNS

Broken sand country overlooking the mouth of the Waikawau Stream at the north-west corner of Limestone Downs, 1993. BARRIE MACDONALD

In further applications of science and technology, staff were trained to take regular spore counts to monitor the risk of facial eczema so that stock could be treated and shifted to new pasture as necessary, and drenching for worms became dependent on the microscopic analysis of faecal samples rather than according to a fixed timetable. Another project suggested that there might be greater returns from shearing ewes once, rather than twice, a year. Although the gross wool returns from shearing twice were greater, the net return was lower once all shearing, crutching and associated costs were taken into account. Against this, ewes heavy in wool had greater difficulties in lambing. Ram harnesses were increasingly used for marking tupped ewes to identify for culling those that did not conceive in the first two ovulation cycles and whose pregnancies would thus extend the lambing season. As data collection became more systematic, all aspects of stock performance were closely monitored. One of the most significant innovations came in 1984, when Limestone Downs began to use ultrasonic scanning on ewes shortly after mating to identify those bearing twins. This was part of a strategy to establish a high-performance ram-breeding flock. Ultrasonic testing also allowed the identification and much earlier culling of ewes that had failed to conceive, thereby increasing the pasture available for those carrying lambs.[9]

Staff gradually settled into the new regime and departures came to reflect promotion rather than discontent. As a sign of further change in the staffing structure at Limestone Downs, Alf Harwood, who came from Massey University's Tuapaka farm in the Manawatu, was appointed assistant manager early in 1986, with overall responsibility for the day-to-

Romney ewes move to fresh pasture, 1993. MAUREEN MACDONALD

day management of the farm. Inevitably, the new approach to scientific management, the continuing development programme, the need for close control of budgets, pastures and stock and increased reporting had all meant that Warwick Deighton had become increasingly concerned with broader and longer term strategic and planning issues. He also had a growing role in farm extension as farming and educational groups began to visit Limestone Downs on a regular basis, separate from the open days that had become an annual feature. By the mid-1980s, the regular full-time staff had risen from eight to ten, with Doreen Deighton also employed on a part-time basis as clerical assistant. By 1985, only two of the staff who had been on the farm when the New Zealand Committee assumed responsibility remained; they were George Marshall and Dana Hoete, both of whom had spent all of their working lives on or near Limestone Downs. The other staff, arriving when the results of change could be seen, were more easily convinced of the wisdom of new directions. Farm facilities had also improved. A staff tennis court had been built next to the swimming pool and plans were approved for new single staff quarters to replace the old 'community house' built by Charles Alma Baker in 1927. In all, the resident Limestone Downs community now numbered forty-five, including children.

With major developments completed, and future earnings seemingly assured, the New Zealand Committee and its parent trust began to consider the distribution of profits in accordance with the trust deed. The matter was discussed in February 1983 during one of the English trustees' regular supervisory visits to New Zealand. Any allocation for scholarships or research would extend the development period of the farm, but the trustees had been anxious to make a start with scholarships at least. Accordingly, at the end of 1983 applications had been invited for C. Alma Baker Study Awards for students with farm experience to complete an agricultural diploma, C. Alma Baker Postgraduate Scholarships for one student from New Zealand to study for a year in Britain and for a C. Alma Baker Travel Award for an agriculturalist to undertake a study tour abroad, all of which were to be

The wool goes out from Limestone Downs; view from the manager's residence, late 1980s.
WARWICK DEIGHTON

offered annually.[10] A year later, the committee established criteria for competitively awarded research grants, to be offered annually for projects contributing to agricultural research and education. In the first year, grants totalling $84,000 were made. All awards became the responsibility of a sub-committee chaired by Sir Alan Stewart who, having played a decisive role in setting up the new venture from the university's point of view, remained a driving force within the New Zealand Committee.

By 1985, most of the major features of the development programme had been completed, which was as well because the 1984 Labour government embarked upon removing all subsidies from the rural sector. Supplementary minimum prices and commodity stabilisation funds, both of which had helped to sustain and smooth farm income during the development period, were early casualties in reforms implemented by Finance Minister Roger Douglas, who was determined to see rural industries subject to strict market forces. Tax concessions and incentives for farm development and increased production were also abolished. But although these moves may, in the longer term, have encouraged the development of more efficient industries, the suddenness of the changes, coming at a time of falling export prices, caused a widespread loss of confidence in farming. By 1986, New Zealand was suffering from a rural crisis, with plummeting land values and many farmers on the brink of bankruptcy.

Having no debt and, as a charitable trust, not having been eligible for or become dependent on, tax concessions, Limestone Downs was less affected than most properties.

Even so, it was necessary to slow the final stages of the development programme, to leave vacated staff positions unfilled and to make substantial reductions in fertiliser application. Gross farm income fell well below $1 million, and profits, the funds available for dispersal for charitable and research purposes, fell from about $500,000 to $100,000. Over the second half of the decade, net farm profit recovered to average about $340,000. At this time, the property was carrying twelve stock units per hectare, which was what had been projected in 1981, but the presence of increasing numbers of young stock, which could not be pressed too hard, and a couple of hard seasons, suggested that a greater margin should be allowed. The trend for beef production to increase at the expense of sheep production was driven largely by comparative returns (beef returns per stock unit were three times those of sheep in some seasons) but also gave added flexibility, since bulls could be sold off as feed became short, or carried through a second winter if it was plentiful.

To a large extent, the farm (the revised management strategy meant that 'station' was no longer an appropriate description) had entered a fine tuning phase. By 1991, the last of the big paddocks had been subdivided, giving a total of 169 paddocks with an average size of 16.5 hectares for the cleared portion of the farm, and water was reticulated to all paddocks. The last of the ewes inherited in 1981 had been sold in 1985, and almost all of the cattle by 1986. In 1988 and 1989 performance for lambing was 107 per cent and for calving 91 per cent, both records for the property. Because of the cost savings, the application of single superphosphate had given way to rock phosphate, supplemented towards the end of the decade with granulated sulphur. Horses had largely given way to motorcycles, then to three-wheelers and finally to the safer four-wheeled farm bikes. Virtually all staff were linked to one another by radio telephone mounted on their vehicles. The farm now had three sets of permanent sheepyards, two sets of cattleyards and the portable Pratley yards used for docking, drenching and other tasks undertaken in the paddock without moving stock to fixed yards. Roads and tracks had been improved, and the system of stock lanes extended. The numbers of permanent full-time staff had stabilised at nine, with contractors still used for shearing, permanent fencing, and heavy machinery work. Baker's community house, known, for most of its life, as 'the single men's quarters', was renamed Baker Lodge and refurbished as a recreation and holiday centre in partnership with the Police Staff Benevolent and Welfare Fund. (A name change would have been needed anyway, with the 1986 appointment of Hannah Schmidt, the first female shepherd to work on Limestone Downs.) Open days, some attracting as many as 200 farmers, had become a major extension activity for Limestone Downs and a community event for the district.

The ending of the main redevelopment period meant that more funds were available for charitable purposes. Between 1981 and 1991, some $1.9 million was granted in a range of categories developed by the New Zealand Committee in association with the English trustees. By far the largest proportion of money, $1.3 million, was allocated for research projects for 'the furtherance of the science of agriculture', with the committee favouring applied projects that would have immediate on-farm benefits. Many, but by no means all, of the grants went to scientists at Massey University. Of the balance, some $400,000 was directed to a range of scholarships, study awards and travel grants to assist both established and student scientists in their work.

One of the most popular schemes was an exchange arrangement for young farmworkers between New Zealand and Britain with the New Zealand Committee and the parent trust in England sharing costs. Working with the National Federation of Young Farmers Clubs, the English trustees have, since 1987, sent four young farmworkers each year to New Zealand where they spend three months working as farm hands on Limestone Downs and then a month travelling elsewhere in the country. Young New Zealand farmworkers are similarly placed on farms in England and Wales. The reports of those working at Limestone Downs emphasise their surprise at the size of its operations, the scientific approach to animal health and farm management, the efficiency of large stock operations such as docking and drenching, stock values that are one-third of those in Britain, and the expectation that they, men and women alike, would be expected to kill and dress old and injured stock for 'dog tucker'.

In all, some $1.6 million had been invested in the redevelopment plan, but by 1993 the increased income had recovered that investment and was beginning to show a return over and above what might have been expected if Limestone Downs had been farmed conventionally. In constant dollar terms, the value of the property as a 'going concern' had been increased by 73 per cent in a decade (to $6.3 million in 1991) and, more important, the annual earning capacity had been enhanced by some $465,000 a year at 1991-92 prices. Towards the end of the 1980s, stock units stabilised at about 35,000-36,000, with the emphasis on improving stock performance, rather than increasing the numbers of stock units carried. As a measure of the success of the decade of development, feed consumed annually by stock had increased by 50 per cent, a comment on the improvement of pasture quality and management. The balance of farm activity has also changed. Sheep numbers reached a high of 30,000 at mid-decade and had dropped to less than 15,000 by 1993; cattle numbers doubled from 2,000 to 4,000 in the same period. Lambing performance had been held at about 107-108 per cent, and calving at 90-91 per cent. In 1980-81, wool accounted for 38 per cent of farm income, cattle for 45 per cent and sheep for 15 per cent; in 1991-92, wool and sheep sales each accounted for only 20 per cent of farm income, while cattle sales had risen to 60 per cent, most of it from the highly profitable bull beef operation. The changes had been driven by considerations of profitability, rather than theory, but the flexible management strategy means that, without buying in any replacement stock, cattle numbers could be reduced, and 25,000 breeding ewes carried within two years.[11]

In effect, the redeveloped farm offers a net return on capital that is twice what it would have been under conventional management. If, rather than being a charitable trust, the enterprise had been taxed, then the relative financial advantages from the redevelopment programme would have been even greater because of the write-offs that would have been allowed. For Kevin Lowe and Warwick Deighton, and for the New Zealand Committee and the English trustees who had backed their judgement, the experiment had been a success. They had proved that intensive management techniques could be applied to a large property and, more important, could enhance profitability over traditional station practice.

In 1992, Limestone Downs carried 1,100 cows, 820 calves, 1,400 bulls and steers and 15,000 sheep, compared with the 1,400 cattle and 500 sheep that had been on the property when it was bought by Charles Alma Baker in 1926. The transformation that had taken place in the 1980s was as great as that wrought by Baker himself in the late 1920s. Warnock's observation that, 'as a result of the progressive policy adopted, the prospects of this estate have been altered and it promises to become a valuable and well-known property' was as apt for the 1990s as it had been in 1927.

RETROSPECT

When, in old age, Charles Alma Baker looked back, he felt he had lived 'a long and full life'. Even as a younger man, before he had the wealth to pursue his hobbies and interests, he had been drawn to the frontiers within New Zealand where he could lead a rugged, independent, outdoors life. Through his surveying he was also able to accumulate capital that allowed him to realise his social ambitions. In these years, Baker consciously built an image and personality that lifted him above his origins and enabled him to move easily within the upper levels of colonial society. He married well, acquired the manners of a gentleman and, as a contract surveyor in Malaya, found the wealth that secured his social position.

But Baker was seldom content with what he had, and was always looking for a new challenge that he could tackle in an innovative way. As an investor in tin mining, he introduced new technologies, as a rubber planter he ignored the orthodoxies of his day and looked to soil conservation strategies that were ahead of their time and, throughout his later life, he invested, speculatively but modestly, in mining ventures and mechanical inventions. He tried, without notable success, to design or modify machinery for agricultural use and could always be relied upon to buy the latest gadget on the market. He always preferred to develop something new, rather than to maintain something already established. His interest therefore tended to shift from one activity to the next as soon as the initial challenge had been overcome.

What set Baker aside from most of his contemporaries was the imperial framework within which he operated. Although imperial fervour was not uncommon, especially in war or when there was an external threat to Britain or its colonies, Baker's career as an international, imperial investor was certainly unusual for its time. The imperial idea gave shape and meaning to much of Baker's life. Whether he was raising funds for the defence of Britain, commenting on the deficiencies of 'de-natured foods' or arguing the case for biodynamic agriculture, Baker couched his statements in the language of empire, urging imperial and colonial parliaments, as well as individuals, to act in the future interests of the British Empire.

Although Baker's ceaseless travel in later years was designed partly to avoid malaria in

Charles Alma Baker. ROBIN BOYES

Malaya and winters anywhere, and to allow him to fish, it also enabled him to supervise his various interests in England, Malaya, Australia and New Zealand. Baker's surveying, mining investments and plantations brought him substantial wealth; his campaigns for aircraft, healthier foods, biodynamic farming and the tourism potential of big game fishing all contributed to contemporary public awareness and debate. Despite this willingness to engage in public debate, Baker remained a very private man, revealing little of himself either to the public or to his immediate friends and family. Although seeming always remote, even austere, in personal relationships, he was generous with his money in the support of others and showed a lifetime concern for his daughter's future.

Baker was proud of his achievements, even vain on occasions. He was not averse to leaving personal monuments and memorials – aircraft carrying his name, the Alma Reel, the Alma Rustless Swivel, the newspaper reports that recorded his activities, the photographs signed 'C. Alma Baker, C.B.E.'. It is reasonable to suppose, then, that he would not have objected to the use of his residual estate, after the death of his daughter, to establish the C. Alma Baker Trust. It would have been even more to his liking that the trust was concerned primarily with agricultural research and education, and that Limestone Downs was at the heart of its activities. This property had been Baker's last major investment but, despite the money poured into its development, it fell well short of reaching its potential, or of breaking even, during his lifetime. The property now has a dual function – to generate income that will help fulfil the charitable purposes of the trust, and to demonstrate the application and test the profitability of new technologies and management techniques. So, although in no way encompassing the complexity of Baker's life or recognising the diversity of his interests and achievements, it is a fitting memorial to a remarkable man.

NOTE ON CURRENCY AND MEASUREMENT

Generally, financial details have been expressed in the currency of the time and country to which they refer. Where clarification has seemed necessary, especially with regard to the Federated Malay States where the value of the local dollar fluctuated against the pound, equivalent values have been expressed in sterling. For the years since the Second World War, amounts given are in New Zealand pounds and then dollars, unless otherwise stated. Both imperial and metric measurements have been used, depending on context and on sources. Throughout, measurement and currency have been matched to the conventions of the time and place under discussion.

NOTE ON SOURCES

Apart from drawing on published works and newspapers that are acknowledged in the references, much of this book is based upon primary resources in collections related, directly or indirectly, to the estate of Charles Alma Baker or found in the archives of government departments and agencies with which he, his agents, or executors conducted business. Photographs have also been used extensively in the research, as well as for illustrations in the text. For the latter, the source of the published photograph has been given, but it has not always been possible to identify either the photographer or ultimate ownership; any such inadvertent infringement of copyright is regretted. The major archival collections consulted are as follows:

1. Papers held by Warren Boyes and Archer and the C. Alma Baker Trust, Huntingdon, England. These are referred to in the notes as being located in the Huntingdon Archive. These papers have been acquired by Frederick, Norman and Robin Boyes, in their various capacities of solicitor to Charles Alma Baker, executors of his will, or trustees of the C. Alma Baker Trust. The main series are:

    English Correspondence
    Malayan Correspondence
    New Zealand Correspondence
    Australian Correspondence
    Wills and Probates Series
    Trust Papers.

2. Papers accumulated by A.E. Warnock and E. Cummane in their respective roles as attorney and accountant for Baker and the Baker estate in New Zealand. These papers have been sorted, listed and lodged in the Massey University Library, Palmerston North, by the New Zealand Committee of the C. Alma Baker Trust. These documents all carry the prefix LD (Limestone Downs) in the notes.

3. Papers accumulated by Edward C. Blomfield, Trevor Sparling and John Sparling as solicitors to Baker and the Baker estate in New Zealand. These papers are held by the Massey University Library, Palmerston North, with permission of Mr John Sparling. These documents all carry the prefix SP (Sparling Papers) in the notes.

4. Papers of the New Zealand Committee of the C. Alma Baker Trust. These documents cover the activities of the committee and the management of Limestone Downs for the period since 1981. The papers are in held at Massey University in the possession of the secretary of the committee and are identified in the notes as 'NZ Committee' with sub-series LD (Limestone Downs) or BT (Baker Trust).

5. Arkib Negara Malaysia (National Archives of Malaysia, Kuala Lumpur). The papers of

the Kinta Lands Office at Batu Gajah represent one of the few pre-war collections of administrative documents from the Federated Malay States to survive the Second World War. The archive includes a great deal of material on the early tin and rubber industries as well as the surveying of land to facilitate mining and agricultural development. Documents from this source carry the prefix KLO (Kinta Lands Office) in the notes.

6. National Archives of New Zealand, Wellington. A number of series have been used, notably those from the Departments of Lands and Survey, Tourist and Publicity and Public Works. Documents from this source are identified as NANZ.

7. New Zealand Oral History Archive. In the early 1980s, the New Zealand Committee of the C. Alma Baker Trust commissioned Judith Fyfe of the New Zealand Oral History Archive to interview people who had known Charles Alma Baker or worked at Limestone Downs, to evaluate the available archival sources and to gather secondary material relating to Baker's life and times. The material from this collection is now held at the Oral History Centre of the Alexander Turnbull Library, Wellington. Tapes are cited as NZOHA, together with serial number.

REFERENCES

Chapter 1 – Born in Otago

1 These family details are derived from the baptismal and confirmation records of St Pauls Anglican Church, Dunedin, supplemented by information supplied by various descendants of Andrew and Matilda Baker and certificates of births, deaths and marriages.

2 William Rout, MS Autobiography – ATL q MS Rout, 1889-1909; *Nelson Examiner*, 11 June 1853.

3 *Otago Witness*, 27 August 1853.

4 Deeds Index, Reference B 157-8 – Department of Survey and Land Information, Dunedin.

5 Crown Grant Record Map, Suburban Central – Hocken Library.

6 *Otago Witness*, 25 February 1854, 4 November 1854.

7 *Otago Witness*, 5 February 1859.

8 A.H. McLintock, *The Port of Otago*, Dunedin: Whitcombe & Tombs, 1951, Chapter 3; *Otago Harbour Development: From Maori Canoe to Ocean Liner*, Dunedin: Otago Daily Times, 1934.

9 *Otago Witness*, 23 June 1860.

10 *Otago Witness*, 23 June 1860.

11 These details are drawn from the standard North Otago histories, the best of which is K.C. McDonald, *White Stone Country: The Story of North Otago*, Oamaru: North Otago Centennial Committee, 1962. See also K.C. McDonald, *History of North Otago*, Oamaru: North Otago Centennial Committee, 1940; W.H.S. Roberts, *The History of Oamaru and North Otago, New Zealand, from 1853 to the end of 1889*, Oamaru: Andrew Fraser, 1890.

12 Norris Brocklebank and Richard Greenaway, *Oamaru*, Dunedin: John McIndoe, 1979, Notes 65-72.

13 *Oamaru Times*, 1 September 1864.

14 Erik Olssen, *A History of Otago*, Dunedin: John McIndoe, 1984, pp. 56-60.

15 Roberts, *The History of Oamaru and North Otago*, p. 105.

16 McDonald, *White Stone Country*, pp. 82-3; *Oamaru Times*, 1 September 1864, 27 October 1864, 26 January 1865.

17 Crown Grants Application Book No. 1 – Department of Survey and Land Information, Dunedin.

18 Robert Pinney, *Early North Otago Runs*, Auckland: Collins, 1981, pp. 63-4.

19 E. Simeon Elwell, *The Boy Colonists: or, Eight Years of Colonial Life in Otago, New Zealand*, London: Simpkin, Marshall & Co., 1878, pp. 76-8.

20 *Oamaru Times*, 11 January 1866.

21 Most of this information is derived from births, deaths and marriage records, and local directories and almanacs, supplemented by information supplied by members of the Baker family, especially Mrs A.F. Curtin, Auckland, Mrs V. Grey, Auckland and Mr H. Harland-Baker, Taupo.

22 Nola Easdale, *Kairuri: The Measurer of Land*, Petone: Highgate/Price Milburn, Chapter 1.

Chapter 2 – The Handsome CAB

1 Much of this section is based on R.J.C. Stone's *Makers of Fortune: A Colonial Business Community and its Fall*, Auckland: Auckland University Press/Oxford University Press, 1973, which provides a superb overview of Auckland's commercial development in this period.

2 W.H. Oliver, entry on Whitaker in A.H. McLintock (ed.), *An Encyclopaedia of New Zealand*, Wellington: Government Printer, 1966, Vol. 3, p. 652. See also, Stone, *Makers of Fortune*, Chapter 10, *passim*.

3 See Hazel Riseborough, *Days of Darkness: Taranaki 1878-1884*, Wellington: Allen and Unwin, 1989, Chapter 2; Alan Ward, *A Show of Justice: racial 'amalgamation' in nineteenth century New Zealand*, Auckland: Auckland University Press/Oxford University Press, 1973, Chapter X.

4 This information is based on those of Baker's survey plans that could be traced in the Auckland, Gisborne and Hamilton offices of the

Department of Survey and Land Information.

5 See L.P. Lee, 'History of the New Zealand Survey System', in J.A. McRae (ed.), *The Surveyor and the Law*, Wellington: New Zealand Institute of Surveyors, 1981; Easdale, *Kairuri*, Chapter 2.

6 *New Zealand Herald*, 1 September 1884.

7 *Observer*, 14 January 1882.

8 Stone, *Makers of Fortune*, p. 67.

9 *New Zealand Herald*, 10, 11 June 1887.

10 Stone, *Makers of Fortune*, p. 127; *New Zealand Herald*, 18, 31 December 1888.

11 Moss to Thurston, 24 January 1891, Moss Papers, Binder 2, B103 – Auckland Museum.

12 Fieldbook A641 – Department of Survey and Land Information, Auckland.

13 Most of the information on Pita Baker given here has come from registers of births, deaths and marriages supplemented by family information supplied by Ms Kahukore Baker, Pita Baker's granddaughter, and by the records of Te Aute College. An obituary of Pita Baker can be found in the *Opotiki Times*, 6 September 1984.

14 Register of Maori Land Plans, ML 6225, 6227 – Department of Survey and Land Information, Auckland.

15 Surveys of New Zealand, Report for 1888-1889 – AJHR, 1889, C.1A, p. 39; 1889-1890 – AJHR, 1890, C.5, p. 45.

16 *New Zealand Herald*, 24 March 1890; Roderick Whitaker, interview with Judith Fyfe, 6 June 1985 – NZOHA, CAB 91.

Chapter 3 – Planting Stones

1 *Perak Pioneer*, 19 September 1894; 22 September 1894.

2 See John G. Butcher, *The British in Malaya, 1880-1941: The Social History of a European Community in Colonial South-East Asia*, Kuala Lumpur: Oxford University Press, 1979, pp. 28-9. See also Arnold Wright and H.A. Cartwright (eds), *Twentieth Century Impressions of British Malaya: its History, People, Commerce, Industries, and Resources*, abridged edition, London, 1908, reprinted Singapore: Graham Brash Ltd, 1989.

3 For general background on these developments, see Yip Yat Hoong, *The Development of the Tin Mining Industry of Malaya*, Kuala Lumpur: University of Malaya Press, 1969.

4 Chai Hon-Chan, *The Development of British

Malaya, 1896-1909, Kuala Lumpur: Oxford University Press, 1967, p. 126.

5 Roderick Whitaker, interview with Judith Fyfe, 6 June 1985 – NZOHA, CAB 94.

6 Perak Annual Report, 1895, p.4 – Arkib Negara Malaysia, A/Suk 1.

7 Collector of Land Revenue to Baker, 15 June 1897 – KLO 953/97.

8 Collector of Land Revenue, Minute, 23 June 1898 – KLO 959/97; see also KLO 953/97, 1020/97.

9 Collector of Land Revenue to District Magistrate, 8 November 1897 – KLO 953/97. It should also be noted that the value of the Malayan dollar fluctuated but for most of the period under review it was worth about 2s 4d sterling.

10 *Perak Pioneer*, 29 August 1894.

11 *Times of Malaya*, 7 March 1912, quoted in Butcher, *The British in Malaya*, p. 84.

12 *Perak Pioneer*, 31 January 1903.

13 See *Perak Pioneer*, August 1894 (Special Racing Issue), 5 December 1894; *Times of Malaya*, 15 June 1908.

14 Roderick Whitaker, interview with Judith Fyfe, 6 June 1985 – NZOHA, CAB 96.

15 *Perak Pioneer*, 20 March 1895.

16 Butcher, *The British in Malaya*, p. 41.

17 *Perak Pioneer*, 29 August 1894.

18 *Perak Pioneer*, 24 December 1894, 9 January 1895.

19 Minute by Hume, 10 June 1893; Hume to Resident, 3 January 1898 – KLO 1020/97.

20 Irving to District Magistrate, 13 August 1895 – KLO 1020/1897.

21 Baker to District Magistrate, 15 November 1896 – KLO 1020/97.

22 Hume to Resident, 3 January 1898 – KLO 1020/97.

23 Birch to Secretary to Government, 23 August 1906 – KLO 1047/1906.

24 The report and evidence have not survived but the contents of both can be inferred in general terms from related correspondence in KLO 953/97, 959/97 and 1020/97.

25 Baker to Birch, 7 August 1906 and subsequent correspondence in KLO 1117/97.

Chapter 4 – A Fortune from Gunong Lano

1 Baker to Resident, 14 October 1902, and subsequent correspondence in KLO 741/1903. See also, KLO 90/1903, 91/1903.

2 Calculated from material in KLO 1901/1903, 1051/1904, 469/1909.

3 Report on leases 3492, 4497 – KLO 1055/1920.

4 The term Sakai was used as a collective term for the aboriginal peoples of the Malay Peninsula.

5 Assistant District Officer to District Officer, 12 October 1903 – KLO 1554/1903.

6 Assistant District Officer to District Officer, 12 October 1903 – KLO 1554/1903.

7 Baker to Collector of Land Revenue, 26 April 1905 – KLO 595/1904.

8 Roderick Whitaker, interview with Judith Fyfe, 6 June 1985 – NZOHA, CAB 95.

9 Warden of Mines to Assistant District Officer, 9 February 1905 – KLO 72/1905.

10 Warden of Mines to District Officer, 22 March 1905 – KLO 360/1905.

11 District Officer, Kinta, to Secretary to Resident, 13 March 1905 – KLO 1102/1904.

12 Assistant District Officer to District Officer, 22 March 1905 – KLO 1102/1904.

13 District Officer to Aylesbury & Garland, 2 January 1906 – KLO 1047/1906.

14 Minute by District Officer, nd – KL0 1047/1906.

15 Birch to Secretary, 23 August 1906 – KLO 1047/1906.

16 Details on Mining Lease 4846 – KLO 1055/1920.

17 Details in KLO 635/1913, 438/1914, 1051/1904, 1055/1920.

18 Baker to District Officer, 5 May 1913 – KLO 635/1913.

19 Baker Memorandum, received 25 March 1916 – KLO 708/1916.

20 Senior Warden of Mines to Secretary to Resident, 13 May 1916 – KLO 708/1916.

21 Senior Warden of Mines to Secretary to Resident, 13 May 1916 – KLO 708/1916.

22 District Officer, Kinta, to Secretary to Resident, 27 April 1916 – KLO 708/1916.

Chapter 5 – The Most Wonderful of all Trees

1 C. Alma Baker, 'Personal Experiences with Hevea Brasiliensis Planting in Malaya, 1895-1941' – NZOHA, CAB 87, pp. 1-3.

2 N.H. Ridley, 'Malay Peninsula: Gardens and Agriculture (1906)', quoted in J.H. Drabble, *Rubber in Malaya, 1876-1922: The Genesis of the Industry*, Kuala Lumpur: Oxford University Press, 1973, p. 8.

3 Baker, 'Personal Experiences with Hevea Brasiliensis', p. 1.

4 Ridley Notebooks, quoted in Drabble, *Rubber in Malaya*, p. 8.

5 Baker, 'Personal Experiences with Hevea Brasiliensis', p. 4.

6 Baker to Resident, 20 March 1906 – KLO 400/1906.

7 Birch to District Officer, Kinta, 30 June 1906 – KLO 770/1906.

8 Drabble, *Rubber in Malaya*, pp. 61-64, Appendix I.

9 Secretary to Resident to Baker, 5 June 1908 – KLO 233/1908.

10 Baker to Secretary to Resident, 14 June 1908 – KLO 233/1908.

11 District Officer, Kinta, to Secretary to Resident, 13 June 1908 – KLO 233/1908.

12 Minute by District Officer, 26 May 1908 – KLO 233/1908.

13 Baker to Collector of Land Revenue, 11 June 1908 – KLO 535/1908.

14 Drabble, *Rubber in Malaya*, Appendix VII.

15 Baker, 'Personal Experiences with Hevea Brasiliensis', pp. 5-6.

16 Inspector of Coconut Plantations to Resident, 2 July 1909 – KLO 1438/1909.

17 The sources are contradictory. In *The Soil and Its Products* (1938), Baker refers to his *Instructions Rubber Planting* (1903), of which no copy has been found, and in 'Personal Experiences of Hevea Brasiliensis', which has been used here, he quotes from *Rubber Estate Management* (also not sighted), for which no date is given.

18 R.N. Whitaker, 'Charles Alma Baker' – NZOHA, CAB 88, p. 4.

19 The chronology is not exactly clear. Reminiscing in old age, Baker gives dates for a number of events that cannot be reconciled with contemporary records. In such cases, the most reliable source is used (usually government land records). In 'Personal Experiences with Hevea Brasiliensis' Baker states that he bought Pondok Tanjong Estate in 1905; in a recorded interview with Judith Fyfe (NZOHA, CAB 96), Roderick

Whitaker, who managed the estate for twenty years, indicated that he found this 'hard to believe'. The evidence overall suggests that Pondok Tanjong was bought in about 1910. This estate was in the Larut District of Perak, for which land records do not survive.

20 Baker, 'Personal Experiences with Hevea Brasiliensis', p. 5; Inspector of Coconut Plantations to Resident, 2 July 1909 – KLO 1438/1909.

21 Drabble, *Rubber in Malaya*, p. 147, Appendix I.

22 Minute dated 1 August 1921 – KLO 332/1921.

23 Baker to Collector of Land Revenue, 20 June 1919 – KLO 450/1919; Pondok Tanjong Estate, Accounts for 1941, Comparative Crop Statements – Malayan Correspondence, Huntingdon Archive.

24 Great Britain, *Colonial Office List*, 1920, p. xx.

Chapter 6 – In Defence of Empire

1 Butcher, *The British in Malaya*, p. 27.

2 Brade to Birch, 5 March 1915 – C. Alma Baker, *Souvenir of the Malayan and Australian Battle Planes, 1914-1918*, London: Field Press, for private circulation, 1920.

3 Appeal of 24 April 1915 – Baker, *Souvenir*, p. 44-5.

4 Appeal of 9 May 1915 – Baker, *Souvenir*, p. 47.

5 See, for example, Appeal of 2 May 1915 – copy held by Mrs A.F. Curtin, Auckland.

6 *Times of Malaya*, 30 August 1915.

7 Roderick Whitaker, Interview with Judith Fyfe recorded on 4 June 1985 – NZOHA, CAB 97.

8 *Times of Malaya*, 29 May 1919.

9 Army File 20772, Pita Heretaunga Baker – Defence Headquarters, Wellington.

10 First Australian Appeal, 12 July 1916 – Baker, *Souvenir*, p. 118.

11 Baker, *Souvenir*, pp. 131, 133-5.

12 Baker, *Souvenir*, p. 121.

13 'Carry On' – Baker, *Souvenir*, p. 147.

14 Baker to Under-Secretary of State for the Colonies, 27 February 1917 – Baker, *Souvenir*, p. 32.

15 Reprinted in Baker, *Souvenir*, *passim*.

16 *Times of Malaya*, 30 March 1916.

17 Colonial Office, Series 448, Volume 12/58556; Volume 14/11146, 22857.

18 Colonial Office, Series 448, Volume 18/2314.

19 Colonial Office, Series 448, Volume 21/54261.

20 Baker to Birch, incorporated in Birch to War Office, 22 August 1919 – Colonial Office, Series 448, Volume 21/54261.

21 *New Zealand Herald*, 19 January 1926.

Chapter 7 – The Finest of all Sea Sports

1 Last Will and Testament of Charles Alma Baker, 28 June 1920 – Wills and Probate Series, Huntingdon Archive.

2 C. Alma Baker, *Rough Guide to New Zealand Big Game Fishing*, Glasgow: Robert Maclehose, for private circulation, 1937, p. 26.

3 *New Zealand Herald*, 20 April 1923.

4 *New Zealand Herald*, 20 April 1923.

5 Baker, *A Rough Guide to New Zealand Big Game Fishing*, p. 8.

6 *Hardy's Catalogue of Big Game Fish and Sea Fishing Tackle*, 2nd edition, Alnwick: Hardy Bros, 1937, pp. 46-7; see also Neil Illingworth, *Fighting Fins: Big Game Fishing in New Zealand Waters*, Wellington: Reed, 1961, p. 21.

7 Tourist and Publicity, Series 1, 40/33, NANZ.

8 Bryn Hammond, Introduction to Zane Grey, *Tales of the Angler's Eldorado: New Zealand*, Auckland: Halcyon Press, 1989.

9 *New Zealand Herald*, 20 January 1926.

10 *Smith's Weekly*, 5 February 1927 – copy in Tourist and Publicity, Series 1, 40/33, NANZ.

11 See, for example, Noel Holmes, 'A Question of Respect', *Bay of Islands Swordfish Club Yearbook*, Diamond Jubilee Edition 1924-84, pp. 17-21; Bryn Hammond, Introduction to Zane Grey, *Tales of the Angler's Eldorado*; Mrs A. Harris, Bay of Islands, personal communication.

12 *New Zealand Herald*, 16 February 1926.

13 See, for example, G.A. Buddle's letter in the *New Zealand Herald*, 18 March 1926.

14 *New Zealand Herald*, 25 March 1926. See Buddle's reply to Baker (*New Zealand Herald*, 30 March 1926), and a further letter from Baker (*New Zealand Herald*, 7 April 1926). For Mitchell's comments, see *New Zealand Herald*, 14 April 1926.

15 Illingworth, *Fighting Fins*, p. 24; see also *New Zealand Herald*, 3 January 1927.

16 Roderick Whitaker, 'Charles Alma Baker' – NZOHA, CAB 88.

17 Roderick Whitaker, Interview with Judith Fyfe, 4 June 1985 – NZOHA, CAB 94; Mrs A. Harris, Bay of Islands, personal communication; Illingworth, *Fighting Fins*, p. 21.

18 James L. Hardy, personal communication; Hardy Brothers Catalogue, various years.

19 See, for example, *New Zealand Herald*, 19, 20 January 1926.

20 *New Zealand Herald*, 19 January 1926.

21 Fred Rivers, Waiomu, personal communication.

22 Grey, *Tales of the Angler's Eldorado*, p. 183.

23 Hammond, Introduction to Grey, *Tales of the Angler's Eldorado*.

24 Grey, *Tales of the Angler's Eldorado*, pp. 25, 101, 183, 187.

25 Curtis Herberts, Memorabilia Chairman of the Tuna Club of Avalon, Catalina, personal communication.

26 Florence Baker to Warnock, 23 July 1928 – LD 1/1/2 (11/2).

Chapter 8 – Te Karaka and Limestone Downs

1 *AJHR*, 1894, D 10B, Promotions within the Railway Department; *AJHR*, 1897, D3, Members of the Railway Department, p. 12.

2 Eric Baker, 'Te Karaka and Limestone Downs', G.A. Tait (ed.), *Farms and Stations of New Zealand*, Auckland: Cranwell Publishing Company, 1957, Vol. 1, pp. 114-5.

3 Memorandum … in regard to disposal of Baker and Peak's farm, 1926 – SP 2/4/1; A.H. Johnstone, Opinion – In the matter of the Estate of Charles Alma Baker, 10 November 1950 – LD 1/5.

4 Mrs A.F. Curtin, personal communication.

5 For the early history of the Te Akau Block and its Maori ownership, see the Report of the Royal Commission on the Te Akau Block – *AJHR*, G 1, 1904.

6 Alison Drummond (ed.), *The Waikato Journals of Vicesimus Lush, 1864-8, 1881-2* , Christchurch: Pegasus, 1982.

7 C.W. Vennell and Susan Williams, *Raglan County: Hills and Sea, A Centennial History, 1876-1976*, Auckland: Wilson and Horton, 1976; Stone, *Makers of Fortune*, p. 181.

8 H. Bullock-Webster, *Memories of Sport and Travel Fifty Years Ago: From the Hudson's Bay Company to New Zealand*, Auckland: Whitcombe and Tombs, 1938, pp. 123, 130-1.

9 *Ibid.*, p. 131.

10 Hugh K. Jones (Alfred Buckland and Sons) to Baker, 10 May 1926 – LD 1/1/2 (1/2).

11 Deed of Agreement, 21 May 1926 – LD 1/5.

12 Warnock to Blomfield, 17 August 1926 – LD 1/1/2 (1/5).

13 *New Zealand Herald*, 5 January 1927.

Chapter 9 – Farm Development

1 See, for example, Blomfield to Warnock, 4 August 1927 – SP 2/1/2 (1/A1).

2 Eric Baker to Warnock, 1 June 1926 – LD 1/1/2 (1/3).

3 Warnock to Eric Baker, 3 August 1926 – LD 1/1/2 (1/3).

4 Warnock to Eric Baker, 10 September 1926 – LD 1/1/2 (1/3).

5 Eric Baker to Warnock, 13 September 1926 – LD 1/1/2 (1/3).

6 Warnock to Eric Baker, 22 October 1926 – LD 1/1/2 (1/3).

7 Jones to Warnock, 20 December 1926 – LD 1/1/2 (2/4).

8 Baker to Williams, 7 January 1927 – LD 1/1/2 (2/8).

9 Warnock to Raglan County Council, 11 January 1927, 19 January 1927, 22 January 1927 – LD 1/1/2 (3/5).

10 Warnock to Minister of Public Works, 17 August 1927 – LD 1/1/2 (6/11); and reply, 20 September 1927 – LD 1/1/2 (6/15).

11 Ledgers – LD 1/2/4; Baker to Eric Baker, 24 February 1927 – LD 1/1/2 (2/4).

12 Warnock to Union Bank of Australia, 16 March 1927 – LD 1/1/2 (2/2).

13 Baker to Warnock, 4 May 1928 – LD 1/1/2 (10/2).

14 Florence Baker to Warnock, 23 May 1927 – LD 1/1/2 (5/2).

15 Warnock to Wright Stephenson, January 1927 – LD 1/1/2 (3/8).

16 Telegrams, Baker to Warnock, April-May 1927 – LD 1/1/2 (4/3).

17 Rough Draft on Further General Notes on Cattle and Sheep Breeding, 24 November 1927 – LD 1/1/2 (7/2).

18 Baker to Managers, 25 March 1927 – LD 1/1/2 (1/1).

19 Dalgety and Co. to Warnock, 22 March 1927 – LD 1/1/2 (2/6).

20 Bucklands to Warnock, 4 March 1927 – LD 1/1/2 (2/5); Warnock to Dalgety & Co., 16 March 1927 – LD 1/1/2 (2/6).

21 Baker to Eric Baker, 16 January 1927 – LD 1/1/2 (2/4).

22 Warnock to Eric Baker, 11 February 1927; Warnock to Newman, 11 February 1927 – LD 1/1/2 (2/4).

23 Warnock to Cumming, 15 July 1927 – LD 1/1/2 (6/5).

24 Baker, Rough Notes Re Timber, 22 February 1927 – LD 1/1/2 (9/2).

25 Rough Report on Duncan McGill's Timber, 16 April 1928 – LD 1/1/2 (9/2).

26 Colin Barlow, *The Natural Rubber Industry: Its Development, Technology, and Economy in Malaysia*, Kuala Lumpur: Oxford University Press, 1978, pp. 58-60, 440.

27 Warnock to Newman, 1 June 1928 – LD 1/1/2 (10/7).

28 Warnock to Eric Baker, 5 July 1928 – LD 1/1/2 (10/3).

29 Baker to Warnock, 9 February, 1929 – LD 1/1/2 (13/2).

30 Warnock to Eric Baker, 27 June 1929 – LD 1/1/2 (15/2).

31 Newman to Warnock, 28 February 1929 – LD 1/1/2 (13/9).

32 McArthur to Julitha Baker, January 1927 – LD 1/1/2 (3/2).

33 Warnock to Ward (NZ Loan & Mercantile Agency Co.), 26 March 1928 – LD 1/1/2 (9/7).

34 Florence Baker to Warnock, 23 July 1928 – LD 1/1/2 (11/2).

35 *New Zealand Herald*, 24 April 1929.

36 Judy Pottinger to Warnock, 19 June 1929 – LD 1/1/2 (15/8).

37 Blomfield to Parr, 5 June 1929 – LD 1/1/2 (15/10).

Chapter 10 – Coping with the Depression

1 Newman to Warnock, 26 June 1930 – LD 1/1/2 (20/6).

2 Blomfield to Minister of Public Works, 2 December 1930 – SP 2/1/2 (3/H1).

3 Eric Baker to Warnock, 10 July 1930 – LD 1/1/2 (20/2).

4 Blomfield, file note, 23 February 1932 – SP 2/1/2 (3/J1).

5 Eric Baker to Baker, 20 February 1932 – SP 2/1/2 (3J1).

6 Newman, Report on Limestone Downs, July 1933 – LD 1/1/2 (23/5).

7 Newman, Report on Limestone Downs, August 1933 – SP 2/3/2 (1/3).

8 Baker to Coates, draft nd [January or February 1933]; see also Blomfield to Macmillan, Minister of Public Works, 6 February 1933 – SP 2/1/2 (3/J1).

9 Memorandum of Agreement between C. Alma Baker and Woolsey Allen, 17 February 1933 – SP 2/4/7.

10 Newman, Reports for Limestone Downs, April, June, July 1935 – SP 2/3/2 (1/5).

11 Baker to Sir Thomas Wilford (New Zealand High Commissioner, London), 14 December 1933 – LD 1/1/2 (25/13).

12 Florence Baker to Warnock, 30 June 1932 – SP 2/1/1 (1/3).

13 Roderick Whitaker, Interview with Judith Fyfe, 4 June 1985 – NZOHA, CAB 98.

14 Report of Inquest, 20 February 1934 – J COR 46/1934/342, NANZ.

15 Roderick Whitaker, Interview with Judith Fyfe, 4 June 1985 – NZOHA, CAB 98.

16 C.R. Boyes, Huntingdon, personal communication.

Chapter 11 – Compost and Cosmic Forces

1 Charles E. Curtis, *Practical Forestry and its Bearing on the Improvement of Estates*, London: Crosby Lockwood & Son, 1908; the other two items were packages including lantern slides and a book of commentary, both prepared by the International Harvester Company, Chicago, 1915.

2 See, for example, David Jayne Hill, *Genetic Philosophy*, New York: Macmillan, 1893, pp. 372-3.

3 Hill, *Genetic Philosophy*, p. 75.

4 *De-Vitaminised and De-Mineralised Foods*, as reprinted in C. Alma Baker, *Peace with the Soil: The World Power of Agriculture*, Glasgow: Robert Macelhose & Co., 1939, p. 69.

5   *De-Vitaminised and De-Mineralised Foods*, p. 69.

6   *De-Vitaminised and De-Mineralised Foods*, p. 80.

7   C. Alma Baker, *The Soil and Its Products: the foods we eat versus life-giving foods*, Glasgow: Robert Maclehose & Co., 1938, p. 2.

8   *De-Vitaminised and De-Mineralised Foods*, p. 81.

9   C. Alma Baker, *The Soil and Its Products*, p. 20; see also Imperial Conference: Summary of Proceedings, AJHR 1924, 1927, 1931, A6; the only relevant piece of legislation in this period, the United Kingdom Food and Drugs (Adulteration) Act of 1928 is a consolidating measure dealing with minimum standards for patent medicines rather than the issues raised by Baker.

10 Baker to Managers, nd – LD 1/1/1 (- /1); see also Frank P. Underhill, *The Physiology of the Amino Acids*, New Haven: Yale University Press, 1915.

11 Baker referred often to this work, and gave copies of Rothamsted reports to his farm managers. See A.D. Hall, *The Book of the Rothamsted Experiments*, second edition, London, John Murray, 1919; E. John Russell, *Soil Conditions and Plant Growth*, Sixth Edition, London: Longmans, Green and Co., 1932.

12 Albert Howard and Yeshwant D. Wad, *The Waste Products of Agriculture*, London: Oxford University Press, 1931.

13 *Peace with the Soil*, p. 10.

14 *The Soil and Its Products*, p. 17.

15 *The Soil and Its Products*, p. 16-17.

16 *The Soil and Its Products*, p. 27.

17 *The Soil and Its Products*, p. 17-18.

18 For a general account see Johannes Hemleben, *Rudolph Steiner: A Documentary Biography*, Old Woking: Henry Goulden, 1975.

19 *The Soil and Its Products*, pp. 9-10.

20 Ehrenfried Pfeiffer, *Short Practical Instructions in the use of the Biological-Dynamic Methods of Agriculture*, London: Rudolph Steiner Publishing Co., 1935.

21 Steiner, Rudolph, *The Agricultural Course*, London: Rudolph Steiner Publishing Co., 1938.

22 Guenther Wachsmuth, *The Etheric Formative Forces in Cosmos, Earth and Man: A Path of Investigation into the World of the Living* (translated by D. Wannamaker), London: Anthroposophical Publishing Company, 1932.

23 *Peace with the Soil*, p. 13.

24 Baker to Warnock, 7 August 1928 – LD 1/1/2 (10/2).

25 *Peace with the Soil*, p. 38.

26 L. Whitaker to N. Boyes, 25 November 1959 – Malayan Correspondence, Huntingdon Archive.

27 Blomfield to Fraser, 5 December 1940 – LD 1/1/4 (1/3).

28 Baker to Newman, 20 February 1940 – LD 1/1/3.

29 Limestone Downs Report, March 1938 – LD 1/1/2 (2/2).

30 Baker to Bensusan, 29 September 1939 – Wills and Probate Series, Huntingdon Archive.

31 Baker to Gunson, 27 May 1940 – SP 2/1/3.

32 *The Labouring Earth*, p. 109.

33 Baker to Bensusan, 29 September 1939 – Wills and Probate Series, Huntingdon Archive.

34 Baker to Bensusan, 29 September 1939 – Wills and Probate Series, Huntingdon Archive, p. 209.

Chapter 12 – In the Twilight of a Long and Full Life

1   Newman, Limestone Downs Report for April 1938 – SP 2/3/2 (2/3).

2   Eric Baker, Te Karaka Report for April 1938 – SP 2/3/4 (1/3).

3   Newman, Limestone Downs Report for February 1938 – SP 2/3/2 (2/2).

4   Newman, Limestone Downs Report for June 1939 – SP 2/3/2 2/4).

5   Report for December 1939, in Cummane to Baker, 6 March 1940 – SP 2/3/2 (1/2).

6   Cummane to Blomfield, 9 May 1940 – SP 2/2/3 (1/2).

7   Baker, *Rough Guide to New Zealand Big Game Fishing*, p. 6.

8   Baker, letter to *New Zealand Herald*, 18 April 1940.

9   Chartered Bank of India, Australia and China to Boyes, 19 June 1941 – Wills and Probate Series, Huntingdon Archive.

10 *Straits Times & Echo of Malaya*, 14 September 1940; *Malay Mail*, 14 September 1940.

11 *Straits Echo & Times of Malaya*, 15 August 1940.

12 N. Sievwright to Frederick Boyes, 17 February 1941 – Wills and Probate Series, Huntingdon Archive.

13 L. Whitaker to Harington, 25 June 1941 – Malayan Correspondence, Huntingdon Archive.

14 A.N. Kenion, quoted in J.B. Wilson, Ministry of Aircraft Production, to Neville Sievwright, 23 June 1941 – Wills and Probate Series, Huntingdon Archive.

15 Harington to G. Sievright, 20 April 1941 – Wills and Probate Series, Huntingdon Archive.

Chapter 13 – A Kind-Hearted Generous Man

1   George Sievwright to Boyes, 21 September 1939 – Wills and Probate Series, Huntingdon Archive.

2   Boyes to Baker, January 1941, Wills and Probate Series, Huntingdon Archive. For a summary of events, see Frederick Boyes, C. Alma Baker, deceased. Instructions to advise the English executors on various points arising under his Wills, 29 December 1941 – Wills and Probate Series, Huntingdon Archive.

3   Kennedy to Blomfield, 3 May 1941 – SP 2/1/5 (1/ B1).

4   For an obituary of Pita Baker, see *Opotiki Times*, 6 September 1984.

5   Abbott to Boyes, 17 September 1941, 7 March 1944, 29 January 1945 – Australian Correspondence, Huntingdon Archive.

6   Boyes to H.J. Howells & Co., 29 August 1941 – Wills and Probate Series, Huntingdon Archive.

7   L.H.E. Whitaker to N.S. Sievwright, 9 May 1941 – Malayan Correspondence, Huntingdon Archive.

8   Roderick Whitaker, Interview with Judith Fyfe, 4 June 1985, NZOHA, CAB 1038-1039.

9   Blomfield to Boyes, nd (received 15 December 1941) – New Zealand Correspondence, Huntingdon Archive.

10 Eric Baker to Boyes, 7 November 1944 – New Zealand Correspondence, Huntingdon Archive.

11 Sparling to Boyes, 1 September 1942 – New Zealand Correspondence, Huntingdon Archive.

12 Harington to George Sievwright, 17 March 1942 – English Correspondence, Huntingdon Archive.

13 Harington to Boyes, 15 December 1942 – English Correspondence, Huntingdon Archive.

14 Harington to Norman Boyes, 13 February 1945 – English Correspondence, Huntingdon Archive.

15 Most of this section has been based on L.H.E. Whitaker, Report on Property belonging to the Estate of Late C. Alma Baker, C.B.E., 18 April 1946 – Malayan Correspondence, Huntingdon Archive.

16 Rehabilitation Finance Board to Secretary, Kinta Valley Estate, 24 May 1948 – Malayan Correspondence, Huntingdon Archive.

17 Whitaker to Boyes, 7 November 1948; see also Whitaker to Judy Pottinger, 1 July 1948 – Malayan Correspondence, Huntingdon Archive.

18 Whitaker to Boyes, 10 November 1949 – Malayan Correspondence, Huntingdon Archive.

19 Sydney Palmer to Whitaker, 11 December 1949 – Malayan Correspondence, Huntingdon Archive.

20 Hugh K. Jones, Alfred Buckland and Sons, to Manager, Union Bank, Valuation and Report on Limestone Downs as at 9 June 1944, 6 November 1944 – New Zealand Correspondence, Huntingdon Archive.

21 Hugh K. Jones, Alfred Buckland and Sons, to Manager, Union Bank, Valuation and Report on Te Karaka as at 9 June 1944, 6 November 1944 – New Zealand Correspondence, Huntingdon Archive.

22 Eric Baker to Boyes, 20 December 1946 – New Zealand Correspondence, Huntingdon Archive; Boyes to Whitaker, 10 October 1947 – Malayan Correspondence, Huntingdon Archive.

23 Eric Baker to Judy Pottinger, 4 September 1949 – English Correspondence, Huntingdon Archive.

24 Sparling to Boyes, 28 July 1953; A.H. Johnstone, Opinion … in the matter of a devise of Te Karaka Station to Eric Bertie Baker – New Zealand Correspondence, Huntingdon Archive.

Chapter 14 – A Dream Come True

1   Much of this chapter is based on annual farm reports and summary accounts in LD 1/1/2 and LD 1/1/4, and on recorded interviews with those familiar with developments at Limestone Downs, notably Claude Cartier, Geoff Chitty, Ben Hoete, Harry Harlick, Jim Kelly, George Marshall, Elsie O'Connell, Bill Parsons, Ike Thompson (Ihaka Tamihana) (all with Judith Fyfe of the Oral History Archive of New Zealand); Dan O'Connell (with Robin Boyes); Ray McCraw (with the author).

2   L.H.E. Whitaker, Memorandum of Visit to England and New Zealand, 2 February 1956 – Malayan Correspondence – Huntingdon Archive.

3   O'Connell to Sparling, 11 June 1963 – New Zealand Correspondence, Huntingdon Archive.

4   Roderick Whitaker, Memoirs (private account prepared by Joan Whitaker), 1984.

5   Gardiner, 'Notes on Kinta Valley Estate Ltd,

1964' – Malayan Correspondence, Huntingdon Archive; Harington to Boyes, 21 May 1964, 28 November 1964 – English Correspondence, Huntingdon Archive.

6   H.R. Crawford, 'Kinta Valley Estate Ltd', 12 December 1964; Gardner to Boyes, 11 December 1964; Weatherley to Boyes, 14 December 1964 – English Correspondence, Huntingdon Archive.

7   Harington to Boyes, 14 December 1967 – English Correspondence, Huntingdon Archive.

8   Harington to Boyes, 26 March 1975 – English Correspondence, Huntingdon Archive.

9   Interview of Elsie O'Connell with Judith Fyfe – NZOHA, CAB 1735.

10 New Zealand had switched to decimal currency in 1967, £1 = $2.

Chapter 15 – The C. Alma Baker Trust

1   Baker, English Will – Wills and Probate Series, Huntingdon Archive.

2   Opinion by John P. Whittaker, Lincoln's Inn, 13 April 1976 – Trust Correspondence, Huntingdon Archive.

3   Order by Master Cholmondeley Clarke, Chancery Division of the High Court, 1977 B 4447, 23 November 1978 – Trust Correspondence, Huntingdon Archive.

4   Boyes to Sparling, 21 September 1979 – LD 1/1/2 (7/11). As well as using the available documentation, this discussion of development of the new trust relies on the recollections of the various people involved, in particular, Norman Boyes, Robin Boyes, the Hon. Les Gandar, Christopher Horton, Kevin Lowe and Sir Alan Stewart.

5   Sparling, Memorandum of meeting at Massey University, 12 May 1979 – LD 1/1/2 (7/11).

6   Boyes to Sparling, 21 September 1979 – LD 1/1/2 (7/11).

7   Gandar to Boyes, 23 May 1980; Whittaker, C. Alma Baker, Deceased, Proposed Scheme, 7 August 1980 – Trust Correspondence, Huntingdon Archive.

8   Treasury Solicitor to Warrens (Boyes), 11 September 1980 – Trust Correspondence, Huntingdon Archive.

9   Charity Commission to Warrens, 10 October 1980 – Trust Correspondence, Huntingdon Archive.

10 Legal opinions by John P. Whittaker, 13 April 1976, Charles Hutchinson, 20 July 1976 – English Correspondence, Huntingdon Archive.

11 C. Alma Baker Trust Deed, 6 July 1981 – Trust Correspondence, Huntingdon Archive.

Chapter 16 – A Valuable and Well-known Property

1   For a brief history and summary of the Riverside venture see W.J. Parker and K.I. Lowe, *Riverside: A Study of Sheep farm Development in the Wairarapa*, Riverside Farm Publication, No. 1, Massey University, nd [1979].

2   Preliminary Estimates 1981/82 and Outline of Three-Year Development Programme – NZ Committee, LD 81/2; Minutes, 16 July 1981.

3   Stud Cattle – NZ Committee, LD 81/10, with attached papers.

4   Proposed Mating Management of Beef Cattle on Limestone Downs – NZ Committee, LD 81/7, Appendix.

5   *Limestone Downs 1986/87*, C. Alma Baker Trust Series, No. 5, p.7.

6   Johnstone to N. Boyes, 19 October 1981 – Sparling Papers, BK/2.

7   Clarke to Lowe, 21 September 1981 – NZ Committee, LD 81/8; Clarke to Lowe, 8 July 1983 – NZ Committee, BT 83/19.

8   New Zealand Committee, Minutes, 12 April 1983 – NZ Committee, BT 83/10.

9   Massey University Fertilizer and Lime Research Centre, Report to the C. Alma Baker Trust … Increasing the Efficiency of Fertilizer Use, June 1984 – NZ Committee, BT 84/18; R.M.W. Sumner, Whatawhata Hill Country Research Station, The Effect of Frequency of Shearing on Production at Limestone Downs – NZ Committee, BT 84/21; Limestone Downs Annual Report – 1/7/83 to 30/6/84 – NZ Committee, BT 84/23; J. Lockhart, Limestone Downs, Winter Grazing Management – NZ Committee, BT 84/24; Report on period 5/6/84 – 23/8/84 – NZ Committee, BT 84/26.

10 C. Alma Baker Trust Awards – NZ Committee, BT 83/34.

11 On management strategies, financial policies and research grants, see [Kevin Lowe] *Limestone Downs: Ten Year History*, Palmerston North: C. Alma Baker Trust Series, No. 10, 1993, together with the annual returns and financial statements for Limestone Downs.

INDEX